Mexico's Second Agrarian Reform

Transformation of Rural Mexico Series, 1
Ejido Reform Research Project
Center for U.S.–Mexican Studies
University of California, San Diego
David Myhre, Series Editor

Other Titles in the Series

- Rural Transformations Seen from Below: Regional and Local Perspectives from Western Mexico

- Mexican Sugarcane Growers: Economic Restructuring and Political Options

- Viva Zapata! Generation, Gender, and Historical Consciousness in the Reception of Ejido Reform in Oaxaca

- Rebellion in Chiapas: Rural Reforms, Campesino Radicalism, and the Limits to Salinismo

- Rural Reform in Mexico: The View from the Comarca Lagunera

- The End of Agrarian Reform in Mexico: Past Lessons, Future Prospects

- Economic Restructuring and Rural Subsistence in Mexico: Corn and the Crisis of the 1980s

- Printed with the assistance of The Ford Foundation

- Additional support for this volume from Proyecto SARH–CEPAL

Mexico's Second Agrarian Reform

Household and Community Responses, 1990 – 1994

Alain de Janvry

Gustavo Gordillo

Elisabeth Sadoulet

EJIDO REFORM RESEARCH PROJECT
CENTER FOR U.S.–MEXICAN STUDIES
UNIVERSITY OF CALIFORNIA, SAN DIEGO | LA JOLLA

HD1289
.M6
D4
1997
i 1878367307

Printed in the United States of America

Cover: Linoleum block print by Annika Nelson

Library of Congress Cataloging-in-Publication Data

De Janvry, Alain.
    Mexico's second agrarian reform : household and community
responses, 1990–1994 / Alain De Janvry, Gustavo Gordillo,
Elisabeth Sadoulet.
        p.   cm. — (Transformation of rural Mexico series ; 1)
    Includes bibliographical references (p.).
    ISBN 1-878367-30-7 (pbk.)
    1. Ejidos—Mexico. 2. Land reform—Mexico. 3. Agriculture,
Cooperative—Economic aspects—Mexico. I. Gordillo, Gustavo.
II. Sadoulet, Elisabeth, 1945– . III. Title. IV. Series :
Transformation of rural Mexico ; no. 1.
HD1289.M6D4 1997
333.3'172—dc21
                                                                97-8991
                                                                CIP

NB: The information and analyses presented herein are the
    responsibility of the authors.

Contents

List of Tables and Figures

TABLES

Chapter 4

Chapter 5

Chapter 6

Chapter 7

Chapter 8

Chapter 9

Chapter 10

Chapter 11

Chapter 12

Chapter 13

Chapter 14

Chapter 15

FIGURES

Chapter 2

Chapter 5

Chapter 12

Chapter 15

Preface

In 1991, Mexico's President Carlos Salinas de Gortari initiated a bold program of agrarian reform with the objective of making the social sector of agriculture participate in the political and economic liberalization that had already been pursued at the national level for several years. In so doing, he reopened one of the most socially sensitive and politically explosive subjects in Mexico: the existence of the *ejido* system, the cornerstone of the political settlement that followed the peasant-led revolution of 1910. By 1991, agriculture was in a serious economic crisis: production was stagnant, poverty among households in the social sector was extensive, and the system of political controls over peasants had become increasingly ineffective, anachronistic, and the cause of costly economic inefficiencies. While the cornerstone of the reforms was the rewriting of Article 27 of the 1917 Constitution, allowing eventual privatization of the land under individual ownership, the reforms occurred in the context of a bewildering array of policy and institutional changes that affected the agricultural sector and the economy as a whole. These reforms ranged from implementing a package of macroeconomic reforms—including trade liberalization and descaling of the role of the state in the economy—to sectoral policies with a major redefinition of the public institutions servicing agriculture, and elimination of the subsidies that had been the hallmark of the relationship between state and peasants.

In 1990, Mexico's Ministry of Agriculture (SARH) and the Economic Commission for Latin America and the Caribbean (Spanish acronym CEPAL) had conducted an extensive nationwide survey of the ejido sector, giving a detailed picture of the household-level implications of the ancien régime of state controls, economic subsidies, and institutional support through specialized parastatals. To assess the impact of the reforms, the Ministry of Agrarian Reform (SRA) and the University of California, Berkeley conducted in 1994 a follow-up survey on a subset of the ejidos covered in 1990. Together, these two surveys give a detailed description of the households and communities in the social sector and a measure of the nature of the changes that affected these households and institutions in the intervening years as a consequence of changes in the global context and the progress of the agrarian reforms. In this book, we provide a detailed analysis of these two data sources to identify early successes and failures in the implementation of the reforms. With the reforms barely initiated, no attempt is made to judge the value of the objectives sought or the expected ultimate outcomes. By 1994, the main visible impact of the reforms had been liberalization of the ejido from extensive state controls within a general context of economic crisis for agriculture and institutional gaps created by withdrawal of the state. Land titling and direct income transfers to agriculture had not yet been implemented.

More time must pass before the value of the reforms can be assessed. In the meantime, the objectives of this book are (1) to provide a detailed quantitative characterization of the households and communities that constitute the social sector, a type of quantitative characterization that is available in dispersed case studies but not with a systematic national coverage, and (2) to provide an assessment of household and community responses to the reforms already in progress. From these characterizations and early responses, a set of guidelines for improvement of the reforms in progress can be derived, suggesting areas where remedial action may be possible.

The 1990 survey was used by SARH–CEPAL for two types of analyses: a characterization of *ejidatario* households by geographical regions, and a typology of ejidatarios in four broad categories based on observed behavior. These results are reported in two documents: "Primer informe nacional sobre tipología de productores del sector social" (1992) and "Tipología de productores agrícolas de los ejidos y comunidades en México" (1994).

The 1994 survey was conducted with personnel from the Ministry of Agrarian Reform and with financial support from the Office of the Agrarian Attorney General of Mexico (Procuraduría Agraria). Technical assistance was provided by CEPAL–Mexico under the leadership of Samuel Lichtensztejn. Research support was provided by grants from the Ford Foundation, the Kellogg Foundation, the Ejido Reform Research Project of the Center for U.S.–Mexican Studies at the University of California, San Diego, the UC–MEXUS project of the University of California, and the College of Natural Resources of the University of California, Berkeley. Design of the questionnaire and data entry were done with the participation of J. Fuentes Maya, Eunice Pérez, and Benjamín González. Numerous individuals provided invaluable assistance to data collection and data analysis. Collaborators were the following:

Ministry of Agrarian Reform–CEPAL team:

Víctor Hugo de Lafuente, Leticia Manzanera, Rosa María Barba Pacheco, Fernando Vera Sánchez, Mario del Roble, Martín González, Enrique Arriaga, Miguel Angel López Bracho, Eduardo Caro, Fernando Rascón, Daniel Covarrubias, Enrique Muñoz Ruiz, Maximiano Bautista, Noé Durán, Misael Chávez, Francisco Javier Perales, J. Santana, Juan Diego Zamarripa, Germán Hernández, Mauro Valle, Fernando Sánchez, Carlo Varela, Tania Castro, Marbel Cortez, José Juan Arreola, Raymundo Yáñez, Juventino Trejo, Arturo García Reyes, Rafael Barrera, Sergio Mora, Mauricio Soberanes, Domingo Páramo, and Antolín Flores.

University of California, Berkeley team:

Benjamin Davis, Kenneth Leonard, Nigel Key, Kevin Seidel, Nancy McCarthy, and David Runsten.

We are indebted to these collaborators as well as to the donors who made this study possible. A special thanks goes to David Myhre for his continuous assistance through the Ejido Reform Research Project of the Center for U.S.–Mexican Studies at the University of California, San Diego, as well as his direct assistance in helping us prepare this book.

1

Origins of the Ejido System

The Mexican *ejido* was conceived as a compromise to serve simultaneously as an instrument of political control, a means for the organization of production, and a body of peasant representation. The primary intellectual founders of the postrevolutionary ejido, Luis Cabrera and Andrés Molina Enríquez, envisioned the ejido as a means of redistributing land to pacify the peasantry while stimulating agricultural production. Presidents Plutarco Elías Calles (1924–28) and Lázaro Cárdenas (1934–40) followed their line of thinking when they implemented this new institutional arrangement (Whetten 1948). At the time, the principal debate was between conceiving the ejido as a transitory form of land ownership that would eventually lead to full private ownership, or as a distinct and permanent form of collective property. Antonio Soto y Gama, an old Zapatista, suggested a compromise by defining the ejido as a form of common property with private appropriation (Córdova 1973). This compromise became a lasting formula and resisted periodic attempts to either privatize or collectivize the ejido. But it was not until Lázaro Cárdenas initiated a period of rapid land distribution that the ejido finally became a permanent form of land tenure in the countryside (Sanderson 1984).

The redistribution of land dismantled the political power of the large landowners and the institutions that supported them. But the political and institutional vacuum that ensued was rapidly filled. The state established a mechanism to control the rural sector by weaving together the affairs of the ejidos' executive committees (*comisariados ejidales*) with various state institutions: intermediary institutions such as the Regional Peasant Committees, the State League of Agrarian Communities, and the National Executive Committee of the National Peasants' Confederation (CNC). It is through this hierarchical network of institutions that the ejido came to play the role of an organization for political control.

However, the state's shaping of the ejido into an instrument of political control happened slowly and unevenly across the country. Ejidos have always been highly diverse and heterogeneous. They differ not only in their natural resource endowments but also in their membership composition and the different trajectories of their struggles for land. While acknowledging this diversity, it is still possible to analyze the model of political control that was applied to all ejidos. This model operated at three levels: a legal framework, political representation, and social reproduction. All these levels operated simultaneously but with varying intensities depending on the time period and the region. While the government's organizations and the forms of state intervention have thus differed, they have all been based on a model of control that was authoritarian, hierarchical, and yet inclusive.

The Ejido's Legal Framework

There were specific legal codes that very strictly regulated the organization of production from within the ejido and secured the rights and obligations of the *ejidatarios*. For example, ejidatarios had to work the land directly; they could not hire wage labor. They could not rent the land or sell it. Absences from the ejido of more than two years led to a loss of right to the land. All ejidatarios had to establish the order of heirs to their land in writing, usually naming a spouse or partner as the preferred successor. Ejidatarios could vote and be elected to the executive committee of the ejido's assembly. They voted for the definition of an internal set of rules that regulated their rights, particularly their access to the community's common lands. Each ejidatario also had the right to an urban lot on which to establish a residence and to a maximum of twenty hectares of land for direct cultivation.

Access to land could be gained in one of four ways. For an indigenous community with legal documentation, access to the land was gained through the right of restitution. If a person lived in a human settlement where land was available for distribution within a certain radius, he or she could obtain land through a grant. If an individual was willing to relocate to another region or state, he or she could obtain land in colonization zones through the creation of new population centers. Finally, existing ejidos could obtain an extension of land and thus incorporate new ejidatarios.[1] In the last decade before the reforms, the government allowed the incorporation of households

---

[1] The legal names for these four processes are *restitución, dotación, nuevos centros de población*, and *ampliación*.

that had the title of ejidatario but without land (*ejidatarios con derechos a salvo*).

A number of mechanisms existed through which the state intervened in the internal life of ejidos to implement the law (Whetten 1948; Fernández y Fernández 1973). First, there were interventions directed at legalizing the ejidos' internal process of decision making. For example, almost all important decisions were made in the ejido assembly: distributing urban lots and land plots for cultivation; approving internal rules; requesting credit and other public support such as schools, running water systems, or roads; regulating access to collectively used lands; and defining forms of work within the ejido. However, to make an assembly valid, the representative of the Ministry of Agrarian Reform (SRA), formerly called the Agrarian Department, had to be present. Furthermore, calling an ejido assembly was only considered legal if a representative of the SRA or of the municipal authority endorsed it. In the case of an extraordinary assembly, the call itself had to be issued by the SRA authority.

Second, the state intervened in ejido arbitration matters. For example, family controversies about the use of land plots or conflicts regarding inheritances had to be settled in state administrative tribunals. These tribunals were part of the structure of the Ministry of Agrarian Reform, and they also settled boundary disputes between ejidos, between ejidos and private landowners, and between ejidos and indigenous communities.

Third, the state controlled the flow of public resources to the ejido. Since the late 1970s, commercial banks have made loans to ejido members, but before that time only official state banks offered this service. In order for an ejidatario to receive credit, an official authorization from the ejido assembly was required. However, the credit was given to the ejido. Thus all its members were co-liable for the total amount of credit received and had to offer their harvest as collateral. In order to secure the harvest as collateral, the official bank established an agreement with the ejido, with each member who had received credit, and with the state organization that marketed the ejido's crop and livestock production. This organization, CONASUPO (the National Basic Foods Company), bought the harvest at an established guaranteed price and issued joint checks for the ejidatario and the official bank. Part of the credit was paid in kind. If the credit was for fertilizer, FERTIMEX, the parastatal for the production and distribution of fertilizers, was responsible for repayment. If the credit was for insecticides, other chemical products, or machinery, the bank established contractual arrangements with the respective private enterprises. In the irrigation districts, an irrigation permit was also required. This permit was issued by the Ministry of Agriculture

(SARH), previously called the Ministry of Water Resources and, before that, the National Irrigation Commission (Gordillo 1988).

Until very recently, all borrowers from the official bank were required to purchase crop insurance from an official institution. There were also state enterprises that operated all along the commercial chain in coffee, cocoa, sugarcane, tropical fruits, and other specialized crops. These parastatals provided credit, purchased the harvest, and supplied technical assistance and inputs as well. In every case, an ejido assembly was required to agree on participation of the ejido in the program. Overwhelmed by so many state requirements, the ejido assemblies could at best only deliberate policies initiated by the government, stifling initiatives that could have emerged from the ejidatarios themselves.

Fourth, there were extensive social welfare and infrastructure interventions. The Ministry of Education (SEP) established schools and provided teachers. Public organizations for health, housing, food aid, roads, ethnic issues, and recreational activities also intervened. This extensive state intervention into social services focused most particularly on the indigenous communities and the poor ejidos, which contributed to the development of a functional distribution of government agencies across ejidos and a deepening of heterogeneity in the rural sector: while the social development agencies concentrated on meeting the needs of poor ejidos and indigenous communities, the agencies promoting production attended to the demands of private producers and the more prosperous ejidos.

Finally, there were pervasive political interventions. Until the mid-1980s, with a few exceptions during the 1950s and 1960s,[2] access to public goods and services required that ejidatarios belong to the National Peasants' Confederation, which in turn was affiliated with the ruling Institutional Revolutionary Party (PRI). Thus, through the ejido assembly or more frequently through the ejido's executive committee decisions, ejidatario membership to both the CNC and the PRI was established.

---

[2]During those years, two major splits occurred in the uncontested political monopoly of the CNC. These splits gave birth to four organizations: the Unión General de Obreros y Campesinos de México (UGOCM), the Central Campesina Independiente (CCI), the Consejo Agrario Mexicano (CAM), and the Central Independiente de Obreros Agrícolas y Campesinos (CIOAC). However, the first three organizations were in subsequent years incorporated in the official political party (PRI). CIOAC, on the other hand, has always been loosely linked to leftist parties.

Political Representation

This second level of the model of political control operated through the different forms of political representation in the ejido. Again, although the model of political control was authoritarian, it was also inclusive. In other words, it did not aim at excluding the rural social sectors; rather, it tried to incorporate them into rural governance. The state accomplished this through three levels of peasant organization.

The first level comprised the corporatist organizations, which were favored by the state. At first these organizations were eminently political because of the links connecting ejido executive committees with regional committees, state leagues, and the CNC. During the 1970s, however, as a consequence of the first substantive modification of the agrarian law in almost thirty years,[3] the economic organization of the ejido came to be the favored form of corporatist organization. That is why, in the 1970s, the first ejido unions and Rural Collective Interest Associations (ARICs) were formed. Since all forms of economic organization had to be promoted by the government and were used to facilitate the implementation of government programs, major efforts were made to include the rural populations through this mechanism. New forms of organization were established to incorporate new social subjects. That is how, during the 1970s, the UAIMs (Agro-Industrial Units for Women) were created. During the 1980s, youth organizations, Community Committees for the Distribution of Foodstuffs (Consejos Comunitarios de Abasto), and specialized organizations for specific products were created, among other organizations, within the ejido. Whenever there was an important new national objective, a new widespread demand in the countryside, or a president's favorite government program, new organizations were established. Even if it was not the original purpose, creating these organizations augmented the negotiating capacity of the ejido, giving birth to a new generation of peasant leaders.

The second level of peasant organization was based on traditional community organizations, which had been present since time immemorial. They were grounded on reciprocity, with organizations for mutual insurance, collective labor, and labor exchange. In most ejidos, these organizations adapted to changing circumstances, but they never disappeared. Since the official criterion to determine whether peasants were organized or not was the number of existing formal organizations, these community organizations were not considered and the assessment was always that peasants were not organized.

---

[3] A new agrarian law was promulgated during the presidency of Luis Echeverría (1970–76).

The third level of peasant organization consisted of entities, previously existing only on paper, that were transformed into representative organizations. There was an explicit process through which existing formal and informal institutions—ejido unions, ARICs, and cooperatives—as well as communitarian forms of organization, could be converted into representative organizations. Usually peasants appropriated an organization and turned it into a representative institution as a result of a mobilization to struggle for ad hoc causes.

Coexistence of these three levels of peasant organization was in large part the result of an unintended separation of functions. Corporatist organizations established the links between state and peasants. Community organizations guaranteed solidarity relationships among members of the community. And representative organizations emerged when traditional channels of demand failed to perform.

Social Reproduction of the Ejido

No model of political control is perfect, especially in the absence of a preestablished plan. Because the model evolved as it was being implemented, many aspects emerged randomly. Several elements of the model contradicted each other, and the instruments of control varied from one presidential regime to the next. There were, however, two features of the model that did not vary. Its inclusive nature was maintained, which means that, rather than excluding new social agents or possible dissidents, the state usually tried to co-opt each group under the preestablished rules. There was also a strong agrarian ideology, which played the role of cement in the structure of the ejido. This ideology was organized around two basic themes: (1) the alliance of peasants and state with the presumed objective of assuring the progress of peasants, and (2) the necessity of resorting to state agents as intermediaries between peasants and the rest of national society.

However, it seems to be a feature of all societies that every state intervention in political or economic markets creates countervailing responses and secondary markets, particularly interventions sustained over a long period of time. The model of state control over the ejido was no exception. For example, the prohibition against selling ejido land created a secondary market (Warman 1980; Gledhill 1991). Widows and permanently migrating ejidatarios were the primary participants in land sales, while sales of surplus lands or parts of an ejidatario's land to resolve severe economic misfortune were the primary sources. The prohibition against renting land created an even more active illegal market, especially in irrigated areas. From the ejidatarios' point of view, the temporary rental of a plot of land was a mechanism for economic recovery in case of hardship. Frequently the illegal rental of ejido land was related to migration (DeWalt 1979). In some cases, the rightful ejidatario migrated for an extended period of time and rented the land to circumvent the rule that prohibited him/her from leaving the ejido for more than two years. In other cases, an old ejidatario or his widow rented the land because they had no children to help work it. Alternatively, wage labor was hired to replace the labor of family members who had migrated. The ejido assembly, which had to be held monthly in the presence of a government official, was frequently conducted without the official's presence, although the latter nevertheless established his presence ex post facto to obtain favors and perquisites. Sometimes assemblies that had never taken place were invented, with the consent of the government representative. In this way, credit, insurance, roads, and schools could be obtained. The method also served to expel ejido members, incorporate new ejidatarios, and dismiss ejido executive commissioners.

The secondary markets generated their own political and economic agents. The state agents who served as intermediaries in the ejidos quickly understood a golden rule that has sustained political elites throughout Mexico's history: if wealth is not inherited, it is acquired through good fortune, and the best good fortune for social mobility is landing a government or political position. Many of the political and economic agents in the secondary markets were commissioners and government agents taking advantage of their good fortune.

Since all black markets break the law, it was necessary for these agents to legalize law breaking. For example, selling a plot of land was legalized through a process of elimination and new assignments (*depuración y nuevas adjudicaciones*). The seller of the plot ceased to be an ejidatario at the time of sale, for any legal reason that would suffice, while the buyer was incorporated as a new ejidatario. Also, a member of the ejido who left for more than two years could be excused from working the land for "health reasons." Without such mechanisms, many of the peasant leaders who had stayed away from the ejido for twenty years would have lost their land. Sometimes an ejidatario would not leave officially but "lend [his land] without compensation" to the ejido executive committee or to a person authorized by the committee, although this was in fact in exchange for some money. The same pattern applied to renting land. To cover for an ejidatario's absence, the ejidatario's name would always appear on the list of those present at the ejido assemblies. Furthermore, the ejidatario was on the credit list of the official bank and even on the list of those who received their insurance from the state firm. To compensate tenants for the short rental period (which was necessary because of the illegality of the transaction), the ejidatarios who rented their land also offered their names to their respective tenants. In this way the tenants had access to official credit, which was subsidized. Some private landowners in northeastern Mexico went so far as to rent not only ejido parcels but entire ejidos.

Some of the secondary markets that emerged from state interventions in economic matters became highly lucrative businesses. For example, the disaster business consisted of feigning damage to the harvest and collecting the crop insurance. In order for this to work, cooperation of an ejido executive committee member was necessary because he or she was the first to be notified of the "disaster." Cooperation on the part of representatives of the Ministries of Agrarian Reform and Agriculture was also necessary. These representatives were responsible for verifying the supposed disaster. Furthermore, insurance company agents, official bank representatives, and, of course, the ejidatario all cooperated in reporting the "disaster." The ejidatario collected the insurance for the "damaged" harvest and then sold the same harvest through regular market channels. For the ejidatario, it was a way of counterbalancing the low guarantee prices or simply a way of making a little extra money. And what did the other participants in the deal gain? This is where the official bank agent came in. Credit had been given to the ejidatario in installments. The last installment paid out before the disaster claim was filed was endorsed over to the official bank agent, who then cashed in the money and distributed it to the whole chain of collaborators in this peculiar business (Rello 1987).

In summary, reproduction of the ejido was supported by secondary, or "black," markets. The secondary markets played an important role in adapting state political and legal interventions to the logic of peasant society and economy. This interaction between two different and frequently contradictory logics affected the way both of them functioned, and it made them compatible if not convergent. But, of course, the efficiency and equity costs were enormous, both in resource wastage and public budget deficits, and in welfare levels for the ejidatarios.

The Ejido as an Organ of Peasant Representation

After examining the complexities and contradictions of political control over the ejido, one wonders how it managed to survive for so long. To answer this question, one must understand how the ejido also functions as an instrument of peasant representation. It is well known that the peasant economy is based on the household as a production and consumption unit and on a series of mutual assistance practices between households in a community. The ejido gave to this peasant economy an institutional arrangement that linked these two crucial elements with a third of equal importance—access to common-property resources.

However, the way the model of political control was implemented distorted the three elements of the ejido peasant economy. The adjudication of land plots to the head of the household, and the almost complete absence of legal rights for the other household members, sowed seeds of conflict. It is apparent, when reviewing ejido conflicts over the past decades, that family disputes were pervasive—conflicts between fathers and sons, between husbands and wives, and among children. These conflicts have escalated due to the enormous demographic transformations that have taken place in the ejidos, particularly since the 1970s, even though the ejidos have had no flexibility to accommodate these changes. The original ejidatarios have aged, and many new settlers (*avecindados*) have come to the ejido villages (sometimes outnumbering the ejidatarios) even though they could not acquire membership status in the ejido. Another factor is extensive migration to the interior of the country and to the United States.

Traditional peasant production practices based on native seeds, biological control, organic fertilizers, animal traction, and intercropping were degraded by a truncated process of technological modernization that was initiated by government organizations for research and development in agriculture. In fact, until recently, intercropping was expressly excluded from credit support despite its being a cornerstone of peasant farming systems. There were also no clear rules about access to common lands. This has led not only to illegal appropriations of land but to accelerating social differentiation within the ejido and to severe ecological degradation of ejido resources. Thus the ejido sector had become a truncated peasant economy that coexisted with a state model of political control—that is, a repressed peasant economy in the grips of the state. The ejido was both the apparatus that embodied the state's political control over peasants and the organization of production and representation that allowed the peasant logic to be utilized and reproduced. Compatibility between state logic and peasant logic had been achieved through the work of secondary markets that combined controls and subsidies. But inevitably, when this unstable equilibrium started to fall apart, the model of political control was also decisively affected.

Erosion of the Model of Political Control

The reforms in the countryside that were implemented during President Salinas's regime addressed two basic areas: the relationship between rural producers and the state and the relationship among productive agents in the countryside (Gordillo 1992).

During the last twenty years, peasants successfully developed mechanisms of resistance to implementation of public policies in rural areas. The state, with its instruments of intervention and control, was increasingly seen as an enemy by the different social agents in rural areas. Frequently, economic problems became politicized and stirred up confrontations that had paradoxical effects. The very same state policies that suffocated the ejidos also increased the ejidos' demands for more state support.

Due to the debt crisis of 1982 and the subsequent implementation of stabilization and adjustment policies, a rural development strategy based on the pervasive presence of the state ceased to be economically viable. The state had intervened through very diverse means, including selective indirect subsidies, which were usually regressive. This strategy was very costly for the state because it depended on the massive disbursement of subsidies. The model soon became highly inefficient. Subsidies were channeled not only to the ejido sector but also and mainly to the private sector in agriculture. These subsidies had different purposes: for the ejido sector, they were intended to grease the machinery of political control; for the private sector, they sought to stimulate production. It was the private sector that was assigned the classical role of agriculture in an import substitution model, providing foreign exchange and cheap food. The model of political control became inefficient because it was a model for a closed society organized into corporatist segments. The winds of political mobilization, which started to blow strongly in Mexico after the student movement of 1968, began to erode this authoritarian model. The state's legitimacy came to depend increasingly on electoral processes and political opening.

Consequently, state institutional control and economic subsidies decreased, creating an exceptional opportunity for convergence between radical free-market macroeconomic policies and social mobilization. The radical economic policy—which focused mainly on trade liberalization, deregulation, and privatization—converged with the social mobilization objectives, which focused on restructuring peasant representation through political liberalization. This convergence was neither premeditated nor deliberately promoted by government or civil society. On the contrary, economic liberalization was to be accomplished by modifying and using political authoritarianism, not abolishing it. Similarly, the strategy of political liberalization—and in some cases democratization—was meant to preserve the economic privileges gained by state subsidies.

How did these two opposing tendencies manage to converge? There never was an articulated policy that combined both strategies.

Rather, a juxtaposition of policies had created an institutional vacuum. The model of political control depended on state intervention. However, the intervening state enterprises were largely privatized, and controls loosened when they found themselves in financial crisis. The political clientele supported by these enterprises prevented a complete privatization, and many state enterprise assets were instead transferred to rural producers. For example, the basic instruments of political control in the countryside were affected when BANRURAL (National Rural Credit Bank) was in financial crisis and land distribution had ceased. However, peasant resistance prevented the complete disappearance of the official bank and led to the emergence of alternative mechanisms such as PRONASOL's credit without collateral and, more recently, credit unions. Peasant resistance also prevented the cancellation of all land distribution, and it allowed for negotiation about lands still in the process of allocation. This very particular convergence helped remove obstacles, but it did not create new institutions.

The economic reforms sought to abandon the system of guaranteed prices and align internal prices with international ones. But the juxtaposition of the two currents, economic and political liberalization, caused two crucial problems. First, the system of guaranteed prices, which had covered twelve products, disappeared, but the guaranteed prices for corn and beans were maintained. No reasonable adjustment scheme ever accompanied the price alignment and commercial opening, which dramatically changed the marketing of agricultural products and increased peasant indebtedness. At the same time, maintaining guaranteed prices for corn and beans generated extraordinary rents for some producers. The agricultural sector turned en masse toward corn, and agriculture evolved toward monoculture instead of diversification.

The legal reform of Article 27 of the Mexican Constitution in 1991–92 contributed to further dismantle the political control model. Promoters of economic liberalism perceived the legal reforms as a way to free the ejido's production potential and create a market for land. To implement their plans, especially the more unpopular measures, they counted on the effectiveness of the model of political control. Promoters of political liberalism perceived the legal reforms as dismantling the model of political control but not the economic reward scheme that it provided. Both perspectives were utopian. One looked toward decreasing economic intervention while maintaining political control. The other looked toward decreasing political control while maintaining economic intervention. The contradiction between these two erroneous positions created serious institutional gaps that allowed the emergence of an incipient peasant production system but also seriously jeopardized the effectiveness of the reforms put in place.

When using the term "peasant production system," it is necessary to guard against any Chayanovian interpretation of this peasant agriculture, as well as against a reedition of the old peasant polemic that raged in the 1970s. The peasant production system referred to here is characterized by its search for a form of integration in the market system, a position that would be based on the comparative advantage of ejido agriculture vis-à-vis private agriculture. Ejido agriculture has an advantage because of its reliance on household labor, community organization, access to collective resources, strong participation in labor markets, and particularly its reliance on national and international migration. It is the response of this peasant system to the reforms of the Salinas administration that we analyze in this book.

The results of the 1994 ejido survey conducted by the SRA and the University of California, Berkeley, and its comparison with the survey carried out in 1990 by SARH and CEPAL, help characterize the transformations of the ejido sector in the midst of a profound crisis in the entire Mexican agricultural sector. This larger crisis is characterized by adverse economic incentives, shrinking public support, and wide institutional gaps. The ejido transformation that occurred during those years was dominated by three broad features which also guide the quantitative analysis: the organization of a peasant economy liberated from state control and tutelage but also, to a large degree, dispossessed of state support; the emergence of a competitive smallholder sector in spite of the adversity of the economic and institutional context; and the transformation of the ejido into an entity of support for peasant production instead of an instrument of political control.

2

Principal Features of the Ejido Reforms

To understand the impact of the ejido reforms during the 1990–94 period for which we have observations, it is essential to place these reforms in the wider economic context in which they occurred and to relate these reforms to the broader package of reforms that were initiated starting in 1986.

The general economic context was one of recovery from the debt crisis of 1982 and from the severe stabilization and adjustment policies that were implemented to achieve recovery. After having declined and fluctuated between 1981 and 1988, real gross domestic product (GDP) had regained the 1981 level by 1988, and it rose steadily between 1988 and 1994 (figure 2.1). The general macroeconomic context was thus one of modest economic growth, reaching an average annual rate of 3.4 percent between 1990 and 1994, compared to an annual population growth rate of 1.9 percent. Agriculture, however, did not participate in the economic recovery. Real value added in agriculture fell steadily between 1990 and 1994 at an average annual rate of 4.5 percent (Zedillo 1996). This fall in agricultural value added was a monetary phenomenon more than a real phenomenon, reflecting the profitability crisis that agriculture was suffering as a consequence of a continuously appreciating real exchange rate and a falling real price of corn (figure 2.2). The average annual rate of appreciation of the real exchange rate between 1990 and 1994 was 4.9 percent.[1] This is a good indicator of the price incentives for the fruit and vegetable sector with little price intervention. The real price declined at the average annual rate of 11.4 percent for corn, 13.3 percent for beans, and 5.6 percent for wheat. As we shall see, these price declines were accompanied by a marked reduction in subsidies on the factor side.

---

[1] The real exchange rate is measured through the first three quarters of 1994. The peso crisis and large devaluation occurred in December 1994.

The result was a sharp profitability crisis in agriculture during the period under study, not a favorable context for successful structural reforms.

Figure 2.1
Economic Growth, 1988–1994

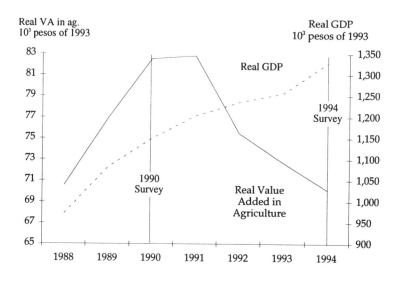

Source: Zedillo 1996.

The source of credit to agriculture shifted from development banks to commercial banks (figure 2.3). Credit available through development banks stagnated while credit available through commercial banks increased in real terms. For the ejido sector, due to lack of land titles that can be used as collateral, credit is largely available through development banks, principally BANRURAL. Credit available through this bank declined very sharply after 1989, particularly for corn and rainfed agriculture. Thus, while overall availability of credit to agriculture increased during the years analyzed, credit available to the ejido sector declined, presaging a serious liquidity crisis and strong barriers hindering the ability to respond to the reforms by modernizing traditional crops and shifting to high-value crops with comparative advantages in an open economy.

Under these conditions, agriculture stagnated (figure 2.2). Production of the ten most important crops (in volume) increased at the

Figure 2.2
Agricultural production and prices, 1986–1994

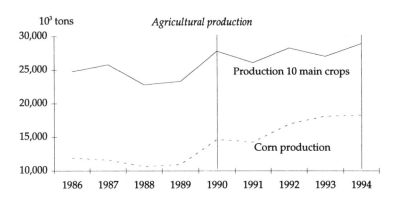

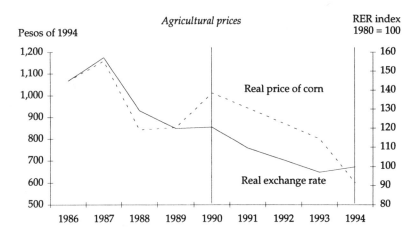

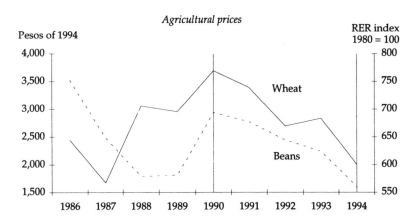

Source: Zedillo 1996.

Figure 2.3
Credit to agriculture by source

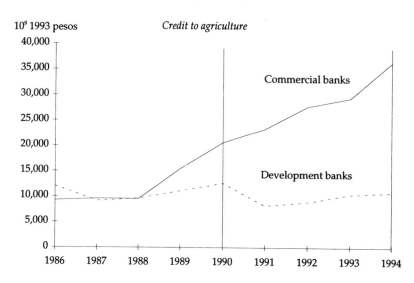

Credit to agriculture

10⁹ 1993 pesos

Commercial banks

Development banks

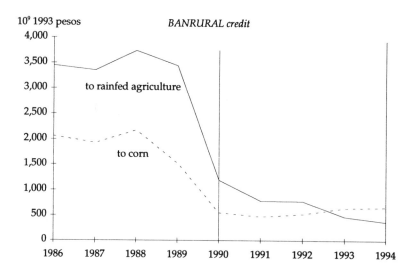

BANRURAL credit

10⁹ 1993 pesos

to rainfed agriculture

to corn

Source: Zedillo 1996.

average annual rate of only 1.2 percent. In spite of the fall in the real price of corn, this crop became relatively more profitable and, importantly, relatively more secure than other activities given that it was one of the last with guaranteed price support. As a result, despite falling profitability, much of the land was reallocated to corn, and corn production increased at the average annual rate of 7 percent in the 1990–94 period. As background information for the analysis of the ejido in this period, we witness a major expansion of corn production, but it is an expansion in which corn is only a relatively attractive crop and does not provide an escape from the overall profitability crisis of the sector.

There are four main areas that President Salinas's reform project targeted: (1) the relationship between the state and agents in civil society, (2) government institutions, (3) the legal system, and (4) the instruments of agricultural policy.

State and Agents in Civil Society

At the beginning of the Salinas administration, the government and social agents in the rural sector interacted primarily to arrive at a political agreement that would allow the government to introduce far-reaching economic reforms and to create political support for future legal reforms. Consequently, the first step of the reform was to establish institutional mechanisms for negotiation that assured plurality and representation among rural producers. In order to accomplish this, the state adopted a favorable attitude toward the National Peasants' Confederation's initiative to form the Permanent Agrarian Congress (CAP). Similarly, the state intensified its relationship with the National Livestock Confederation (CNG), an organization for all livestock producers in the country; with the National Agriculture and Livestock Council (CNA), the main policy maker for private livestock producers; and with the National Confederation of Rural Producers (CNPR), an organization for the political representation of private landowners. This attempt at strengthening the negotiation process was first accompanied by efforts to reinforce producers' organizations in order to channel resources for agricultural projects directly through them. Later these direct transfers were institutionalized through the National Solidarity Program (PRONASOL) and in particular through its specialized programs such as the National Fund for Solidarity Businesses (FONAES).

Changes in Government Institutions

Strategies for reforming the role of government included deregulating markets, decreasing and changing the nature of state intervention, cutting and redirecting subsidies, liberalizing trade, dismantling and/or transforming development institutions, and creating new government organizations needed to implement the legal reforms. The following is a brief discussion of some of the most important changes in government institutions that affected ejidos and ejidatarios between the 1990 and 1994 surveys.

In the financial sector, the main institutions that changed their modes of operation were the National Rural Credit Bank (BANRURAL) and the Trust Funds for Agriculture (FIRA). They redefined their target populations according to the credit history of borrowers and the profitability of investments. This took place in 1991, when a part of BANRURAL's liabilities were transferred to another institution created for this purpose, FIRCAVEN (Trust Fund to Restructure the Overdue Portfolio), so that a smaller portion of these liabilities would have to be restructured by PRONASOL. On the other hand, FIRA targeted medium-sized and large producers in support of export projects, the production of basic foods, and training. Hence the result was that different economic strata of rural producers received attention from different organizations. The other important financial institution that was transformed was the National Agricultural Insurance Company (ANAGSA), which was closed and replaced by AGROASEMEX due to ANAGSA's history of serious mismanagement and abuse.

National Warehouses (ANDSA), an auxiliary credit organization serving providers of storage services for agricultural products, was eliminated. Most of its functions were transferred to the National Basic Foods Company (CONASUPO) and to a new institution called Support Services for Agricultural Marketing (ASERCA).

PRONASOL was created as a new welfare institution that also assumed financial functions, granting credit without collateral to local institutions. It served as an instrument of rural development, providing credit to producers who were rejected by BANRURAL, and it also provided access to credit for farmers located in high-risk rainfed areas, who, because of their location, were unable to meet the profitability requirements of development and commercial banks.

The state's participation in input and product markets, through guaranteed prices and a vast infrastructure for marketing and storage, was also modified. Two state enterprises that produced inputs, the National Seed Company (PRONASE) and the Mexican Fertilizer Company (FERTIMEX), were affected by the reforms. PRONASE liberalized the improved-seed market, allowing private producers to participate and compete in the market. FERTIMEX privatized its local distribution infrastructure, permanently transferring its branches to the social sector.

CONASUPO maintained its presence in the product market and strengthened its position through support in the marketing of basic grains. CONASUPO's storage infrastructure was maintained while its urban role in subsidized urban food distribution was reduced.

In the livestock sector, the network of enterprises for the production and distribution of animal feed, previously integrated in Balanced Feeds of Mexico (ALBAMEX), was privatized. The marketing of coffee had been dominated by the Mexican Coffee Institute (INMECAFÉ), an organization for the storage, processing, and marketing of coffee, which participated extensively in international markets. The commercial activities of the institute ended in 1990, and its infrastructure for processing was transferred principally to the social sector.

Regarding infrastructure development, the National Water Commission (CNA) was in charge of the construction of water projects and the maintenance and management of irrigation districts. The management of these districts was fully turned over to the users during the second quarter of 1994. Expansion of the irrigated area was linked to a fee system that permitted subsidies to be reduced and reoriented to those areas with the highest productive potential. The Trust Fund for Shared Risk (FIRCO) was organized to promote small-scale infrastructure projects, and it continues to do so today.

The firm Servicios Ejidales S.A., coordinated by the Ministry of Agriculture, was eliminated in 1990. It had been responsible for providing access to heavy machinery and harvest equipment for small producers.

The most important agro-industrial development organizations that were created were the National Fund for Solidarity Businesses (FONAES) and the Capitalization and Investment Fund for the Rural Sector (FOCIR). These agencies emerged when the channels of negotiation between the state and producer groups were reestablished. FONAES is mainly dedicated to the creation of medium-sized and small peasant enterprises through a combination of direct state investment and investment by groups of producers. FOCIR, created in 1993, carries out similar tasks for larger enterprises, including project development.

The National Institute of Forestry, Agriculture, and Livestock Research (INIFAP) is in charge of agricultural and forestry research. It started operating under new modalities to generate resources for its research, adaptation, and diffusion of technology for the agricultural sector.

Modifications of the Legal System

The reform of Article 27 is the fundamental element of the rural reforms supporting modernization of the ejido sector (Cornelius 1992). This legal reform formally ended the process of land redistribution. The concentration of land in large estates remains forbidden. A legal mechanism was created to distribute individual landholdings in excess of the legal size limits. In addition, a time limit was set for implementing the land distributions still in progress. The reform gave social organizations and individuals freedom in making decisions, and it made definitive the rights of ejidatarios and community members.

The new legislation established a flexible policy for defining ejido property. A distinction was made between parceled farm land, land used in common, and land for human settlement. In the land designated for human settlement, lots occupied by members of the ejido can be sold; the remainder (public service facilities) is inalienable, indispensable, and unseizable. Common land cannot be appropriated individually, although it can be assigned individually to achieve commercial and production objectives. Parceled farm lands remain social property, but a parcel can be transferred temporarily or permanently to an individual and either maintain its community status or be privatized if the ejido assembly authorizes it.

The new Article 27 allows investment companies to buy land through shares. The limit for the amount of land purchased is twenty-five times the limit established for private individual use. Civil societies can also own rural land.

In order to implement the new legal framework, the Office of the Agrarian Attorney General was created. This institution was decentralized from the Ministry of Agrarian Reform. Its main function is to mediate agrarian conflicts by attempting to reconcile diverging interests and by providing advice to peasant groups about legal recourse compatible with the new legal framework. It plays a very important role in implementing the Program for the Certification of Ejido Land Rights and the Titling of Urban House Plots (PROCEDE), a program through which land rights in the social sector are being regularized (INEGI 1990–92).

The Superior Agrarian Court was founded along with local courts to resolve land tenure conflicts and implement the new agrarian law. In addition, the National Agrarian Registry (RAN) was created to issue titles and certificates for ejido land, as well as to register and certify social organizations so they could be legally recognized.

Agricultural Policy Reforms

Along with reorganization of the institutional apparatus came the introduction of an array of agricultural policy reforms geared toward opening markets to international competition. They also redefined the allocation of subsidies to account for the heterogeneity of Mexican agriculture and of rural producers' groups.

The new regulations emphasized trade liberalization and market openness. They sought to eliminate the distortions that originated in the extensive involvement of parastatal enterprises, and they gradually introduced conditions of access to factors of production and services through market forces. These policy modifications also sought to prevent the rise of monopoly power in domestic agricultural markets. The decision to modify the relative price structure was very important. Crops with high social value, such as corn and beans, remained protected by guaranteed prices. In this way, CONASUPO maintained the Support Program for Ejido Marketing (PACE), through which subsidies for reducing transaction costs, such as discounts for transportation fees, were channeled. The collection and storage of corn and beans were also subsidized through this program.

The decision to develop a scheme of forward prices, which implies an agreement between agricultural producers and industrial processors of sorghum, wheat, soybeans, and rice, had a large economic impact on the industrialization of basic goods for final consumption. ASERCA is the government institution that manages this scheme, with the explicit purpose of gradually evolving toward the organization of future markets in these commodities.

Access to public-sector credit was modified, with respect to both the interest rate and the restructuring of delinquent loans. This gave rise to a stratification of producers according to their qualifications in accessing credit. The financial sector became specialized to service four distinct groups of producers: (1) producers in rainfed and marginal areas, attended by PRONASOL; (2) low- and medium-income producers with production potential, financed by BANRURAL and FIRA at preferential interest rates; (3) producers with a higher level of organization and production capacity, financed by credit unions with BANRURAL or FIRA resources; and (4) commercial producers attended directly by FIRA, the National Development Bank (NAFIN), the Trust Fund for Marketing (FIDEC), and the National Bank for Foreign Trade (BANCOMEXT).

The availability of technical assistance services was sharply reduced. The remaining services were decentralized, and they were contracted directly by producers, with the selective economic support of institutions like FIRCO and FIRA.

However, the most important change in the channeling and targeting of income transfers was the creation of PROCAMPO in response to the gradual elimination of price subsidies in accordance with NAFTA (the North American Free Trade Agreement). During its initial two-year phase, the fifteen-year program supported the income of 3.3 million producers of nine basic crops through direct payments per hectare based on historical areas planted. Payments were decoupled from yields and sales of a marketed surplus. Small farmers consequently received a share of PROCAMPO transfers equal to their share of area planted in these crops, despite the fact that they achieved very low yields and may never have marketed any of their production. The program is thus remarkably progressive about the distribution of income among farm producers. The program's medium-term objectives are the reconversion of land according to comparative advantages in an open economy, compensation for subsidies received by producers in countries from which Mexico is importing competitive crops, incentives for the emergence of marketing organizations, consumer access to cheaper food, increased competitiveness of the livestock sector, and a reduction of environmental degradation. However, because it consists of income transfers, it is more a welfare program than a program to help agriculture modernize and diversify. This program made its first payments after the 1994 survey, which was carried out during the first three months of the year. As a consequence, it had no visible effects on the results of this study.

3

The 1990 and 1994 Ejido Surveys

The data analyzed in this study are from two surveys of households in the social sector that include ejidatarios and members of indigenous communities.[1] The first survey was carried out by SARH–CEPAL in 1990. It was designed by INEGI (the National Institute for Statistics, Geography, and Informatics) to be representative of the ejido sector at the national, state, and rural development district (DDR) levels. This was a nationwide survey, including 5,007 ejidos and 35,090 ejidatarios and community members. The questionnaire asked for information about the following topics:

- Household: composition, age, gender, education, occupations.
- Land: size, tenure, irrigated area, rainfed area.
- Land use: crops, natural pastures, forests.
- Agricultural production: area planted, area harvested, production, destination of production, prices received, marketing channels for each crop, the technology used for corn, beans, and the main crop other than corn and beans.
- Technology: use of improved or local seeds, fertilizers, chemicals, mechanization, animal traction, manual labor.
- Farm assets: ownership of machinery, instruments, infrastructure and buildings (mills, animal pens, wells, etc.), work animals.
- Access to credit, insurance, technical assistance, modern inputs.
- Animal production and backyard production, production of perennial and tree crops.

---

[1] In the following, the term ejido will be used as a generic name for ejidos and indigenous communities when the distinction between the two is not important.

- Membership in organizations and objectives sought in joining these organizations.
- Activities external to the farm, use of family labor.

This survey was analyzed by SARH–CEPAL. It was used to give a structural description of the ejido sector and to construct a typology of producers, contrasting producers specialized in production for their own consumption, producers focused on animal production, producers with a commercial orientation, and diversified producers (SARH–CEPAL 1994).

A follow-up survey was conducted in 1994 with two principal objectives:

- To identify the differentiated impact of the reforms at the ejido and the ejidatario levels, given their specific characteristics.
- To add a series of important topics to the 1994 survey to assist agricultural policy design.

Topics that were added include the following:

- A complete annual accounting of the sources of access to corn and the ways in which this corn was used by each ejido family.
- A detailed characterization of the sources of access to credit and the uses of the credit obtained.
- A detailed characterization of the use of family labor and hired labor in the production of corn, beans, and the main crop other than corn and beans.
- A characterization of the migratory experience of the family members who live in the household, the children of the household head who have left the household, and the brothers and sisters of the household head.
- A quantification of family income and its sources, including gross agricultural, livestock, and forest income, income derived from the labor market and microenterprises, and migrant remittances.
- The use of common-property land.
- A characterization of the transaction costs in accessing markets and public services and the potential role of organizations in reducing these costs.

A questionnaire at the ejido level was also added, to be answered by the ejido leader. This questionnaire included information about the decision-making mechanisms at the ejido level, the participation of its members, and the management of the ejido's collective resources.

The sampling design was based on a two-step procedure, with a stratified sampling of ejidos and random choice of households within the chosen ejidos. The variable used for the stratification of ejidos was the average area of agricultural land per household in the ejido. The 1990 survey had been designed to be representative at the district level, with a precision of 10 percent at a 95 percent confidence level on the per-household agricultural area. In 1994, a subsample of 275 of the ejidos chosen in 1990 was drawn for representativity at the state level only.

Before initiating this second survey, a visit was made to each ejido. There was a discussion with the leaders to inform them of the survey's objectives and to gain familiarity with the characteristics of the ejido and its situation in the context of the reforms. The survey was conducted and carried out by SRA personnel. (It was not possible to carry out the survey in the state of Chiapas due to the political events at the beginning of 1994.) In each of the selected ejidos, the same number of families was surveyed as in 1990. These families were selected randomly, but they were not necessarily the same ones that had been surveyed in 1990. This survey included 1,548 ejidatarios.

To compare the 1990 and 1994 surveys, the data set for the 275 ejidos surveyed in 1994 was extracted from the survey taken in 1990. Because we do not have two observations over time on the same families, analysis on an individual level is not possible. Thus the analysis of change between 1990 and 1994 has to be done on pseudo panels, in terms of household categories, using classificatory variables that were observed in both years, such as land assets, human capital, and social capital. In this study, land area is used as the main classifying variable, with land homogenized for its productive potential in national rainfed equivalent (NRE) hectares.

Given the stratified sample design, sampling weights (expansion factors) by state and ejido class were used to correct for unequal representation of ejidos in the survey. These expansion factors were applied to all the calculations reported in this book.

4

Design of a Typology of Ejidatarios and Land Tenure

Definition of the Typology

A variety of typologies have been developed to characterize the Mexican peasantry. In the agricultural and livestock censuses of 1940, 1950, and 1960, the typological division that was used compared the ejidos to private farms of less than five hectares (ha) of cultivated land and to private farms of more than five hectares. Based on this division, the distribution of farms in the 1960 census was as follows:

Ejidos	57%
Private farms 5 ha	29%
Private farms > 5 ha	14%

Under the influence of the CIDA (Inter-American Committee for Agricultural Development), farm categories labeled infrasubsistence, subfamily, family, and multifamily were introduced with size limits of approximately 0 to 5 ha, 5 to 15 ha, 15 to 50 ha, and more than 50 ha of rainfed land, respectively (Osorio et al. 1974: 206). Using these categories, in 1960 the farms were distributed as follows:

Infrasubsistence	0–5 ha	50%
Subfamily	5–15 ha	33%
Family	15–50 ha	13%
Multifamily	> 50 ha	4%

Schejtman (CEPAL 1982), using the agricultural and livestock census of 1970 and transforming cultivated area into national rainfed equivalents (NRE), proposed the following categories:

Infrasubsistence peasants	0–5 ha NRE	54.7%
Subsistence peasants	4–8 ha NRE	15.9%
Stationary peasants	8–12 ha NRE	6.4%
Peasants with surplus	> 12 ha NRE	8.1%
Other producers		14.9%

Finally, the SARH–CEPAL study based on the ejido survey of 1990 used the limits listed below for the cultivated area of individual plots of ejidatarios (SARH–CEPAL 1994). The ejidatarios are distributed among these categories as follows:

< 2 ha	19.0%
2–4 ha	37.6%
4–10 ha	33.6%
10–20 ha	8.3%
20–30 ha	1.0%
> 30 ha	0.5%

In the present study, the focus is on ejido households and not just on the cultivated area that ejidatarios use. Therefore, the survey gave information on the total land area, which includes rainfed land, irrigated land, natural pastures, and forests. This area includes private land and rented land, but it does not include land rented out to others.

As in Schejtman's study, an adjustment is made to convert land to a national rainfed equivalent (NRE) using the following methodology: the standard that defines a hectare of national rainfed equivalent (ha NRE) is the average national corn yield on rainfed land ($\bar{R}$) where corn is planted in pure stands, thus excluding intercropped corn and corn planted in association with other crops. In the spring–summer seasons of 1990 and 1994, an average yield of 1.08 tons of corn per hectare was observed. The ejidos are grouped in five agro-ecological regions:

Regions	*% of Mexico's Agricultural Area*
Humid tropical	9.4
Subhumid tropical	27.5
Humid temperate	0.1
Subhumid temperate	16.4
Arid and semi-arid	31.8
Other regions	15.3

On individual ejido farms, most of the land has potential agricultural use, since "bad" land is usually part of the ejido's collective land. At any particular point in time, natural pastures are considered to be part fallow land, in rotation with corn, and part land with potential for corn cultivation. Every observed hectare of rainfed corn, which produces an average of 1.08 tons per hectare, requires an additional area of fallow land to sustain this yield. For example, with the widely used "año-y-vez" rotation system, where land is planted in corn every other year, one hectare of fallow land would exist for every hectare planted in corn (Foster 1942). Therefore, in this case the effective yield of corn for an average hectare of rainfed land would equal 0.5 times 1.08 t/ha. Yet fallow land serves as natural pasture, so it also has a yield as forage for animal production. To adjust for this yield of fallows, we use a fallow coefficient of 0.75 instead of 0.50 to transform hectares of rainfed corn and natural pastures in the national rainfed equivalent of corn land. Using the following definitions,

R_{ti} = average yield of rainfed corn in agro-ecological zone i,

R_{ri} = average yield of irrigated corn in agro-ecological zone i,

$\bar{R}$ = average national yield of corn on rainfed land = 1.08 tons per hectare,

W_i = adjustment coefficient in agro-ecological zone i,

the adjustment coefficients for each type of land use and agro-ecological zone i are the following:

Cultivated land, irrigated $W_i = R_{ri}/\bar{R}$

Cultivated land, rainfed $W_i = 0.75 \times R_{ti}/\bar{R}$

Natural pastures $W_i = 0.38 \times R_{ti}/\bar{R}$

Forest land $W_i = 0.2 \times R_{ti}/\bar{R}$.

In table 4.1, we give the values that were obtained for these adjustment coefficients. All the land used by an ejidatario is thus transformed into area measured in ha NRE.

The threshold of five hectares, which has traditionally been used in Mexico, is applied to group the ejidatario farms into classes (but in NRE units). Intervals of farm sizes are then defined to ensure a reasonably uniform distribution of the observations so that calculated indicators within each class are based on a sufficient number of cases and thus have statistical validity. We work with the following farm groups, where the percentages indicate how the ejidatarios are distributed in the 1994 survey:

< 2 ha NRE	22.8%
2–5 ha NRE	34.4%
5–10 ha NRE	19.2%
10–18 ha NRE	16.6%
> 18 ha NRE	7.1%

Table 4.1
Construction of national rainfed equivalent (NRE) area

	Avg. yield of corn [a]		NRE Coefficient			
	Rainfed (t/ha)	Irrigated (t/ha)	Rainfed land [b]	Irrigated land [c]	Natural pastures [d]	Forests [e]
Agroecological zones						
Humid tropical	1.02		0.94		0.36	0.19
Subhumid tropical	1.19	1.97	1.10	1.82	0.42	0.22
Humid temperate	1.29		1.19		0.45	0.24
Subhumid temperate	1.13	1.62	1.05	1.50	0.40	0.21
Arid and semi-arid	0.66	1.70	0.61	1.57	0.23	0.12
National	1.08	1.70				

[a] Average of spring-summer, monocropped corn yields observed in 1990 and 1994.
[b] Yield of rainfed corn/national yield of rainfed corn.
[c] Yield of irrigated corn/national yield of rainfed corn.
[d] 0.38 x (yield of rainfed corn/national yield of rainfed corn).
[e] 0.2 x (yield of rainfed corn/national yield of rainfed corn).

For certain types of analysis we confine ourselves to two groups of ejidatarios—smaller and larger—as follows:

< 5 ha NRE	57.1%
> 5 ha NRE	42.9%

In other cases, it is of interest to analyze the middle class, and we use three classes of farms—small, medium, and large—as follows:

< 2 ha NRE	22.8%
2–10 ha NRE	53.6%
> 10 ha NRE	23.7%

For certain types of analyses, such as land concentration, migration, access to markets, and the distribution of poverty, it is also informative to use a typology by geographical region. The five geographical regions, and the percentage of households in each region, are defined as follows:

- *Region 1*: North (Coahuila, Chihuahua, Durango, Nuevo León, San Luis Potosí, Tamaulipas, and Zacatecas), 23.3%.
- *Region 2*: North Pacific (Baja California, Baja California Sur, Nayarit, Sinaloa, and Sonora), 8.4%.

- *Region 3*: Center (Aguascalientes, Distrito Federal, Guanajuato, Hidalgo, Jalisco, México, Michoacán, Morelos, Puebla, Querétaro, and Tlaxcala), 33.1%.

- *Region 4*: Gulf (Campeche, Quintana Roo, Tabasco, Veracruz, and Yucatán), 18.6%.

- *Region 5*: South Pacific (Colima, Guerrero, and Oaxaca [Chiapas is not included in the survey]), 16.6%.

Land Distribution by Class of Ejidatario and Region

It is important to note that the principal objective of the 1990 and 1994 surveys was not to measure changes in the distribution of land by farm size; much larger samples or census data would need to be used for that purpose. The percentage distribution of land between farm classes is very sensitive to the random drawing of large farms in the sample. With a relatively small sample, the total land covered by the surveys is affected by such random variations. However, given this caveat, the data are useful for observing certain changes in how the land was used, and the data also provide information about the distribution of farms by farm size.

Table 4.2 gives the distribution of land across the five farm categories in the typology as well as between small (≤ 5 ha NRE) and large (> 5 ha NRE) farms. It is evident that land is unequally distributed in the ejido sector.[1] During the four years surveyed, important changes in the total area in farms could not have occurred. We use the observation that there indeed was no significant change in average farm size between 1990 and 1994 as validation of the comparability of the information contained in the two surveys: average farm size was 7.6 ha NRE in both 1990 and 1994.

While there were no changes in overall average farm size, there were systematic changes in the distribution of land across classes of farm size: the distribution of land shifted from the smallest toward the middle-sized farms, and natural pastures were reallocated to cultivated rainfed land. For all farm categories, the average area in natural pastures fell from 3.74 ha NRE in 1990 to 2.95 ha NRE in 1994, and at the same time the average area of cultivated rainfed land increased from 4.19 to 5.13 ha NRE. The average irrigated area per farm did not change. Conversion of natural pastures to cultivated rainfed land principally reflects the expansion of corn cultivation to marginal

---

[1]Substantial inequality in landholdings, often the result of illegal appropriations by more powerful members, is documented in DeWalt 1979 and Hewitt de Alcántara 1976.

Table 4.2
Typology of ejidatarios by farm size, 1990 and 1994

	Farm size (ha NRE)							
	All	*< 2*	*2–5*	*5–10*	*10–18*	*≥ 18*	*≤ 5*	*> 5*
1990								
Distribution								
of farms (%)	100	28.8	27.9	18.8	18.1	6.3	56.7	43.3
Farm size (ha NRE)	7.59	1.17	3.42	7.27	13.61	38.89	2.27	14.56
Irrigated (ha)	0.98	0.06	0.37	1.48	2.08	3.16	0.21	1.98
Rainfed (ha)	4.19	1.54	3.94	4.82	6.15	9.87	2.72	6.12
Natural								
pastures (ha)	3.74	0.04	0.33	1.66	7.25	31.60	0.21	8.40
Forests (ha)	0.38	0.01	0.07	0.63	0.72	1.77	0.04	0.83
1994								
Distribution								
of farms (%)	100	22.8 – –	34.4 ++	19.2	16.6	7.1	57.1	42.9
Farm size (ha NRE)	7.59	1.19	3.26 – –	7.24	13.86	35.42	2.44 ++	14.46
Irrigated (ha)	0.96	0.12 ++	0.29	1.09 – –	2.14	3.82	0.22	1.95
Rainfed (ha)	5.13 ++	1.54 – –	3.92	5.68 ++	6.52	17.85 ++	2.97 ++	8.02 ++
Natural								
pastures (ha)	2.95	0.00	0.29	1.95	7.10	18.40 – –	0.17	6.66
Forests (ha)	0.29	0.00	0.06	0.11 – –	0.70	1.87	0.03	0.63

Note: the signs indicate a significant statistical difference between 1994 and 1990. Significance at the 95% level is indicated by two signs and at the 90% level by one sign. A blank indicates that the difference is not significant.

The significance tests of the differences in all tables are the following: For 0,1 variables, chi-square test is used. The null hypothesis is rejected if chi-square > 3.84 (2 tails, 10%) or 5.02 (2 tails, 5%). For continuous variables, t test is used. The null hypothesis is rejected if t > 1.65 (2 tails, 10%) or 1.96 (2 tails, 5%).

lands, as well as reduction in the length of the fallow cycle of rainfed land. This intensification of land use through a decline in natural pasture area occurred on the largest farms (farms above 18 ha NRE): these farms had a higher ratio of pasture area to total area in 1990 and were therefore able to reallocate a larger portion of their pastures to corn cultivation.

Finally, in table 4.2 a decrease in the number of the smallest farms (below 2 ha NRE) can be noted, along with a displacement of land toward the 2–5 ha NRE category. This shows that the smallest farms, where households were below subsistence level, are being abandoned and that land is being consolidated into more viable small farms. It is therefore important to analyze the relationship of this process to migration and to characterize the regions of the country where this process of abandonment of small farms is occurring most rapidly.

The distribution of different farm sizes by geographic zone is shown in table 4.3. In 1994, 71 percent of the smallest farms (0 to 2 ha NRE) were in the Center and South Pacific regions, where the *minifundio* problem is most severe. There has been an abandonment of these smallest farms in almost every region of the country, as land is shifted to farms between 2 and 5 ha NRE, except in the South Pacific, where it becomes concentrated into the larger farm categories.

The changes in the distribution of land by geographic region are also analyzed in table 4.3 using three producer classes: 0 to 2, 2 to 10, and above 10 ha NRE. A pattern similar to the one mentioned above is revealed in the Center region, where land was displaced from the smallest farms to the medium-sized farms. In the Gulf region, land was also displaced to the medium-sized group but starting from the larger farms. In this case the peasant family economy was consolidated at the expense of the larger farms, presumably accompanied by a decrease in pastures and an increase in rainfed area. Finally, in the South Pacific the land was displaced from the smallest farms to the largest farms, which was accompanied by a decrease of peasant cultivation and an increase in pastures.

In table 4.4, the distribution of land by types of use in 1994 is analyzed among different farm sizes. Not surprisingly, pastures were more important on larger farms: they occupied 41.5 percent of the area on the largest farms and less than 0.1 percent on the smallest. What is most important about the information is the access to irrigation. It is surprising that the smallest plots had less access to irrigation as a percentage of their cultivated area. The cultivated irrigated area was only 15 percent of total area in the two smallest farm classes. By contrast, the three largest farm classes had irrigated areas of 30.3, 41.4, and 32.6 percent, respectively. The inverse relationship between farm size and extent of cultivated land, which falls from 99.9 percent on the smallest to 57.4 percent on the largest farms, does not apply as strongly to irrigated land. For enterprises that had access to irrigation, the portion of irrigated land is quite constant across farm sizes, declining from 89.9 percent on the smallest to 84.6 percent on the largest farms.

As expected, irrigation is less important in humid zones and very important in arid and semi-arid regions. However, irrigation is more unequally distributed in the zones where it is more important. Thus in the arid zone, where 45.3 percent of all farms had irrigation, only 28.8 percent of the farms below 5 ha NRE had access to irrigation, in contrast to 79.5 percent of the farms over 5 ha NRE.

Finally, it can be observed that irrigation is most prevalent in the North Pacific, where 66.2 percent of all farms have irrigation. However, the distribution of access to irrigation is most unequal in the North Pacific, followed by the Center and North regions.

Table 4.3
Typology of ejidatarios by geographic zone, 1990 and 1994

	N	% of obs.	< 2	2–5	5–10	10–18	≥ 18	≤ 5	> 5
			Farm size (ha NRE)						
1990									
Distribution of farms in each geographic zone (%)									
North	364	100	21.6	34.2	23.0	10.3	10.8	55.9	44.1
North Pacific	147	100	11.3	13.6	25.6	44.3	5.1	25.0	75.0
Center	514	100	43.8	30.8	15.6	4.7	5.1	74.6	25.4
Gulf	291	100	13.3	19.8	20.3	42.6	4.0	33.1	66.9
South Pacific	256	100	36.8	30.6	13.9	13.0	5.7	67.4	32.6
Distribution of farms among geographic zones (%)									
North		23.2	17.3	28.4	28.3	13.2	39.6	22.8	23.6
North Pacific		9.4	3.7	4.6	12.7	22.9	7.6	4.1	16.2
Center		32.7	49.7	36.1	27.1	8.5	26.4	43.0	19.2
Gulf		18.5	8.5	13.1	19.9	43.6	11.7	10.8	28.7
South Pacific		16.3	20.8	17.9	12.0	11.7	14.7	19.3	12.3
1994									
Distribution of farms in each geographic zone (%)									
North	348	100	15.7 –	40.9	23.5	8.7	11.3	56.6	43.4
North Pacific	126	100	8.2	20.1	26.5	37.1	8.2	28.3	71.7
Center	494	100	35.9 – –	39.9 ++	13.2	6.9	4.1	75.8	24.2
Gulf	278	100	6.7 –	30.1 ++	23.5	34.5	5.1	36.8	63.2
South Pacific	248	100	32.0	26.1	16.7	16.3	8.9	58.1 – –	41.9
Distribution of farms among geographic zones (%)									
North		23.3	16.1	27.7	28.5	12.2	37.0	23.1	23.6
North Pacific		8.4	3.0	4.9	11.6	18.9	9.7	4.2	14.1
Center		33.1	52.1	38.4	22.7	13.8	19.1	43.9	18.7
Gulf		18.6	5.5	16.3	22.8	38.8	13.4	12.0	27.4
South Pacific		16.6	23.3	12.6	14.4	16.3	20.8	16.9	16.2

Note: the tests of difference of means compare 1990 and 1994.

Table 4.4
Distribution of land by types of farm and types of use, 1994

	N	%	Farm size (ha NRE)	Distribution by use (% of total farm)			Distribution of cult. land (% of cult. ha NRE)		Ejidatarios w/ irrigation (%)	Distribution among those w/ irrigation	
				Natural pastures	Forests	Cultivated land	Irrigated area	Rainfed land		Irrigated area	Rainfed area
All	1493	100	7.6	30.0	0.8	69.2	30.0	70.0	23.2	82.9	17.1
Farm size (ha NRE)											
≤2	340	22.8	1.2	0.1	0.0	99.9	15.0	85.0	14.8	89.9	10.1
2–5	513	34.4	3.3	6.4	0.4	93.3	15.0	85.0	17.5	75.7	24.3
5–10	287	19.2	7.2	20.0	0.3	79.7	30.3	69.7	32.4	81.4	18.6
10–18	247	16.5	13.9	38.6	1.0	60.4	41.4	58.6	31.1	84.2	15.8
> 18	106	7.1	35.4	41.5	1.1	57.4	32.6	67.4	34.0	84.6	15.4
Geographic region											
North	348	23.3	8.6	19.9	0.2	79.8	32.3	67.7	33.6	75.8	24.2
≤5 ha	197	56.6	2.7	1.6	0.0	98.4	23.2	76.8	23.9	79.2	20.8
>5 ha	151	43.4	16.2	24.0	0.3	75.7	34.9	65.1	46.2	75.2	24.8
North Pacific	127	8.5	10.8	10.3	0.0	89.7	81.8	18.2	66.2	98.5	1.5
≤5 ha	36	28.3	2.8	17.9	0.0	82.1	34.3	65.7	27.0	98.0	2.0
>5 ha	91	71.7	14.0	9.7	0.0	90.3	85.3	14.7	81.7	98.5	1.5
Center	493	33.0	5.2	26.8	0.2	73.0	27.1	72.9	22.8	80.6	19.4
≤5 ha	374	75.9	2.2	3.5	0.1	96.4	14.8	85.2	17.9	79.7	20.3
>5 ha	119	24.1	14.3	38.3	0.3	61.4	36.6	63.4	38.2	80.9	19.1
Gulf	277	18.6	9.0	48.2	2.2	49.6	0.7	99.3	1.8	49.5	50.5
≤5 ha	102	36.8	3.0	10.7	1.2	88.1	2.2	97.8	3.6	52.9	47.1
>5 ha	175	63.2	12.6	53.5	2.3	44.2	0.2	99.8	0.8	42.3	57.7
South Pacific	248	16.6	7.8	40.2	1.0	58.8	6.0	94.0	11.2	41.8	58.2
≤5 ha	144	58.1	2.0	6.2	0.5	93.3	6.3	93.7	8.9	56.4	43.6
>5 ha	104	41.9	15.8	46.2	1.1	52.7	5.9	94.1	14.3	38.4	61.6

Land Tenure

Due to the reform of Article 27 at the beginning of 1992, there were important changes in land tenure that occurred between the 1990 and 1994 surveys. The ultimate objective of these reforms is to allow ejidatarios to receive individual titles to the land parcels that they currently cultivate in usufruct. Ultimately this could lead to the titling of up to 4.6 million agricultural parcels. The program is managed by PROCEDE, with INEGI surveying and preparing the maps and titles, the National Agrarian Registry storing and updating maps and titles, and the Agrarian Attorney General helping ejidos organize to carry out the land-titling program and arbitrating land disputes. In 1994, the PROCEDE program had already made significant advances. While no private titles had been granted to ejidatarios in the sample, other measures permitted by the reforms had affected land use, particularly the rights to rent land and to form joint ventures with agents inside or outside the ejido without prior approval of anyone, including ejido authorities. These reforms dynamized the land market as land rental transactions (which were previously illegal even if widely practiced) increased, even when land sales could not yet take place. These land transactions are part of the process of consolidation of minifundia into larger farms that we observed in table 4.2.

In table 4.5, land tenure is characterized by plots. On average, the number of plots by ejidatario did not change (1.8 in 1990 and 1.7 in 1994). The portion of plots under individual ownership decreased from 95.0 percent to 93.8 percent between 1990 and 1994, while cultivated plots that were not owned (rented, in partnerships, loaned, or under concession) rose from 5.0 to 6.2 percent. Parcels under communal ownership declined while individual, private, and rented plots increased.

In the characterization of land tenure by ejidatario (table 4.6), it can be observed that neither ejidatarios who own land (98.7 percent in 1994) nor the average cultivated area owned (9.8 ha in 1994) changed significantly. The number of ejidatarios who used land that was not their own increased from 4.7 percent in 1990 to 8.5 percent in 1994. The number of ejidatarios who rented land to others also increased, from 1.4 to 4.9 percent. Both of these changes reflect the increased dynamism of the land market that was achieved through contractual arrangements, even if this land market remains small. Among the forms of access to other people's land, the two most common were rental (3.0 percent in 1994) and land loans (2.4 percent in 1994).

Land movements by farm size and geographical region are detailed in table 4.7. Larger farmers were more actively involved in the land market: they were more engaged in renting land from others and

Table 4.5
Forms of property in use, by plot, 1990 and 1994

	1990		1994		
Forms of property (%)	100.0		100.0		
Owned (%)	95.0	100.0	93.8	100.0	
Ejido		85.6		88.0	++
Communal		11.5		8.1	--
Private		2.9		3.9	++
Public		0.0		0.0	
Rented, loaned, etc. (%)	5.0	100.0	6.2	100	
Ejido		63.0		74.4	++
Communal		19.3		12.3	--
Private		16.0		10.2	-
Public		1.6		1.7	
Number of plots per ejidatario		1.8		1.7	

to others. Thus the portion of ejidatarios who use land that belongs to others ranged from 3.3 percent on the smallest farms to 23.1 percent on the largest farms in 1994. Also, the number of ejidatarios who rented land to others varied from 0.4 percent on the smallest farms to 10.3 percent on the largest. It is not surprising that the large farmers rented more land to others. It is interesting, however, that the largest farmers also rented more land from others. This means either that those who had the most land could rent more land (for example, because they had more access to credit or more machinery) or that those who rented land ended up having enough land for their direct use to put them in the largest farm classes.

The land market was most active in the Gulf, Center, and North regions, where the more commercially oriented ejidos are located. The market was least developed in the South Pacific region, where very small farms dominate.

Finally, table 4.8 shows how the different types of land tenure are distributed by farm size and by geographic region. Communal land plots are highly atomized. In the smallest farm class (0–2 ha NRE) in 1994, 20.9 percent of ejidatarios had communal land plots, compared to a maximum of 3.9 percent on larger farms (larger than 5 ha NRE). These small, communal farms were principally located in the South Pacific region, where 52 percent of ejidatarios with farms below 5 ha NRE had communal land plots.

Ejidatarios with private land were found mostly in the Center region. While communal tenure was common among small farms, pri-

Table 4.6
Types of land tenure, 1990 and 1994

	1990		1994	
	% of ejidatarios	Average size (ha)	% of ejidatarios	Average size (ha)
Ejidatarios with land				
Owned	98.3	9.8	98.7	9.8
Not owned	4.7	8.4	8.5	5.0
Rented	1.2	5.5	3.0	5.4
In partnership	0.6	5.6	1.1	4.7
Loaned	1.0	4.6	2.4	5.2
Granted	1.2	14.7	0.2	3.6
Other	0.9	7.7	2.0	4.1
Rented to others	1.4	2.6	4.9	4.4

Table 4.7
Land market by farm size and geographic region, 1990 and 1994

	1990 Ejidatarios with land (%)		1994 Ejidatarios with land (%)	
	Not owned	Rented to others	Not owned	Rented to others
Farm size (ha NRE)				
< 2	3.9	0.2	3.3	0.4
2–5	3.5	1.5	8.4	3.5
5–10	3.3	0.8	6.7	0.8
10–18	5.4	1.5	12.0	4.6
≥ 18	15.4	4.3	23.1	10.3
< 5	3.7	0.8	6.3	2.3
≥ 5	6.0	1.6	11.4	3.9
Geographic region and farm size (ha NRE)				
North	8.1	2.0	8.0	3.4
< 5	8.5	2.4	4.2	1.1
≥ 5	7.5	1.4	13.0	6.4
North Pacific	4.6	0.1	6.0	2.7
< 5	7.5	0.3	4.1	1.7
≥ 5	3.6	0.0	6.8	3.1
Center	2.9	1.5	9.3	4.4
< 5	0.4	0.0	6.8	3.1
≥ 5	10.0	5.8	17.1	8.4
Gulf	4.3	0.3	13.1	2.1
< 5	2.5	0.0	17.7	5.0
≥ 5	5.2	0.4	10.3	0.3
South Pacific	4.0	0.9	3.9	0.7
< 5	5.3	1.3	0.6	0.0
≥ 5	1.5	0.0	8.6	1.6

Table 4.8
Forms of land tenure, 1990 and 1994

	1990 % of ejidatarios with			1994 % of ejidatarios with		
	Ejido land	Communal land	Private land	Ejido land	Communal land	Private land
Ejidatarios who own land	91.5	9.7	2.5	91.6	8.6	4.8
Farm size (ha NRE)						
< 2	80.9	19.8	2.7	77.8	20.9	5.7
2–5	91.2	9.9	4.0	93.2	7.8	5.4
5–10	97.1	3.6	1.8	96.6	3.4	1.1
10–18	99.7	0.7	0.4	99.2	1.4	2.6
≥ 18	100.0	9.3	4.1	98.9	3.9	15.4
< 5	85.9	14.9	3.3	86.8	13.2	5.5
≥ 5	98.6	3.1	1.5	97.9	2.7	3.7
Geographic region and farm size (ha NRE)						
North	98.6	1.4	0.2	99.0	1.5	2.9
< 5	98.7	1.3	0.0	98.9	1.1	1.6
≥ 5	98.9	1.1	0.5	99.0	2.3	5.2
North Pacific	96.5	4.1	0.0	95.5	4.9	0.0
< 5	85.3	14.7	0.0	85.3	16.4	0.0
≥ 5	100.0	0.8	0.0	98.9	1.1	0.0
Center	92.7	9.6	7.1	95.2	5.3	9.3
< 5	91.0	10.0	7.3	94.1	6.5	9.5
≥ 5	97.7	8.9	6.9	100.0	1.6	5.9
Gulf	100.0	0.0	0.1	100.0	0.0	1.8
< 5	100.0	0.0	0.0	100.0	0.0	3.8
≥ 5	100.0	0.0	0.2	100.0	0.0	0.8
South Pacific	66.2	36.2	0.6	63.5	35.5	4.8
< 5	51.8	50.5	0.5	46.2	52.0	3.2
≥ 5	94.1	8.7	0.6	89.8	10.4	7.4

vate property was more frequent among ejidatarios with the largest farms. At a national level, 15.4 percent of those who had farms above 18 ha NRE also had private land. There was no other category of farm size where this number exceeded 5.7 percent. Between 1990 and 1994, the number of ejidatarios with private land increased from 2.5 to 4.8 percent for all ejidatarios, and for those in the category of the largest farms it increased from 4.1 to 15.4 percent. This increase was not caused by the privatization of ejido land, which had not happened by the time of the survey, but by ejidatarios' access to private land outside the ejidos. Like the increase in land rental, greater access to private land was evidence of the land market's increased dynamism.

5

The Ejido Household and
Its Occupations

Demographic Characteristics

In the 1994 survey, information was collected about four types of individuals:

- *The head of household.* In 1994, this person was a man in 96 percent of the cases.
- *The direct family.* This includes the household members who live in the household or study. Average family size, including the household head, decreased from 5.5 persons in 1990 to 5.1 persons in 1994.
- *The children of the household head who do not live at home.* In general these are adults who have left the household and started their own families. The combination of the household heads, other family members who live in the household, and these children of the household head make up the biological family.
- *The siblings of the household head.* This information was gathered mostly to measure the social migration capital of each household and community. Adding these individuals to the direct family constitutes what we call the extended family.

The 1990 survey included information about 5,889 adults in direct families. In 1994, we had information about 5,267 adults in direct families and 9,216 adults in extended families. Adults are defined as individuals more than 14 years old.

In table 5.1, we contrast the characteristics of ejido households in 1990 and 1994. The table shows that average direct family size de-

Table 5.1
The ejido household and its occupations, 1990 and 1994

	1990	1994	Test
Family size (direct family)	5.5	5.1	– –
All adults (over 14 years)			
Number of individuals	5889	5267	
Percentage of men	56.9	55.6	
Average age	36.4	35.7	
Men	36.3	36.4	
Women	36.4	34.8	– –
Test of difference men/women		– –	
Years of education	4.2	4.8	++
Men	4.3	4.9	++
Women	4.0	4.8	++
Test of difference men/women	– –		
Adults' occupations [a]			
Percentage of adults who "work"	57.0	56.4	
Men			
% of men among those who "work"	90.1	89.9	
Distribution of activities among men who work			
Principal activity (%):			
Agriculture, livestock, and forestry	81.5	81.7	
Wage labor			
Agriculture	8.0	7.3	
Construction	1.1	1.4	
Industry	0.8	2.6	++
Commerce	2.0	3.5	++
Other sectors	4.9	2.3	– –
Total	16.9	17.1	
Secondary activity (%):			
Agriculture, livestock, and forestry		10.3	
Wage labor		11.8	
Women			
% of women who do housework	78.1	79.2	
% of women among those who "work"	9.9	10.1	
Distribution of activities among women who work (%):			
Agriculture, livestock, and forestry	54.6	25.2	– –
Wage labor			
Agriculture	3.2	4.4	
Construction	0.5	1.0	
Industry	1.3	8.0	++
Commerce	16.4	22.1	
Other sectors	18.1	17.4	– –
Total	39.4	53.0	

[a] Excludes houseworkers, students, and nonactive population.

creased as a consequence of migration. The share of adult women in the ejido population grew because more men than women participate in migration. The percentage of men thus fell from 56.9 to 55.6 between 1990 and 1994, even though the average age of adults did not change significantly in this time period (36.4 and 35.7 years, respectively). The average age of women declined significantly from 36.4 to 34.8 years, reflecting an increase in the participation of women in migration.

Average number of years of education is very low among adults, but it rose from 4.2 to 4.8 years. Therefore, the group of family members that reached adulthood between 1990 and 1994 had a higher level of education than the group that was already adult in 1990. In 1990, adult men had on average more years of education than women, with 4.3 years for men and 4.0 years for women. However, the level of education rose faster among women than among men, so that in 1994 there was no difference in educational level between genders.

The ejidatarios' occupational structure shows few significant changes between 1990 and 1994. On average, excluding houseworkers, students, and those without occupation, the proportion of "working" adults was close to 57 percent in both years. Ninety percent of these working adults were men. Women, in contrast, declared housework as their principal occupation in 79 percent of the cases. As a result, only about 10 percent of women were "working" in both years.

Analyzing separately the activities of adult working men shows that agriculture, livestock raising, and forestry were the principal activities for 82 percent of ejidatarios in both 1990 and 1994. Also, there was no significant change in the total number of ejidatarios whose principal activity was wage labor, equal to 17 percent in both 1990 and 1994. There were some changes in the categories of wage labor, with a fall in agricultural wage labor and a higher participation in the industrial and commercial labor markets. Wage labor was a secondary occupation for 11.8 percent of the men in 1994, so that a total of 29 percent of adult men derive income from labor market activities.

For the women, who constitute 10 percent of the work force in each survey year, the dominant activity was wage labor (53 percent of "working" women in 1994), and the principal wage occupation was commerce (22 percent). Industrial-sector wage labor increased strongly from 1.3 percent in 1990 to 8 percent of adult women in 1994.

Participation in Migration

Migration is a widespread activity among ejidatarios. Not only is it an important source of income and liquidity for the households, but migration also conditions land use, technological choices, and investment in cattle raising. This can be seen in table 5.2: 14.5 percent of all adults in the direct family, 18.8 percent of all adults in the biological family (see table 5.4), and 37.8 percent of the household heads have participated in migration during their lifetime. Of course, higher participation in migration of household heads is explained by their more advanced age. Their average age is 49, compared to 29 for the other adults in the family. Among the latter, only 5 percent have migrated. In their youth, many household heads participated in the Bracero program to work in U.S. agriculture (before the program was canceled in 1964). This is reflected in the relative age of adults and household heads who have migrated to the United States vis-à-vis those who have migrated within Mexico. Those who have gone to the United States are older: on average, adults who went to the United States are 47 years old and household heads are 51 years of age. Adults who migrated somewhere else in Mexico are younger, with an average age of 42 for adults and 47 for household heads.

Figure 5.1 analyzes the frequency distribution by age of household heads who have and have not migrated. There are two age groups where migration is most frequent: between the ages of 30 and 40 and the ages 50 and 55. The first are younger men who use migration as a complementary source of income; the second are older men who migrated in their youth, between the ages of 20 and 25, to take advantage of the Bracero program.

The frequency distribution of household heads by age is shown in figure 5.2. The 1990 distribution has been shifted by four years to coincide with the second survey's observations. The 1990+4 curve indicates the age distribution that would have existed in 1994 if the heads of families from 1990 had not migrated or died. Thus the population "deficit" by age reflects the categories where migration and/or deaths have taken place. The migratory deficit is evident in the age group between 20 and 30 years old. The deficit in the over-60 age group is due to deaths. In the age group between 20 and 25 years, 21 percent of the population is missing, which can be attributed to increased migration between 1990 and 1994.

It is also interesting to analyze the difference in education between those who migrate and those who do not, as well as the difference in education between those who go to the United States and those who go to the rest of Mexico. The data from table 5.2 show that those who did not migrate have more education, namely, 5.0 years of instruction, compared to 3.9 years of instruction for those who did migrate.

Table 5.2
Characteristics of migrants, 1994

	Have not migrated for work	Have migrated for work	Test	Migrated for work to Mexico	Migrated for work to US	Test
Adults in the direct family						
All adults in direct family	4569	772		453	292	
Percentage of migrants		14.5		8.5	5.5	
Age	34.3	43.8	++	42.0	47.2	++
Years of education	5.0	3.9	− −	4.2	3.7	− −
% with fewer than 3 years				36.0	30.2	
% with 3 to 6 years				28.3	40.3	++
% with more than 6 years				38.7	29.7	− −
Know how to read (%)	85.6	87.9	+			
Know how to write (%)	85.3	87.7	+			
% Men	49.6	91.1	++			
% Women	50.4	8.9	− −			
Head of household	960	583		339	243	
Percentage of migrants		37.8		22.0	15.7	
Age	50.3	48.7		46.6	51.3	
Years of education	3.1	3.4		3.5	3.3	
% with fewer than 3 years				42.9	34.5	
% with 3 to 6 years				28.6	43.1	
% with more than 6 years				28.5	22.4	
Know how to read (%)	79.4	85.8	++			
Know how to write (%)	79.1	85.5	++			
% Men	94.3	98.8	++			
% Women	5.7	1.3	− −			
Adults, not head of family	3608	189		114	49	
Percentage of migrants		5.0		3.2	0.9	
Age	30.0	28.6		28.5	27.9	
Years of instruction	5.5	5.6		6.0	5.9	
Destination of those who migrated [a]						
Adults in direct family (%)				58.6	32.7	
% who cannot read				71.8	20.3	
% who can read				56.5	34.2	
Test of difference				− −	++	
% who cannot write				70.2	22.1	
% who can write				56.7	34.0	
Test of difference of means				− −	++	
Men (%)				57.6	34.8	
Women (%)				66.6	9.2	
Test of difference of means				++	− −	
Head of household (%)				58.3	41.7	
% who cannot read				76.6	21.5	
% who can read				54.7	38.1	
Test of difference				− −	++	
% who cannot write				74.7	23.4	
% who can write				54.9	37.8	
Test of difference of means				− −	++	

[a] The complement to 100 migrates to the US and Mexico or to unknown destinations.

Figure 5.1
Head of household migration by age category

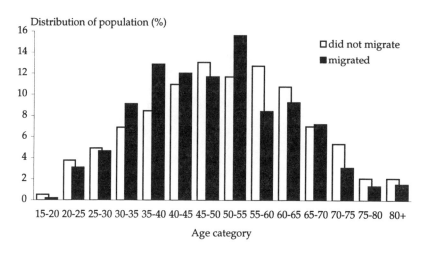

Figure 5.2
Age distribution in 1994 of the population of both surveys

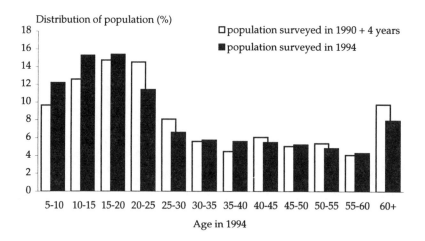

Nonetheless, the percentage of individuals who can read and write is higher for migrants than for those who do not migrate (88 percent of those who have migrated can read, compared to 86 percent of those who have not migrated). This observation suggests that better educated people are less likely to migrate. However, those who migrate do have a basic education; they know how to read and write. It can also be observed that those who migrate to the rest of Mexico have more years of education (4.2) than those who migrate to the United States (3.7). This pattern was already noted by J. Edward Taylor, who explained that education (at levels observed in rural areas) is more valuable in the Mexican labor market than it is in the United States (Taylor 1984).

Those who migrate to the rest of Mexico are at both extremes of the distribution of educational levels. Most of those with fewer than three years of education migrate nationally. Individuals with between three and six years of instruction, the category that is able to read and write, clearly migrate more to the United States. In contrast, those with more than six years of education migrate more often nationally. This same pattern is observed among household heads. We thus conclude that international migration is more difficult for the least educated ejidatarios and is less desirable for those with the highest educational levels.

Looking at migration by gender, it can be seen that only 9 percent of the adults who have migrated were women, and among household heads who have migrated only 1 percent were women.

The destination of members of the direct family who migrated is also analyzed in table 5.2. Of those who have migrated, 59 percent stayed within Mexico and 33 percent went to the United States. Women who have migrated tended to stay in the country: 67 percent of women migrants went elsewhere in Mexico, and 9 percent went to the United States. Men, in contrast, migrated within Mexico in 58 percent of the cases, and in 35 percent of the cases they went to the United States.

It can also be seen in table 5.2 how those who can and those who cannot read are distributed by migration destination. In both cases, there is a higher probability that a person who is not able to read or write has moved to a destination in Mexico, while a literate person is more likely to have moved to the United States. For example, 70 percent of the migrants who could not write moved within Mexico; only 57 percent of the migrants who could write did the same. This difference in destination by literacy is also observed among household heads.

The Ejido Household by Farm Size

Table 5.3 analyzes the ejido household by farm size, the most important asset for an ejidatario household. Education is markedly higher among ejidatarios with larger farms, a difference that is also observed among household heads and among the other adults in the household. Clearly, education cumulates with land ownership to increase a family's assets and thus its capacity to generate both on- and off-farm income.

Table 5.3
The ejido household by farm size, 1990 and 1994

	< 5 ha NRE	≥ 5 ha NRE	Test
Age (years)			
All members			
1990	27.2	26.4	– –
1994	26.6	27.0	++
All adults			
1990	36.8	35.7	– –
1994	35.9	35.2	
Household head			
1990	49.2	48.6	
1994	49.5	49.7	
Adults (excluding household head)			
1990	32.1	31.0	– –
1994	30.1	29.7	
Education (years of education)			
All members			
1990	3.3	4.1	++
1994	3.8	4.5	++
All adults			
1990	3.8	4.7	++
1994	4.4	5.3	++
Household head			
1990	2.5	3.0	++
1994	2.9	3.7	++
Adults (excluding household head)			
1990	4.3	5.2	++
1994	5.0	5.9	++

Migration is also related to farm size. The data in table 5.4 show an interesting contrast across farm sizes between migration to any destination and migration to the United States. Migration to all destinations does not vary with farm size, neither for adults in the extended family nor for those in the biological family. In contrast, migration to

Table 5.4
Migration by farm size, 1994

	% of ejidatarios who have migrated	% of those who have migrated who have gone to the U.S.
All adults in the extended family [a]		
Farm size (ha NRE)		
< 2	18.8	38.6
2–5	20.5	49.4
5–10	21.2	65.1
10–18	18.7	61.3
≥ 18	21.8	57.4
< 5	19.8	45.6
≥ 5	20.3	62.4
All	20.1	53.1
All adults in the biological family		
Farm size (ha NRE)		
< 2	18.0	40.3
2–5	20.5	49.8
5–10	19.6	60.6
10–18	16.1	55.3
≥ 18	17.3	61.1
< 5	19.6	46.5
≥ 5	17.9	58.9
All	18.8	51.4

[a] The extended family includes the absent children and the head of household's siblings.

the United States is biased toward farms larger than 10 ha NRE, expectedly because these households can finance the costs and assume the risks of migration and satisfy the minimum literacy requirements for international migration. By reverse logic, this indicates that households with the least land migrate more to destinations in Mexico. Smaller amounts of land are associated with a greater incidence of poverty and illiteracy.

For those who have migrated, there is a high incidence—no less than 53 percent—of migration to the United States. In the 5–10 ha class, where migration to the United States is most frequent, this number reaches 65 percent. This implies that in this farm class 14 percent of all adults have gone to the United States to work. International migration is evidently an important phenomenon in the economics and dynamics of the ejido sector.

Indigenous Population in the Social Sector

At the ejido level, ejidatario households can be categorized into three groups according to the type of institution to which they belong (table 5.5):

Ejidos with a majority of mestizo population	78.0% of all households
Ejidos with a majority of indigenous population	12.5% of all households
Indigenous communities	9.5% of all households

This categorization allows us to identify household characteristics by ethnicity. For example, households in ejidos with a mestizo majority are principally located in the Center and North regions. Ejidos with an indigenous majority are principally found in the Gulf, Center, and South Pacific, while indigenous communities are overwhelmingly found in the South Pacific. The land area under individual control is larger in mestizo ejidos (7.9 ha NRE) and indigenous ejidos (7.5 ha NRE) when compared to indigenous communities (2.5 ha NRE). This last figure reflects the higher land fragmentation that exists in the indigenous communities, where land can be divided between heirs, a procedure that is legally forbidden in the ejido.[1] These data also underestimate access to land in the indigenous community because cultivable land in fallow and in natural pastures reverts to common land in the community, while it is still part of individual plots in the ejido. This is significant when subsistence corn plots are in the slash-and-burn system. The differential is reflected in the larger total ejido area (in ha NRE) per household in the indigenous community relative to both the mestizo and the indigenous ejido: in 1994, there were 33 ha NRE per household in the indigenous community, compared to 21 in the mestizo ejido and 22 in the indigenous ejido.

Nonetheless, there is clearly a higher incidence of poverty and marginalization among households in indigenous communities. Less land is planted in corn, both rainfed and irrigated, than in the ejidos. Production systems are more frequently intercropped, which is characteristic of subsistence farming. Members of indigenous communities cultivate fewer high-value crops, such as monocropped corn in the fall–winter season, and fruits and vegetables, crops that have higher technical requirements. These households have less access to public credit. They own fewer head of cattle. A larger number of them do not sell corn but are self-sufficient or net buyers of corn. The level

---

[1] The mechanisms of land redistribution among community members are described in Hinton 1972 and Cancian 1992.

of educational capital for adults in these households is, in general, lower.[2] There is also less participation in the labor market as a primary activity: each indigenous community household on average has 0.20 adult members in this category, compared to 0.53 for mestizo ejidatarios. Indigenous families are consequently primarily dedicated to farming. However, more of them use the labor market as a secondary source of income, with 0.42 adults per family, compared to 0.29 for mestizo ejidatarios. They also participate more in migration than do households in indigenous ejidos. These indigenous community households are the type of family where the strategy of subsistence agriculture combined with migration dominates. Production is more oriented toward family self-sufficiency and, for those who have the capacity to capitalize, cattle raising through access to common land.

Migration by Origin and Destination

In table 5.6, we analyze the 950 members of the direct and extended ejidatario families who have migrated to the United States. There is a strong concentration in the places of origin of these migrants: ten states located in the Center, North Pacific, and North contribute 75 percent of migration to the United States. In some of these states, migration is a highly prevalent phenomenon. In Jalisco, Durango, Nayarit, and Michoacán, more than 20 percent of adults have migrated to the United States; in Guanajuato, San Luis Potosí, Tamaulipas, and Zacatecas, more than 15 percent have done so. In some of these states the incidence of international migration is accelerating.

To analyze the change over time in the importance of migration, a contrast is made between the migratory history of adults over and under 35 years of age. In the last column of table 5.6, we observe that the region where migration has accelerated most is the South Pacific. In Guerrero, the percentage of adults who migrated increased by 86 percent between those under and those over 35 years of age. In Oaxaca this increase was 25 percent. These two states alone constitute 10.3 percent of total migration (table 5.7), and this contribution is rapidly increasing, raising the ethnic component of international migration. Even in states with the highest levels of migration, migration is still accelerating, suggesting that the practice is far from reaching an equilibrium point. In Durango, Jalisco, Nayarit, Michoacán, and Tamaulipas,

---

[2] The indicator of educational capital for adults older than 14 years of age is calculated as follows:

1.06^i when $i \leq 6$, where i=years of instruction,

$(1.06)^i (1.12)^{i-6}$ when $6 < i \leq 12$,

$(1.06)^i (1.12)^7$ when $i > 12$.

The coefficients are taken from Schultz 1993.

Table 5.5
Characteristics of the indigenous population, 1990 and 1994

	1990					1994				
	Ejido with mestizo majority	Ejido with indigenous majority	Test	Indigenous community	Test	Ejido with mestizo majority	Ejido with indigenous majority	Test	Indigenous community	Test
Number of households	1257	206		152		1204	193		146	
(percentage)	77.8	12.8		9.4		78.0	12.5		9.5	
Distribution by geographic region (%)										
North	27.4	12.0	– –	3.1	– –	28.5	11.1	– –	2.3	– –
North Pacific	10.9	1.7	– –	6.8	++	10.8	1.7	– –	7.6	++
Center	36.2	18.6	– –	19.2	– –	36.1	21.9	– –	17.0	– –
Gulf	15.3	49.2	++	9.8	++	14.7	44.5	++	10.7	++
South Pacific	10.1	18.6	++	61.1	++	9.9	20.8	++	62.4	++
Area of ejido (ha NRE per household) [a]	20.8	23.8		34.0	++	20.7	22.4		32.7	++
Land in individual use (ha NRE)	7.71	8.41		3.33		7.87	7.47		2.91	– –
Rainfed (ha)	4.46	3.13	– –	2.18	– –	5.27	4.84	– –	2.68	– –
Irrigated (ha)	1.15	0.45	– –	0.00	– –	1.16	0.15	++	0.03	– –
Pasture (ha)	3.28	6.98	++	2.06	– –	2.83	4.52	++	0.94	– –
Forest (ha)	0.34	0.69		0.15	–	0.23	0.74	++	0.04	– –
Distribution by farm size (%)										
≤ 2 ha NRE	28.3	24.7		58.7	++	20.6	27.5	++	60.8	++
2–10 ha NRE	49.5	29.6	– –	33.7		55.3	43.6	– –	34.3	–
> 10 ha NRE	22.2	45.7	++	7.6	– –	24.1	28.9		5.0	– –
Land in corn (ha)										
Monocropped, rainfed	2.24	2.66		1.01	– –	2.59	2.77		0.77	– –
Monocropped, irrigated	0.30	0.05	– –	0.00	– –	0.50	0.03	– –	0.01	
Intercropped, rainfed	0.29	0.15		0.24	+	0.40	0.45		0.63	
Intercropped, irrigated	0.01	0.02		0.00		0.02	0.00		0.00	
Producers of fruits and vegetables (%)	12.2	30.6	++	7.2	– –	14.7	42.1	++	5.2	– –
Producers of monocropped corn, fall-winter (%)	9.6	42.1	++	11.0	– –	13.6	39.6	++	11.4	– –

	(1)		(2)		(3)		(4)		(5)		(6)
Balance of corn use											
% who buy							22.7	++	37.1	++	46.2
% who neither buy nor sell							30.3	--	28.4	--	41.9
% who sell							32.3	--	22.3	--	8.9
% who buy and sell							14.7	--	12.2	--	2.9
Credit											
Public							27.5	--	16.3	--	10.4
Private formal							2.2		1.0		0.0
Other							4.7	--	1.0	--	3.3
Animals (number)											
Cattle	4.8	++	4.3	--	1.9		6.4	--	4.1	--	2.9
Pigs	1.8	++	3.0	--	1.2		1.8	++	2.7	++	1.1
Family											
Size of family	5.5	++	6.1	--	5.2		5.0		5.0	--	5.4
Number of adults	3.7	++	3.7	--	3.4		3.6		3.0	--	3.2
Age of head of the household	49.5	--	48.1		46.1		51.1	++	44.9		45.0
Educational capital/adult[c]	1.35	--	1.26	--	1.33		1.42	++	1.38		1.35
Employment - number of adults who											
Work at home	1.40	+	1.53	--	1.35		1.36	--	1.21	++	1.43
First job outside the farm	0.50	--	0.20		0.51		0.53	--	0.18	--	0.20
Second job outside the farm							0.29	++	0.26	++	0.42
Wage labor	0.45	--	0.19		0.46		0.48	++	0.15	--	0.14
Migrated							0.54	++	0.28	++	0.47

[a] Total area adjusted by the regional coefficient of rainfed corn.
[b] There are two tests of difference of means: (1) ejido with indigenous majority against ejido with mestizo majority and (2) indigenous community against indigenous majority.
[c] Defined in the text.

Table 5.6
Migration by state of origin, 1994

	All adults [a]			Adults > 35			Adults < 35			
	% who have migrated	% of migrants who have gone to the U.S.	% who have migrated to the U.S.	% who have migrated	% of migrants who have gone to the U.S.	% who have migrated to the U.S.	% who have migrated	% of migrants who have gone to the U.S.	% who have migrated to the U.S.	% who migrate to the U.S. (< 35 / > 35)
Center										
Jalisco	27.1	86.0	23.3	25.0	80.3	20.1	28.9	90.3	26.1	130
Michoacán	27.5	77.9	21.4	27.3	75.9	20.7	27.6	79.8	22.0	106
Guanajuato	23.5	76.1	17.9	27.9	66.2	18.5	18.1	95.2	17.2	93
North Pacific										
Nayarit	25.6	84.2	21.6	23.6	83.1	19.6	27.4	85.1	23.3	119
Sinaloa	12.7	44.6	5.7	19.4	42.5	8.2	5.6	52.5	2.9	36
North			0.0						0.0	
Zacatecas	31.0	48.7	15.1	35.6	44.1	15.7	26.7	54.7	14.6	93
Tamaulipas	30.1	56.2	16.9	30.7	54.1	16.6	29.4	58.5	17.2	104
San Luis Potosí	24.8	71.5	17.7	30.5	73.8	22.5	18.8	67.3	12.7	56
Durango	24.1	96.3	23.2	21.8	93.2	20.3	26.3	98.6	25.9	128
Chihuahua	18.1	58.4	10.6	24.9	67.8	16.9	12.4	42.7	5.3	31
South Pacific										
Guerrero	22.1	45.6	10.1	19.6	35.1	6.9	24.2	52.9	12.8	186
Oaxaca	15.7	32.1	5.0	14.9	29.6	4.4	16.3	33.9	5.5	125
Others	15.8	27.5	4.3	19.0	28.8	5.5	13.3	26.0	3.5	63

[a] Includes head of family, adults present in the family, children of head of family (present or absent), and head of family's siblings.

where the highest frequency of migration is observed, the incidence of migration for those under 35 years is higher than for those over 35 years of age. With increasing participation of states in the South Pacific, the points of origin of migration are becoming more broadly distributed geographically. An extrapolation of these tendencies suggests simultaneously a deepening of migration in those states that are already more involved in migration and a diffusion of migration toward new states, even those that are far from the border and have little migratory tradition.

In table 5.7, migration is organized by state of origin in Mexico and region of destination in the United States. It is observed that the destinations are even more concentrated than the points of origin: 56 percent of all migrants go to California and 23 percent go to Texas. The rest are dispersed, in decreasing order of importance, over the Midwest, South, Southwest, and Northwest. Interestingly, the states with the highest participation in migration are those with the most concentrated destinations. So Jalisco, Michoacán, Nayarit, Guerrero, and Oaxaca send nearly all of their migrants to California. By contrast, Tamaulipas, Durango, and Chihuahua, states with a lower participation in migration, have more dispersed destinations. This observation confirms the theory that strongly established social networks at the points of destination facilitate the migratory process by reducing its costs and risks and thus attract more migration in a cumulative process (Durand and Massey 1992).

Comparing the migratory history of those below and above 35 years of age indicates that over time the processes of both concentration and geographical diffusion have increased. California increased its absorption of migrants from 48 percent for those over 35 years of age to 58 percent for those under 35. The concentration process is accompanied by a growing participation of migrants in nonagricultural activities, especially in the tertiary sector. By contrast, the relative absorption of migrants in Texas and the Southwest and Northwest declined. In Texas, this loss of relative importance was in part a result of the mechanization of agriculture. The diffusion process is observed in the increasing importance of more disperse destinations, especially to the Midwest and South.

We thus conclude that migration is a very important element in the ejido peasant economy. It is simultaneously deepening in the states that are already involved in migration and extending toward new states, especially in the South Pacific. This indicates that the peasant economy emerging in the ejido sector is strongly involved in the labor market and in international migration. Migration influences the organization of production in the ejido economy because it affects the availability of labor on ejido land. Migration also reduces the entrepreneurial capacity of the ejido and its potential for modernization

Table 5.7
Matrix of Mexico-U.S. migration, 1994

	California	Texas	Southwest	Northwest	Midwest	South	Others	Total
All adults								
Central								
Jalisco	16.0	0.4	0.0	0.7	1.6	0.0	0.0	18.7
Michoacán	12.0	0.0	0.0	0.4	0.7	0.0	0.0	13.1
Guanajuato	0.6	4.0	0.0	0.3	0.0	2.8	0.4	8.1
North Pacific								
Nayarit	6.0	0.0	0.0	0.2	0.0	0.1	0.0	6.3
Sinaloa	0.9	0.0	0.0	0.0	0.0	0.0	0.0	0.9
North								
Zacatecas	1.5	1.7	0.0	0.0	0.4	0.0	0.0	3.6
Tamaulipas	1.3	2.0	0.0	0.0	0.0	2.5	0.3	6.1
San Luis Potosí	0.9	4.7	0.5	0.0	0.9	0.6	0.0	7.6
Durango	4.6	0.0	1.5	0.0	2.3	0.0	0.2	8.6
Chihuahua	0.2	0.2	1.5	0.7	0.0	0.0	0.0	2.5
South Pacific								
Guerrero	4.7	0.2	0.0	0.4	0.0	0.2	0.2	5.7
Oaxaca	3.9	0.2	0.0	0.0	0.3	0.0	0.2	4.6
Others	3.1	9.3	0.0	0.0	0.4	0.3	1.1	14.2
Total	55.7	22.6	3.5	2.7	6.6	6.5	2.4	100
Adults > 35 years								
Central								
Jalisco	15.7	1.1	0.0	0.5	0.0	0.0	0.0	17.3
Michoacán	10.0	0.0	0.0	0.0	0.0	0.0	0.0	10.0
Guanajuato	2.1	8.0	0.0	1.3	0.0	1.3	0.0	12.7
North Pacific								
Nayarit	7.2	0.0	0.0	0.5	0.0	0.0	0.0	7.7
Sinaloa	1.7	0.0	0.0	0.0	0.0	0.0	0.0	1.7

	C1	C2	C3	C4	C5	C6	C7	Total
North								
Zacatecas	0.8	1.6	0.0	0.0	0.0	0.0	0.0	2.4
Tamaulipas	1.2	3.2	0.0	0.0	0.0	1.2	0.0	5.6
San Luis Potosí	0.5	8.6	0.0	0.0	2.1	0.0	0.0	11.2
Durango	4.8	0.0	1.6	0.0	0.0	0.0	0.0	6.4
Chihuahua	0.0	0.6	3.6	1.4	0.0	0.0	0.0	5.6
South Pacific								
Guerrero	0.8	0.0	0.0	0.0	0.0	0.9	0.0	1.7
Oaxaca	0.8	0.0	0.0	0.0	0.0	0.0	0.0	0.8
Others	1.9	10.4	0.0	0.0	1.6	1.2	2.1	17.2
Total	47.5	33.5	5.2	3.7	3.7	4.6	2.1	100

Adults < 35 years

	C1	C2	C3	C4	C5	C6	C7	Total
Central								
Jalisco	16.1	0.2	0.0	0.8	2.2	0.0	0.0	19.3
Michoacán	12.7	0.0	0.0	0.5	0.9	0.0	0.0	14.1
Guanajuato	0.0	2.7	0.0	0.0	0.0	3.3	0.5	6.5
North Pacific								
Nayarit	5.6	0.0	0.0	0.1	0.0	0.2	0.0	5.9
Sinaloa	0.7	0.0	0.0	0.0	0.0	0.0	0.0	0.7
North								
Zacatecas	1.8	1.7	0.0	0.0	0.5	0.0	0.0	4.0
Tamaulipas	1.3	1.6	0.0	0.0	0.0	3.0	0.4	6.3
San Luis Potosí	1.0	3.3	0.7	0.0	0.4	0.8	0.0	6.2
Durango	4.5	0.0	1.5	0.0	3.2	0.0	0.3	9.5
Chihuahua	0.2	0.0	0.7	0.5	0.0	0.0	0.0	1.4
South Pacific								
Guerrero	6.1	0.3	0.0	0.5	0.0	0.0	0.3	7.2
Oaxaca	4.9	0.3	0.0	0.0	0.5	0.0	0.3	6.0
Others	3.5	8.9	0.0	0.0	0.0	0.0	0.8	13.2
Total	58.4	19.0	2.9	2.4	7.7	7.3	2.6	100

since many of the more dynamic members of the ejido are away pursuing other activities. On the positive side, it serves as a source of liquidity for consumption, the purchase of inputs, and capitalization in cattle. And, as we shall see, migration is a fundamental source of income for ejido households.

6

Changes in the Use of Cultivated Land, 1990–1994

Aggregate Changes

There were notable changes in the use of cultivated land between 1990 and 1994. In large part, these changes were the consequence of government interventions that maintained guaranteed prices for corn and beans and made these crops relatively more profitable and less risky. Other changes were the increase in cattle raising and the selective expansion of export crops.[1] Table 6.1 details the changes in cultivated area of eleven product categories, which occupy the total cultivated area. Table 6.2 summarizes the percentage changes in the use of cultivated land between 1990 and 1994.

The most notable change is the strong expansion of the area used for corn cultivation. In 1994, monocropped or intercropped corn covered 51.5 percent of the rainfed area, 38.3 percent of the irrigated area,

---

[1] For the analysis that follows, crops are grouped into eight categories: (1) corn, (2) beans, (3) wheat, (4) other grains (sesame, rice, oats, fodder oats, barley, garbanzo beans, lima or navy beans, lentils, sorghum), (5) oil seeds (canola, soybean), (6) fruits and vegetables (spinach, artichoke, hazelnut, eggplant, peanut, squash, pumpkin, vegetable pear, pea, chilacayote, red pepper, dried pepper, green pepper, cilantro, cabbage, spinach, flowers, strawberry, jicama, lettuce, litchi, melon, potato, cucumber, parsley, radish, rapini, watermelon, red tomato, green tomato, tomatillo, carrot, avocado, plum, peach, guava, cherry, rosemary, lime, lemon, lily, century plant, mamey, mandarin tangarine, mango, apple, nanche, orange, nectarine, loquat, nopal, walnut, papaya, pear, peyote, pineapple, pine nut, pistachio, banana, tamarind, lime tea, grapefruit, cassava), (7) fodder (alfalfa, fodder alfalfa, fodder barley, fodder barley for pasturing, fodder garbanzo, fodder corn, grass, hay, sorghum, sorghum for fodder, sorghum for pasture, millet), and (8) traditional exports (cotton, cocoa, coffee, café capulín, cherries, sugarcane, tobacco).

Table 6.1
Use of cultivated land, 1990 and 1994

		1990	1994	Test
Corn, monocropped				
Percentage of farmers	%	70.6	71.1	– –
Average rainfed area	ha	2.25	2.57	+
Average irrigated area	ha	0.25	0.41	++
Percentage of cultivated land				
Rainfed	%	47.4	43.7	n.a.
Irrigated	%	19.8	36.8	n.a.
Total	%	41.6	42.6	n.a.
Corn, intercropped				
Percentage of farmers	%	14.2	20.8	++
Average rainfed area	ha	0.27	0.45	++
Average irrigated area	ha	0.01	0.02	++
Percentage of cultivated land				
Rainfed	%	5.8	7.8	n.a.
Irrigated	%	1.1	1.5	n.a.
Total	%	4.8	6.7	n.a.
Beans, monocropped				
Percentage of farmers	%	17.2	20.7	+
Average rainfed area	ha	0.38	0.59	
Average irrigated area	ha	0.10	0.08	
Percentage of cultivated land				
Rainfed	%	8.1	10.0	n.a.
Irrigated	%	7.9	6.8	n.a.
Total	%	8.1	9.5	n.a.

		1990	1994	Test
Oil seeds, monocropped				
Percentage of farmers	%	5.2	3.1	– –
Average rainfed area	ha	0.32	0.22	
Average irrigated area	ha	0.16	0.09	– –
Percentage of cultivated land				
Rainfed	%	6.8	3.7	n.a.
Irrigated	%	12.8	7.6	n.a.
Total	%	8.1	4.4	n.a.
Fruits and vegetables, monocropped				
Percentage of farmers	%	14.5	18.2	++
Average rainfed area	ha	0.33	0.36	
Average irrigated area	ha	0.14	0.11	
Percentage of cultivated land				
Rainfed	%	6.9	6.2	n.a.
Irrigated	%	10.9	9.9	n.a.
Total	%	7.8	6.8	n.a.
Fodder, monocropped				
Percentage of farmers	%	9.1	11.4	++
Average rainfed area	ha	0.47	0.97	++
Average irrigated area	ha	0.09	0.10	
Percentage of cultivated land				
Rainfed	%	9.9	16.4	n.a.
Irrigated	%	7.4	9.0	n.a.
Total	%	9.4	15.2	n.a.

	Unit			Test
Beans, intercropped				
Percentage of farmers	%	10.6	14.9	++
Average rainfed area	ha	0.12	0.16	++
Average irrigated area	ha	0.01	0.01	
Percentage of cultivated land				
Rainfed	%	2.5	2.7	n.a.
Irrigated	%	0.6	0.6	n.a.
Total	%	2.1	2.4	n.a.
Wheat				
Percentage of farmers	%	5.1	2.8	– –
Average rainfed area	ha	0.02	0.02	
Average irrigated area	ha	0.29	0.17	– –
Percentage of cultivated land				
Rainfed	%	0.4	0.3	n.a.
Irrigated	%	22.9	15.5	n.a.
Total	%	5.1	2.8	n.a.
Other basic grains, monocropped (not corn, beans, or wheat)				
Percentage of farmers	%	9.5	7.5	
Average rainfed area	ha	0.33	0.27	
Average irrigated area	ha	0.12	0.06	
Percentage of cultivated land				
Rainfed	%	6.9	4.5	n.a.
Irrigated	%	9.4	5.0	n.a.
Total	%	7.4	4.6	n.a.
Traditional exports, monocropped				
Percentage of farmers	%	6.3	6.4	
Average rainfed area	ha	0.16	0.18	
Average irrigated area	ha	0.07	0.07	
Percentage of cultivated land				
Rainfed	%	3.4	3.0	n.a.
Irrigated	%	5.3	5.9	n.a.
Total	%	3.8	3.5	n.a.
Other crops, intercropped (not corn or beans)				
Percentage of farmers	%	7.0	11.5	++
Average rainfed area	ha	0.09	0.10	++
Average irrigated area	ha	0.02	0.01	
Percentage of cultivated land				
Rainfed	%	1.8	1.8	n.a.
Irrigated	%	1.9	1.3	n.a.
Total	%	1.9	1.7	n.a.
All crops				
Number of observations		1565	1462	
Average rainfed area	ha	4.74	5.89	++
Average irrigated area	ha	1.26	1.13	
Percentage of cultivated land				
Rainfed	%	100	100	n.a.
Irrigated	%	100	100	n.a.
Total	%	100	100	n.a.

Note: n.a. indicates test of difference not applicable.

and 49.3 percent of the total cultivated area (table 6.1). The strongest expansion was the penetration of corn onto irrigated land. During the 1990–1994 period, monocropped corn on irrigated land augmented by 64 percent, and intercropped corn on rainfed land, which covers 18 percent of the area occupied by pure corn on rainfed land, increased by 67 percent. There was a sharp increase in the number of producers who planted intercropped corn, from 14 to 21 percent of ejidatarios.

Table 6.2
Percentage change in the use of cultivated land, 1990 and 1994

Crop	% change in cultivated area 1990-94		Area in 1994 % of cultivated land
	Rainfed	Irrigated	
Corn, monocropped	14.2	64.0	42.6
Corn, intercropped	66.7	100.0	6.7
Corn, total	19.8	65.4	49.3
Beans, monocropped	55.3	-20.0	9.5
Beans intercropped	33.3	0.0	2.4
Beans, total	50.0	-18.2	11.9
Wheat	0.0	-41.4	2.8
Other basic grains, monocropped (not corn, beans, or wheat)	-18.2	-50.0	4.6
Oil seeds, monocropped	-31.3	-43.8	4.4
Fruits and vegetables, monocropped	9.1	-21.4	6.8
Fodder, monocropped	106.4	11.1	15.2
Traditional exports, monocropped	12.5	0.0	3.5
Other crops, intercropped (not corn or beans)	11.1	-50.0	1.7
All	24.3	-10.3	100

Bean cultivation expanded by 50 percent on rainfed land but fell by 18 percent on irrigated land (table 6.2), where beans, as other traditional crops, are being replaced by corn. The proportion of ejidatarios who cultivate intercropped beans rose from 11 to 15 percent (table 6.1). Corn and beans are overwhelmingly the most important crops, occupying 57 percent of the total cultivated land in the ejido.

Other traditional crops such as wheat, basic grains, and oil seeds were displaced by the expansion of corn on irrigated land and of corn and beans on rainfed land. In irrigated zones, the area in wheat fell by 59 percent, the area in oil seeds by 44 percent, and the area in other basic grains by 50 percent.

There was a very strong expansion in the area planted in fodder on rainfed land (106 percent) and in the share of ejidatarios who cultivate fodder (from 9 to 11 percent). This phenomenon accompanied the expansion of cattle in the ejido sector. The increase in corn cultivation, through the use of stalks as feed, also supported the expansion in cattle raising.

Another important change was an increase in the percentage of ejidatarios who cultivate fruits and vegetables but without change in the area planted. This last information reflects the ejido's difficulty in adopting those crops which, through implementation of NAFTA, have a comparative advantage. The ejido's ability to adapt was limited by lack of access to credit and technical assistance. The net effect was an insignificant change in the area used for the cultivation of fruits and vegetables between 1990 and 1994. The area planted in traditional export crops increased, particularly in irrigated areas, suggesting that agriculture—if the proper conditions apply—can be responsive to market incentives.

For all crops, the cultivated rainfed area increased by 24 percent. As we have seen, this was due to the reduction of natural pastures and fallow land. The change in irrigated area between 1990 and 1994 was not statistically significant.

Changes by Farm Size

In tables 6.3 through 6.6, we analyze the changes in the use of cultivated land by two groups of farms: those above and those below 5 ha NRE, or small and large. The percentage of ejidatarios with larger farms who produced monocropped corn increased, while the percentage of small farmers who produced monocropped corn decreased. The participation of both types of producers in intercropped corn increased, but this increase was much stronger among smaller farmers. In 1994, corn cultivation covered 68 percent of the land on small farms and 42 percent of the land on large farms. Corn and beans together occupied 82 percent of the cultivated area on small farms and 53 percent on large farms.

A detailed analysis of the sources of change in corn cultivation by farm size is carried out in table 6.7. Expansion of the total area planted in corn was 20 percent on rainfed land. This increase originated primarily from the cultivation of monocropped corn (66 percent). Small ejidatarios contributed 35.4 percent of the increase in corn cultivation on rainfed land. On these farms, monocropped corn increased by 10.8 percent, and participation in intercropped corn rose by 24.7 percent. Larger farms were at the origin of the dramatic expansion of corn cultivation on rainfed land: 65 percent of the increase occurred on large farms, 55 percent of it in monocropping and 10 percent in intercropping.

Table 6.3
Use of cultivated land on large farms (> 5 ha NRE), 1990 and 1994

		1990	1994	Test
Corn, monocropped				
Percentage of farmers	%	66.4	73.6	++
Average rainfed area	ha	2.94	3.66	++
Average irrigated area	ha	0.45	0.85	++
Percentage of cultivated land				
Rainfed	%	41.4	38.9	n.a.
Irrigated	%	17.5	36.5	n.a.
Total	%	35.0	38.4	n.a.
Corn, intercropped				
Percentage of farmers	%	8.4	12.0	++
Average rainfed area	ha	0.26	0.38	
Average irrigated area	ha	0.03	0.02	
Percentage of cultivated land				
Rainfed	%	3.6	4.0	n.a.
Irrigated	%	1.0	0.8	n.a.
Total	%	2.9	3.4	n.a.
Beans, monocropped				
Percentage of farmers	%	19.7	23.9	++
Average rainfed area	ha	0.51	0.98	
Average irrigated area	ha	0.21	0.16	++
Percentage of cultivated land				
Rainfed	%	7.2	10.4	n.a.
Irrigated	%	8.0	6.9	n.a.
Total	%	7.4	9.7	n.a.

		1990	1994	Test
Oil seeds, monocropped				
Percentage of farmers	%	10.4	5.7	--
Average rainfed area	ha	0.71	0.48	
Average irrigated area	ha	0.37	0.20	--
Percentage of cultivated land				
Rainfed	%	9.9	5.1	n.a.
Irrigated	%	14.2	8.6	n.a.
Total	%	11.1	5.8	n.a.
Fruits and vegetables, monocropped				
Percentage of farmers	%	21.8	24.1	
Average rainfed area	ha	0.61	0.66	
Average irrigated area	ha	0.25	0.21	
Percentage of cultivated land				
Rainfed	%	8.6	7.0	n.a.
Irrigated	%	9.7	9.2	n.a.
Total	%	8.9	7.5	n.a.
Fodder, monocropped				
Percentage of farmers	%	15.3	18.4	++
Average rainfed area	ha	1.01	2.16	++
Average irrigated area	ha	0.18	0.20	
Percentage of cultivated land				
Rainfed	%	14.2	23.0	n.a.
Irrigated	%	6.9	8.5	n.a.
Total	%	12.2	20.1	n.a.

Beans, intercropped					**Traditional exports, monocropped**			
Percentage of farmers	%	4.7	7.1	++	Percentage of farmers	%	7.8	9.0
Average rainfed area	ha	0.08	0.14	++	Average rainfed area	ha	0.28	0.34
Average irrigated area	ha	0.01	0.00		Average irrigated area	ha	0.13	0.14
Percentage of cultivated land					Percentage of cultivated land			
Rainfed	%	1.1	1.5	n.a.	Rainfed	%	4.0	3.7	n.a.
Irrigated	%	0.6	0.1	n.a.	Irrigated	%	5.1	5.8	n.a.
Total	%	1.0	1.3	n.a.	Total	%	4.3	4.1	n.a.
Wheat					**Other crops, intercropped (not corn or beans)**			
Percentage of farmers	%	9.5	4.6	– –	Percentage of farmers	%	7.2	8.3
Average rainfed area	ha	0.02	0.01		Average rainfed area	ha	0.10	0.09
Average irrigated area	ha	0.65	0.40	– –	Average irrigated area	ha	0.05	0.03
Percentage of cultivated land					Percentage of cultivated land			
Rainfed	%	0.2	0.0	n.a.	Rainfed	%	1.4	0.9	n.a.
Irrigated	%	25.2	17.2	n.a.	Irrigated	%	1.9	1.1	n.a.
Total	%	6.9	3.5	n.a.	Total	%	1.5	1.0	n.a.
Other basic grains, monocropped (not corn, beans, or wheat)					**All crops**			
Percentage of farmers	%	12.7	10.4		Number of observations		677	619
Average rainfed area	ha	0.60	0.51		Average rainfed area	ha	7.11	9.42	++
Average irrigated area	ha	0.25	0.12		Average irrigated area	ha	2.59	2.32
Percentage of cultivated land					Percentage of cultivated land			
Rainfed	%	8.5	5.4	n.a.	Rainfed	%	100.0	100.0	n.a.
Irrigated	%	9.8	5.2	n.a.	Irrigated	%	100.0	100.0	n.a.
Total	%	8.8	5.4	n.a.	Total	%	100.0	100.0	n.a.

Note: n.a. indicates test of difference not applicable.

Table 6.4
Use of cultivated land on small farms (≤5 ha NRE), 1990 and 1994

		1990	1994	Test
Corn, monocropped				
Percentage of farmers	%	73.8	69.3	– –
Average rainfed area	ha	1.71	1.77	n.a.
Average irrigated area	ha	0.09	0.10	n.a.
Percentage of cultivated land				
Rainfed	%	58.6	53.8	n.a.
Irrigated	%	38.8	38.3	n.a.
Total	%	57.1	52.7	n.a.
Corn, intercropped				
Percentage of farmers	%	18.6	27.3	++
Average rainfed area	ha	0.29	0.51	++
Average irrigated area	ha	0.00	0.02	++
Percentage of cultivated land				
Rainfed	%	9.8	15.4	n.a.
Irrigated	%	1.3	6.3	n.a.
Total	%	9.2	14.8	n.a.
Beans, monocropped				
Percentage of farmers	%	15.2	18.3	
Average rainfed area	ha	0.29	0.30	
Average irrigated area	ha	0.02	0.02	
Percentage of cultivated land				
Rainfed	%	9.8	9.1	n.a.
Irrigated	%	7.1	6.7	n.a.
Total	%	9.6	9.0	n.a.

		1990	1994	Test
Oil seeds, monocropped				
Percentage of farmers	%	1.2	1.1	
Average rainfed area	ha	0.03	0.03	
Average irrigated area	ha	0.00	0.00	
Percentage of cultivated land				
Rainfed	%	1.1	0.8	n.a.
Irrigated	%	1.1	1.1	n.a.
Total	%	1.1	0.8	n.a.
Fruits and vegetables, monocropped				
Percentage of farmers	%	8.9	13.9	++
Average rainfed area	ha	0.11	0.14	
Average irrigated area	ha	0.05	0.04	
Percentage of cultivated land				
Rainfed	%	3.8	4.4	n.a.
Irrigated	%	20.7	15.2	n.a.
Total	%	5.1	5.1	n.a.
Fodder, monocropped				
Percentage of farmers	%	4.4	6.3	
Average rainfed area	ha	0.06	0.09	
Average irrigated area	ha	0.03	0.03	
Percentage of cultivated land				
Rainfed	%	2.0	2.6	n.a.
Irrigated	%	11.8	12.4	n.a.
Total	%	2.7	3.3	n.a.

Beans, intercropped				
Percentage of farmers	%	15.2	20.7	++
Average rainfed area	ha	0.15	0.17	++
Average irrigated area	ha	0.00	0.01	++
Percentage of cultivated land				
Rainfed	%	5.1	5.1	n.a.
Irrigated	%	0.7	3.6	n.a.
Total	%	4.8	5.0	n.a.
Wheat				
Percentage of farmers	%	1.7	1.5	
Average rainfed area	ha	0.02	0.03	
Average irrigated area	ha	0.01	0.01	
Percentage of cultivated land				
Rainfed	%	0.8	0.8	n.a.
Irrigated	%	4.1	3.9	n.a.
Total	%	1.0	1.0	n.a.
Other basic grains, monocropped (not corn, beans, or wheat)				
Percentage of farmers	%	7.1	5.4	
Average rainfed area	ha	0.12	0.09	
Average irrigated area	ha	0.01	0.01	
Percentage of cultivated land				
Rainfed	%	4.0	2.7	n.a.
Irrigated	%	6.2	3.8	n.a.
Total	%	4.2	2.8	n.a.
Traditional exports, monocropped				
Percentage of farmers	%	5.2	4.6	
Average rainfed area	ha	0.07	0.06	
Average irrigated area	ha	0.02	0.02	
Percentage of cultivated land				
Rainfed	%	2.3	1.7	n.a.
Irrigated	%	6.9	6.5	n.a.
Total	%	2.6	2.0	n.a.
Other crops, intercropped (not corn or beans)				
Percentage of farmers	%	6.9	13.8	++
Average rainfed area	ha	0.08	0.12	++
Average irrigated area	ha	0.00	0.01	
Percentage of cultivated land				
Rainfed	%	2.7	3.6	n.a.
Irrigated	%	1.5	2.3	n.a.
Total	%	2.6	3.5	n.a.
All crops				
Number of observations		888	843	
Average rainfed area	ha	2.93	3.29	++
Average irrigated area	ha	0.24	0.25	
Percentage of cultivated land				
Rainfed	%	100.0	100.0	n.a.
Irrigated	%	100.0	100.0	n.a.
Total	%	100.0	100.0	n.a.

Note: n.a. indicates test of difference not applicable.

Table 6.5
Percentage change in cultivated land use on large farms (> 5 ha NRE), 1990 and 1994

Crop	% change in cultivated area 1990-94		Area in 1994 % of cultivated land
	Rainfed	Irrigated	
Corn, monocropped	24.5	88.9	38.4
Corn, intercropped	46.2	-33.3	3.4
Corn, total	26.3	81.3	41.8
Beans, monocropped	92.2	-23.8	9.7
Beans, intercropped	75.0	-100.0	1.3
Beans, total	89.8	-27.3	11.0
Wheat	-50.0	-38.5	3.5
Other basic grains, monocropped			
(not corn, beans, or wheat)	-15.0	-52.0	5.4
Oil seeds, monocropped	-32.4	-45.9	5.8
Fruits and vegetables, monocropped	8.2	-16.0	7.5
Fodder, monocropped	113.9	11.1	20.1
Traditional exports, monocropped	21.4	7.7	4.1
Other land, intercropped			
(not corn or beans)	-10.0	-40.0	1.0
All	32.5	-10.4	100

Table 6.6
Percentage change in cultivated land use on small farms (≤ 5 ha NRE), 1990 and 1994

Crop	% change in cultivated area 1990-94		Area in 1994 % of cultivated land
	Rainfed	Irrigated	
Corn, monocropped	3.5	11.1	52.7
Corn, intercropped	75.9	566.7	14.8
Corn, total	14.0	29.0	67.5
Beans, monocropped	3.4	0.0	9.0
Beans, intercropped	13.3	400.0	5.0
Beans, total	6.8	36.4	14.0
Wheat	50.0	0.0	1.0
Other basic grains, monocropped			
(not corn, bean, or wheat)	-25.0	0.0	2.8
Oil seeds, monocropped	0.0	0.0	0.8
Fruits and vegetables, monocropped	27.3	-20.0	5.1
Fodder, monocropped	50.0	0.0	3.3
Traditional exports, monocropped	-14.3	0.0	2.0
Other land, intercropped			
(not corn or beans)	50.0	150.0	3.5
All	12.3	4.2	100

Table 6.7
Change in land used for corn, 1990 and 1994

	1990 Area by ejidatario		1994 Area by ejidatario		Change 1990-1994	
	ha	%	ha	%	%	source
Rainfed area						
Corn, monocropped and intercropped						
All farms	2.55	100.0	3.06	100.0	20.1	100.0
Small farms	1.09	42.8	1.27	41.6	16.7	35.4
Large farms	1.46	57.2	1.79	58.4	22.7	64.6
Corn, monocropped						
All farms	2.27	89.1	2.61	85.2	14.8	65.6
Small farms	0.93	36.6	0.99	32.3	5.9	10.8
Large farms	1.34	52.5	1.62	52.9	21.0	54.8
Corn, intercropped						
All farms	0.28	10.9	0.45	14.8	63.7	34.4
Small farms	0.16	6.2	0.28	9.3	80.0	24.7
Large farms	0.12	4.6	0.17	5.5	42.1	9.7
Irrigated area						
Corn, monocropped and intercropped						
All farms	0.27	100.0	0.45	100.0	67.9	100.0
Small farms	0.05	18.8	0.07	14.8	32.0	8.9
Large farms	0.22	81.2	0.38	85.2	76.2	91.1
Corn, monocropped						
All farms	0.25	94.3	0.43	95.6	70.1	97.4
Small farms	0.05	18.2	0.06	12.3	13.7	3.7
Large farms	0.20	76.1	0.38	83.2	83.6	93.7
Corn, intercropped						
All farms	0.02	5.7	0.02	4.4	30.9	2.6
Small farms	0.00	0.6	0.01	2.5	582.2	5.2
Large farms	0.01	5.1	0.01	2.0	-35.2	-2.6

The cultivation of corn on irrigated land experienced even more spectacular growth: cultivated area grew by 68 percent. Of this increase, 91 percent originated on large farms. This contribution of large farms was almost exclusively in pure stands (93.7 percent), compared to a slight decrease in the intercropped area of 2.6 percent. Small farms only contributed 8.9 percent to the increase in corn cultivation on irrigated land. They gained 3.7 percentage points in monocropped cultivation and 5.2 percentage points in intercropped cultivation. Consequently, the increase in corn production on irrigated land was mostly due to large producers as well.

To summarize, the increases in areas sown with corn by farm size were the following:

> *Corn on Rainfed Land*
> Small farms   16.7%
> Large farms   22.7%
>
> *Corn on Irrigated Land*
> Small farms   32.0%
> Large farms   76.2%

The percentage contribution of each farm class to the increase in area was the following:

> *Corn on Rainfed Land*
> Small farms   35.4%
> Large farms   64.6%
>
> *Corn on Irrigated Land*
> Small farms   8.9%
> Large farms   91.1%

Wheat and oilseeds production fell as larger farmers abandoned these crops for corn, beans, and fodder (table 6.3). The selective expansion of cultivated area for fruits and vegetables is confined to small producers with rainfed land. The number of small-farm ejidatarios who produce these crops increased from 9 to 14 percent (table 6.4). Fodder production increased on rainfed land on large farms. For all crops, the cultivated rainfed area grew by 12.3 percent on small farms. On large farms it grew by 32.5 percent because there was more opportunity for cultivating land previously left fallow or used for pastures.

7

Corn and Bean Cultivation

Production and Yield

In this chapter, the characteristics of corn and bean producers will be analyzed. To characterize their yields and the technology they use, only cases of monocropped cultivation are considered, since inter-cropped corn is a highly heterogeneous farming system that is diffi-cult to compare across observations.

Corn

In table 7.1, we observe that the area sown with corn by each ejida-tario in the spring–summer season increased between 1990 and 1994 from 2.19 to 3.17 hectares (45 percent) on irrigated land and from 3.20 to 3.68 hectares (15 percent) on rainfed land. These numbers reflect the rising importance of corn cultivation. In the fall–winter season, these areas also increased. However, since there are fewer observa-tions, the variance of the observed areas is high and these changes are not significant. In the spring–summer season, yields fell by 21 percent on irrigated land and by 3 percent on rainfed land. The fall in yields was partially due to unfavorable weather in 1994. This hypothesis is supported by comparing the harvested area in relation to the culti-vated area in each year: in 1990 harvested area was 94 percent on irri-gated and 93 percent on rainfed land, but in 1994 it fell to 84 percent on irrigated land and 83 percent on rainfed land. The weather should have had a stronger negative effect on rainfed-cultivation yields, but the equally large decline in yields on irrigated land suggests there was an additional effect of technological retrogression which aug-mented the climatic effect. Irrigated agriculture, which uses more modern inputs, was apparently affected more severely than rainfed

Table 7.1
Corn cultivation, 1990 and 1994

	Spring-summer season			Fall-winter season		
	1990	*1994*	*Test*	*1990*	*1994*	*Test*
Production per ejidatario with monocropped corn						
Cultivated area (ha)						
Irrigated	2.19	3.17	++	3.64	4.05	
Rainfed	3.20	3.68	++	2.24	2.41	
Harvested area (ha)						
Irrigated	2.11	2.67		2.92	4.00	
Rainfed	2.99	2.96		1.74	2.14	++
Production (tons)						
Irrigated	4.93	5.50		5.72	21.84	++
Rainfed	3.46	3.74		2.50	2.24	
Yield (tons/ha)						
Irrigated	1.99	1.58	- -	1.85	3.85	++
Rainfed	1.12	1.09		1.33	1.01	- -
Ratio harvested/cultivated (%)						
Irrigated	94.1	84.2	- -	92.2	98.3	
Rainfed	93.4	83.9	- -	91.6	91.5	
Yields under different technologies (tons/ha)						
Corn, irrigated						
Local seeds						
without fertilizer	1.36	1.37		1.45	0.52	- -
Local seeds						
with fertilizer	2.16	1.69		2.00	2.34	
Test	++	+		++	++	
Improved seeds						
with fertilizer	2.36	1.85		3.14	5.73	++
Test				++	++	
Corn, rainfed						
Local seeds						
without fertilizer	0.84	0.80		1.32	0.99	- -
Local seeds						
with fertilizer	1.19	1.18		1.34	0.89	- -
Test	++	++				
Improved seeds						
with fertilizer	1.93	2.08		2.00	1.68	
Test	++	++			++	

agriculture, which uses more traditional technology. Thus the decline in the use of technology between 1990 and 1994 is reflected in a greater decline in yields on irrigated land.

Comparing the effect of technology in the spring–summer season on corn yield in each year and for each mode of cultivation (irrigated or rainfed), we see that in 1990 the yields under irrigation increased from 1.36 to 2.16 tons/ha with the use of fertilizers, and they increased further with the combined use of fertilizers and improved seeds (from 2.16 to 2.36 ton/ha). On rainfed land, yields also rose, from 0.84 to 1.19 tons/ha, with the adoption of fertilizers, and from 1.19 to 1.93 tons/ha with the joint adoption of fertilizers and improved seeds. This technological regularity was maintained on rainfed land in 1994. The yields increased from 0.80 to 1.18 tons/ha with the adoption of fertilizers and to 2.08 tons/ha with the joint use of improved seeds and fertilizers.

As we have seen, aggregate corn yields have fallen, particularly on irrigated land. The distribution of this decline in yields among farm sizes (table 7.2) on irrigated land differs from rainfed land. On irrigated land, the fall in yields occurred on farms in the interval of 5 to 18 ha NRE. In contrast, on rainfed land, it is the smallest producers (under 2 ha NRE) who experienced the fall in yields, while yields of larger farmers (10–18 ha NRE and > 18 ha NRE) remained constant. This contrast again suggests a negative technological shock on larger, technified, irrigated farms and a negative but weaker shock on smaller, traditional, rainfed farms, probably more weather- than technology-induced.

The Intensity of Labor Use

Since family labor is cheaper than wage labor, small producers use more family labor as a percentage of total labor, and they use more family labor per hectare of a particular crop (Eswaran and Kotwal 1986). In this section, the sources of labor in corn and bean cultivation are analyzed, as well as the intensity of labor per hectare. Labor use on small and large farms is also compared.

The first observation, based on the results presented in table 7.3, is the strong dominance of family labor in ejido agriculture: 64.6 percent of ejidatarios did not use wage labor for any tasks related to corn cultivation. For bean cultivation (not reported in the table), this number was even higher, reaching 77.2 percent. The percentage of ejidatarios who used only wage labor in these two crops were 5.5 and 3.9, respectively.

The second observation is that those who use only family labor for corn use more labor per hectare than those who use only wage labor.

Thus, for all tasks in corn production, median use for those who utilize only family labor was 20 days work per hectare compared to 13.3 for those who use only wage labor, a 34 percent difference. This significant difference is also observed in plowing corn, with a 65 percent difference.

Table 7.2
Cultivated area and yields of corn by farm size, 1990 and 1994
(Ejidatarios cultivating monocropped corn, spring-summer season)

	Farm size (ha NRE)							
	All	< 2	2–5	5–10	10–18	≥ 18	< 5	≥ 5
Cultivated area (ha)								
Corn, irrigated								
1990	2.19	0.81	1.33	2.09	3.88	5.24	1.17	3.08
1994	3.17	0.68	1.49	2.24	2.35	10.93	1.11	5.07
Test	++				− −	++		++
Corn, rainfed								
1990	3.20	1.47	3.24	4.26	4.03	7.26	2.38	4.56
1994	3.68	1.45	3.21	4.27	5.34	7.89	2.58	5.24
Test	++				++		++	+
Yield (tons/ha)			Test	Test	Test	Test	Test	Test
Corn, irrigated								
1990	1.99	1.79	1.91	1.86	2.60	1.90	1.87	2.10
1994	1.58	1.75	1.59	1.07	1.26	2.09 +	1.67	1.49
Test	− −			− −	− −			− −
Corn, rainfed								
1990	1.12	1.18	1.12	1.23	0.97 − −	0.96	1.15	1.08
1994	1.09	0.93	1.14 ++	1.17	1.07	1.08	1.07	1.12
Test			− −					

Comparing farm sizes, it can be seen that small farms used 29 percent more labor per hectare than large farms. This higher labor intensity applies to family labor and, surprisingly, to wage labor as well. For all agricultural labor in corn cultivation, the median days of work paid per hectare were 22.2 on farms below 5 ha NRE and 5.2 on those above 5 ha NRE. For family labor, the median days of work per hectare fell from 21.4 on small farms to 18.9 on large farms. Total labor used, including wage and family labor, was also higher on smaller farms (24.5 as opposed to 19.0 days of work/hectare). This inverse relationship between labor per hectare and farm size was expected, confirming the relative advantage of small farms in the access to cheap family labor.

The higher intensity of use of wage labor on small farms is, however, surprising. Since both family labor and wage labor decreased as farm size increased, the ratio of family labor to total labor per hectare stayed constant (around 94–95 percent) across different farm sizes. This could indicate that wage labor is more efficiently used on small farms than on large ones because stricter supervision is possible with more family labor and fewer employees. It could also suggest that small farms work the land more intensively, using more wage labor and more family labor. More likely, it indicates a technological substitution where, on a per hectare basis, larger producers use more machinery and smaller producers use more labor. Thus the latter use more of all kinds of labor.

Agricultural Technology and Technical Assistance

Overall Access

In general, the use of technology fell very sharply between 1990 and 1994, and the state almost completely stopped providing technical assistance to the social sector.

Technology can be characterized as follows: use of local and improved seeds, use of natural and chemical fertilizers, use of agrochemicals, and access to technical assistance services. These variables were studied for corn and bean cultivation in both seasons and for each farmer's most important crop apart from corn or beans. The different ways in which inputs are acquired—self-provision and social, private, and official sources—will also be analyzed.

In table 7.4, it can be seen that on a global level the use of technology declined sharply between the two years. For example, the percentage of those who use fertilizers was 61 percent in 1990; it fell to 52 percent in 1994, a decrease of 15 percent. The use of improved seeds fell by 24 percent, and farmers used more local seeds as substitutes. In 1990, 53.4 percent of producers used some type of chemical (herbicide, insecticide, or fungicide) in agricultural activities. Four years later this number fell to 44.5 percent, a 17 percent decline. Finally, it is in the availability of technical assistance that the fall was most dramatic. In 1990, 59.6 percent of producers said they received this service. However, by 1994 only 8.6 percent of producers received it, a reduction of 86 percent. The withdrawal of the state's technical assistance services has not been compensated by a private or social supply of these services, leaving the ejidatarios with an alarming vacuum in technological assistance.

It can also be observed that official sources withdrew from the input market. Table 7.4 shows that the frequency with which ejidatarios

Table 7.3
Intensity of labor use in corn by farm size, 1994

| | Use only wage labor | | Use only family labor | | Test: family vs. wage | All Labor | | | |
| | | | | | | Total labor | | Ejidatarios who do not use wage labor (%) | Family labor/total (%) |
	N	Median days work/ha	N	Median days work/ha		N	Median days work/ha		
Plowing									
All producers	91	1.5	689	4.3	++	891	4.4	77.3	90.3
<5 (ha NRE)	49	2.5	382	4.0	++	481	4.3	79.4	90.1
≥5 (ha NRE)	42	0.8	307	5.0	++	410	4.8	74.9	
Test: <5 vs. ≥5		++		++					
Weeding									
All producers	85	4.0	776	4.8		1013	5.0	76.6	92.1
<5 (ha NRE)	42	5.2	415	5.3		526	6.0	78.9	91.4
≥5 (ha NRE)	43	1.8	361	3.5		487	4.0	74.1	
Test: <5 vs. ≥5		++		++			++		
All agricultural labor									
All producers	59	13.3	690	20.0	++	1068	20.5	64.6	94.6
<5 (ha NRE)	28	22.2	381	21.4		557	24.5	68.4	93.6
≥5 (ha NRE)	31	5.2	309	18.9	++	511	19.0	60.5	
Test: <5 vs. ≥5		++		++			++		

had access to technology and technological assistance through official sources fell from 62 percent in 1990 to 9 percent in 1994, an 85 percent decline. The vacuum official sources left was only partly filled by social organizations (different types of organizations within the ejido) and by the private sector. Even though the social sector's participation increased by 30 percent, its role was still modest in 1994. The private sector's participation increased by only 4 percent, but it became the principal source of technology acquisition in 1994, after playing a secondary role in 1990 relative to the official sector.

Corn

Table 7.5 shows that in both seasons the use of technology in corn production declined. (The only exception is the adoption of improved seeds in the fall–winter season.) For example, the percentage of farmers who use chemical products in the fall–winter season fell from 77.4 in 1990 to 66.5 in 1994. With respect to fertilizers, there was no significant decline in the more technified fall–winter season, but in the spring–summer season, when most farmers are cultivating corn, the percentage fell from 61.6 to 53.1. The same pattern is present in technical assistance. In the fall–winter season of 1990, 66.1 percent of producers received assistance. Only 10.0 percent received assistance in 1994. In the spring–summer season, the change in percentage receiving assistance was even more dramatic—falling from 56.5 percent to only 4.2 percent.

However, the number of households producing corn in the fall–winter season rose from 14.6 percent in 1990 to 17.9 percent in 1994 (number of cases reported in tables 7.4 and 7.5). This change reflects the entry of ejidatarios who use more advanced technology into irrigated corn production in the fall–winter season. But only in the increased use of improved seeds was greater technification visible. While access to technical assistance collapsed dramatically (a 56.1 percent drop for the fall–winter season and a drop of 52.3 percent in the spring–summer season), it was always higher among fall–winter than spring–summer producers, indicating the greater commercial orientation of the former.

A similar technological difference across seasons occurred in the use of seeds. In the spring–summer season the percentage of farmers who use improved seeds did not change significantly, but in the fall–winter season the percentage of producers who use improved seeds increased. There was thus a technological differentiation in favor of the producers who cultivate corn in the fall–winter season. The use of fertilizers fell between these periods, but a substitution of natural fertilizer by chemical fertilizer can be observed, particularly in the

Table 7.4

Use of technology and access to technology in the ejido, 1990 and 1994

(In corn, beans, and most important crop other than corn or beans)

	1990	1994	Percentage change 1990-94	Test
Number of cases	1615	1543		
Use of technology				
Percentage of ejidatarios who use each technology or service				
Improved seeds	23.2	17.7	-23.7	– –
Fertilizer	61.0	52.0	-14.8	– –
Natural fertilizer	9.2	3.5	-62.0	– –
Chemical fertilizer	54.9	49.6	-9.7	– –
Chemical products [a]	53.4	44.5	-16.7	– –
Technical assistance	59.6	8.6	-85.6	– –
Access to technology				
Frequency with which each source of acquisition is used				
Self-provision	19.3	8.7	-54.9	– –
Social	11.5	14.9	29.6	++
Private	56.9	59.4	4.4	
Official	62.0	9.3	-85.0	– –

[a] Includes herbicides, insecticides, and fungicides.

Table 7.5

Use of technology, 1990 and 1994

(Number of cases and percentage of ejidatarios using each technology)

	Corn			Beans			Other crops		
	1990	1994	Test	1990	1994	Test	1990	1994	Test
Fall-winter season									
Number of cases	237	276		78	106		163	140	
Improved seeds	4.6	15.5	++	15.3	6.0		68.1	46.0	– –
Fertilizers	50.2	45.2		35.5	29.0		67.1	57.4	
Natural	7.9	3.2		6.5	2.0		4.5	2.9	
Chemical	43.0	42.0		29.0	27.0		64.3	54.5	
Chemical products	77.4	67.0	– –	71.2	49.8	~	58.0	41.5	
Technical assistance	66.1	10.1	– –	60.6	9.3	– –	68.4	19.3	– –
Spring-summer season									
Number of cases	1071	1035		357	419		240	271	
Improved seeds	10.4	8.4	'	6.3	2.3	– –	36.4	18.3	– –
Fertilizers	61.6	53.2	– –	38.1	37.9		52.7	45.1	– –
Natural	8.4	2.8	– –	7.1	3.2	– –	8.1	3.7	– –
Chemical	54.5	50.8		31.2	35.2		48.1	41.4	
Chemical products	39.0	33.6		31.7	29.0		44.2	35.6	– –
Technical assistance	56.5	4.2	– –	57.4	3.1	– –	62.9	6.4	– –

spring–summer season. Among producers who use fertilizers, the composition of use was the following:

Corn	1990	1994	Test of Difference
Fall–Winter Season			
Natural fertilizer	15.7%	7.1%	
Chemical fertilizer	85.7%	92.5%	
Spring–Summer Season			
Natural fertilizer	13.6%	5.3%	—
Chemical fertilizer	88.5%	95.5%	

Similar patterns of technological decline are observed in beans and other crops without, in these cases, even a compensatory increase in the use of improved seeds.

Acquisition of Inputs

In table 7.6, the different sources of input acquisition are analyzed. The strong withdrawal of official sources is obvious, as well as the rise of private suppliers. The withdrawal of official sources is the result of an explicit change in federal government policy, reducing the interventionist role of the state in the countryside. As a consequence, decisions over the acquisition and use of inputs have to be made by producers and not by the state. Producers now have to purchase their own supplies in the private or social sector. However, while government intervention has been sharply reduced, the gap in services has been only partially filled by other sources, resulting in a decline in technological levels.

The rise of the private sector's role in the access to modern inputs is particularly notable in improved seeds, chemical fertilizers, and chemical products. Access to technological assistance from the private sector rose, but the extent of coverage was very small compared to the total number of farmers. Acquisition of improved seeds shifted from the public to the private sector.

With respect to chemical fertilizers, the decline of the official sector and the strong rise in acquisition from private sources reflects the sale and disintegration of FERTIMEX, which helped to create small companies for the commercialization of this input.

In the field of technical assistance, a relative decline in the role of the official sector can be observed among those who received technical assistance. This role is taken up in different proportions by other sources, principally private and social. The fall of the official sector between 1990 and 1994 is from 92.2 percent to 65.6 percent in the

Table 7.6
Sources of acquisition of technology, 1990 and 1994
(Percentage of technology transactions originating from each source)

	Self-provision			Social			Private			Official		
	1990	1994	Test	1990	1994	Test	1990	1994	Test	1990	1994	Test
Corn, spring-summer season												
Local seeds	92.7	91.2		0.6	0.7		6.2	8.0		0.2	0.1	
Improved seeds	9.0	2.4		9.0	10.1		55.0	81.1	++	14.3	6.4	
Natural fertilizer	48.7	55.4		12.8	6.8		37.7	31.0		2.5	0.0	
Chemical fertilizer	3.3	3.1		7.1	9.8		50.6	80.3	++	34.6	5.8	– –
Chemical products [a]	4.3	2.7		7.9	5.4		75.7	88.0	++	9.4	1.5	– –
Technical assistance	6.4	17.4	++	0.8	11.4	++	0.4	5.5	++	92.2	65.6	– –

[a] See Table 7.4

spring–summer season. This reflects the decision by government authorities to include the cost of technical assistance in the financial cost of credit and to eliminate subsidies in this area. The rise of self-provision could be due to a misinterpretation of the questionnaire: when the financial cost of the technical assistance service was included in the cost of their credit, those surveyed believed they were providing their own access to technical assistance simply because they were paying for the service. Moreover, in this case the source was not clearly interpreted since it did not come directly from the social sector, nor from the private or official sectors.

Technology by Farm Size

In table 7.7, the changes in the technology of corn production are analyzed in the context of the producer typology. A contrast is made between small farms under 2 ha NRE, medium-sized farms between 2 and 10 ha NRE, and large farms of more than 10 ha NRE.

The first observation is that ejidatarios with larger farms make more use of technology, in both the fall–winter and spring–summer seasons. In 1994, in the spring–summer season, 2.7 percent of small farmers, 9.0 percent of medium-sized farmers, and 14.8 percent of large farmers used improved seeds. The use of chemical products was 18.1, 41.3, and 61.8 percent, respectively. Technical assistance was very low for all farm groups but higher on medium-sized and large farms compared to small farms. In the fall–winter season, when there are fewer but more technified producers, technological differences across farm sizes were less significant, except in the use of chemical products.

In table 7.5, we have seen that the only input that increased over the four years was improved corn seeds in the fall–winter season. Table 7.7 shows that this increase occurred across farm sizes and especially on large farms, where it rose from 3.9 to 18.2 percent. We can also see that the use of fertilizers declined pretty well across all farm sizes and seasons. Among farmers who use fertilizers, chemical fertilizers increased in the spring–summer season, particularly among small and medium-sized farmers. The few cases of technological progress were thus limited to the use of improved seeds on larger farms and the use of chemical fertilizers among fertilizer users.

The technological decline in other modern inputs such as chemical products affected every class of farmer. There was a general loss in access to technical assistance, and this loss was more severe for small than for large farmers.

Table 7.7
Technology used in corn production by farm size, 1990 and 1994

	Farm size (ha NRE)									
	Corn production, fall-winter					Corn production, spring-summer				
	≤2	2–10	Test [a]	>10	Test	≤2	2–10	Test	>10	Test
Ejidatarios using each technology or service (%)										
Improved seeds 1990	3.0	5.8		3.9		5.6	10.5	++	13.3	
Improved seeds 1994	7.8	14.0		18.2		2.7	9.0	++	14.8	++
% change	160.0	141.4		366.7		-51.8	-14.3		11.3	
Test				++					++	
Chemical products 1990	46.0	87.0	++	76.7		25.6	51.0	++	65.9	++
Chemical products 1994	40.2	69.2	++	69.8		18.1	41.3	++	61.8	++
% change	-12.6	-20.5		-9.0		-29.3	-19.0		-6.2	
Test				– –		– –	– –		– –	
Fertilizers 1990	48.1	50.3		50.6		62.6	61.1		53.7	
Fertilizers 1994	32.4	53.3		37.2		52.9	54.2		40.8	
% change	-32.6	6.0		-26.5	– –	-15.5	-11.3		-24.0	– –
Test										
Chemical fertilizers 1990	94.3	96.1		74.4		88.0	89.8		89.8	
Chemical fertilizers 1994	84.8	93.1		93.9		96.1	94.0		95.7	
% change	-10.1	-3.1		26.2		9.2	4.7		6.6	
Test				++		++	+			– –
Technical assistance 1990	83.4	57.4	–	69.3		41.9	64.4	++	67.1	
Technical assistance 1994	1.0	10.3		11.2		1.2	5.2	++	5.1	
% change	-98.8	-82.1		-83.8		-97.1	-91.9		-92.4	
Test	– –					– –				

[a] The test of difference of means is with respect to the immediately preceding class.

Finally, in table 7.8, irrigated and rainfed agriculture are contrasted with respect to corn cultivation in the spring–summer season. In 1994, a strong relationship is noted between farm size and technology, particularly in the case of rainfed agriculture. It is thus rainfed agriculture that most internalizes the technological dualism between small and large producers.

The technological decline that took place between 1990 and 1994 was omnipresent in irrigated and rainfed agriculture and on small and large farms. However, the magnitude of the change affected producers differently. On irrigated land, as measured by yields, large farmers lost more. The relationship between yield and farm size, which was positive in 1990, turned negative in 1994 with the decline in technological levels. In the case of rainfed agriculture, small farmers lost more and a regressive relationship was established, with yields increasing with farm size. The technological loss was thus larger for farmers who were already using less technology, which made the relationship between yields and farm size change from negative to positive.

Conclusion

As the data from the two surveys show, the ejido suffered a strong decline in technological levels, except in the use of improved seeds for corn in the fall–winter season. This technological decline was particularly sharp in the fall–winter season. During this season, there was some modernization in corn production due to the entry of technologically advanced producers seeking to take advantage of the price incentives. But the few technological gains were limited to farmers with large farms. In contrast, the technological decline in other inputs affected everybody. In rainfed agriculture, it is the small producers who lost more technological capacity and whose yields declined relatively more. In irrigated agriculture, where there is less technological dualism, larger farmers lost more. There is thus an inverse relationship between yield and farm size in irrigated land.

The sources of input supply moved from the public sector to the private sector in the case of corn and to the social sector in the case of beans. The most dramatic fall during the last four years was access to technical assistance, for both large and small farmers. There was only a partial reconversion from public to private sources of assistance. The majority of producers were left in an alarming institutional vacuum precisely at the moment when they needed to diversify and modernize their crops to remain competitive in the context of the broader economic reforms. Unless this institutional vacuum is filled,

Table 7.8
Summary of corn cultivation by farm size, spring-summer season, 1990 and 1994

	Irrigated Corn									Rainfed Corn								
	Farm size (ha NRE)									*Farm size (ha NRE)*								
	All	< 5	≥ 5	Test	≤ 2	2-10	Test	> 10	Test	All	< 5	≥ 5	Test	≤ 2	2-10	Test	> 10	Test
Ejidatarios who use each technology or service (%)																		
Improved seed																		
1990	23.6	3.9	40.9	++	*Insufficient number of observations*					8.7	7.8	10.3		6.7	10.9		6.9	
1994	15.6	7.3	23.3							8.8	5.4	13.7	++	3.8	9.0	+	12.9	+
% change		87.2	-43.0								-30.8	33.0		-43.3	-17.4		87.0	
Test		--																
Chemical products																		
1990	53.5	58.2	49.5							48.7	38.7	65.4		26.7	54.9		67.7	++
1994	27.4	25.3	29.4							44.8	33.2	61.4	++	18.3	45.2	++	67.9	++
% change		-56.5	-40.6								-14.2	-6.1		-31.5	-17.7		0.3	
Test		--										--		--				
Fertilizers																		
1990	71.4	76.3	67.2							60.3	63.9	54.5		65.4	61.9		49.5	
1994	51.4	55.0	48.2							53.7	59.1	45.9		54.4	59.4		39.3	
% change		-27.9	-28.3								-7.5	-15.8		-16.8	-4.0		-20.6	
Test												--		--			--	

Technical assistance

	1	2	3	4	5	6	7	8	9
1990	76.3	71.1	80.8 ++	58.0	52.1	67.9 ++	43.9	64.2 ++	65.3 ++
1994	4.0	0.3	7.3	5.0	4.5	5.7	1.9	6.4 +	4.3 +
% change		-99.6	-91.0		-91.4	-91.6	-95.7	-90.0	-93.4
Test		--	--		--	--	--	--	--

Production results (monocropped corn)

Cultivated area (ha)

	1	2	3	4	5	6	7	8	9
1990	2.19	1.17	3.08 ++	3.22	2.39	4.59 ++	1.47	3.68 ++	4.78 ++
1994	3.17	1.11	5.07 ++	3.62	2.60	5.09 ++	1.46	3.57 ++	5.73 ++
% change		-5.13	64.61		8.8	10.9	-0.68	-2.99	19.87
Test			++		++				+

Yields (tons/ha)

	1	2	3	4	5	6	7	8	9
1990	1.99	1.87	2.10	1.13	1.15	1.09	1.18	1.17	0.96 --
1994	1.58	1.67	1.49	1.09	1.06	1.13 ++	0.92	1.16 ++	1.09
% change		-10.70	-29.05		-7.83	3.67	-22.03	-0.85	13.54
Test			--						+

the reforms threaten the ejido with loss of competitiveness and eventual bankruptcy.

8

Mechanization, Animal Power, and Manual Tasks

Changes in the Degree of Mechanization, 1990–1994

In order to carry out an analysis of the mechanization of agricultural tasks, only producers who answered this part of the questionnaire are considered. The tasks of plowing, sowing, and weeding, the application of fertilizers and agrochemicals, and harvest and post-harvest activities are taken into account. These tasks are analyzed with respect to the technology applied in 1990 and 1994: manual, animal traction, or machinery.

Corn cultivation is analyzed in table 8.1. Only 17 percent of the ejidatarios cultivated corn in the 1994 fall–winter season, compared to 83 percent in the spring–summer season. However, those who cultivated during fall–winter used much more technology, and they usually used irrigation. In contrast, most cultivation during spring–summer was dominated by rainfed production, which uses more traditional technology.

Between 1990 and 1994, there was a strong increase in the mechanization of corn cultivation during the fall–winter season. The proportion of producers who use machinery increased from 7 to 16 percent for sowing, 0.2 to 7 percent for applying chemicals, and 3 to 9 percent for harvesting. The number of ejidatarios who manually carry out these tasks diminished correspondingly. There was no change in the use of animal traction, which is low in this season.

In the spring–summer season, the panorama is very different. Mechanization is lower and it increased only for harvesting. Intermediate technology, including the use of animals in sowing and in applying fertilizers, increased. More manual labor was used for weeding. Thus there was some advance in mechanization, but it was lower than that observed in the fall–winter season because the heterogeneity of corn producers in that season is much higher. In the spring–summer season, technological progress was uneven and heterogeneous.

Table 8.1
Mechanization in corn cultivation, 1990 and 1994
(Percentage using each type of technology)

| | Technology used | | | | | | | | |
| | Manual | | | Animal | | | Machinery | | |
	1990	1994	Test	1990	1994	Test	1990	1994	Test
Corn, fall-winter									
Type of task									
Plowing	55.6	49.1		13.8	14.0		30.2	33.2	
Sowing	88.3	80.6		4.5	3.3		6.7	16.2	++
Weeding	84.7	83.8		5.7	5.9		6.9	8.8	
Applying fertilizers and agrochemicals	86.2	77.6	– –	0.0	0.0		0.2	7.1	++
Harvesting	91.0	89.4		0.0	0.0		3.4	9.4	++
Post harvest	38.8	55.2	++	21.1	10.5	– –	13.6	8.2	
Corn, spring-summer									
Type of task									
Plowing	23.8	25.1		38.7	34.8		37.4	39.2	
Sowing	55.8	48.4	– –	26.7	31.7	++	17.3	19.9	
Weeding	56.6	65.0	++	30.1	22.8	– –	12.0	10.3	
Applying fertilizers and agrochemicals	70.7	62.9	– –	1.1	3.7	++	1.8	2.7	
Harvesting	89.4	85.9		2.4	2.4		3.1	6.3	++
Post harvest	30.8	44.2	++	12.2	11.2		14.1	7.6	– –

The higher mechanization of corn is contrasted with the strong decline in the mechanization of the other most important crop for each farmer, apart from corn and beans (table 8.2). The decline in technological level is quite evident. In the fall–winter and spring–summer seasons, machinery use fell and manual labor increased in almost all tasks. The use of animal traction hardly changed, indicating that it was human labor, not animal traction, that replaced machinery.

These results reflect the consequence of the important incentive differentials offered to corn cultivation. The cultivation of other crops was relatively less profitable and prices were less certain. The stimulus to corn increased the use of inputs for its production to the detriment of other crops. This can be partly explained by the policy of support prices, which guaranteed a minimum price for corn, thus securing not only an acceptable degree of profitability but, more importantly, a level of security that did not exist with other crops.

Table 8.2
Mechanization in the most important crop other than beans or corn, 1990 and 1994
(Percentage using each technology)

| | | | | *Technology used* | | | | | |
| | *Manual* | | | *Animal* | | | *Machinery* | | |
	1990	1994	test	1990	1994	test	1990	1994	test
Other crop, fall-winter									
Types of task									
Plowing	2.2	9.4		20.0	15.5		76.6	75.2	
Sowing	22.1	37.4	++	21.5	14.0		55.2	48.6	–
Weeding	34.5	58.5	++	13.8	7.1		21.2	15.9	
Applying fertilizers									
and agrochemicals	37.6	49.5	++	0.0	1.7		31.0	20.6	– –
Harvesting	39.2	56.2	++	1.2	1.6		46.6	35.1	– –
Post harvest	8.9	33.9	++	5.4	7.9		45.5	21.2	– –
Other crop, spring-summer									
Types of task									
Plowing	13.7	21.6	++	21.1	27.0		63.1	51.2	– –
Sowing	45.2	42.1	+	14.8	26.9	++	39.0	30.9	– –
Weeding	40.1	61.3	++	16.3	18.2		22.5	8.5	– –
Applying fertilizers									
and agrochemicals	51.4	54.6		0.2	3.0		21.4	11.1	– –
Harvesting	50.4	75.2	++	6.4	1.3		35.2	17.3	– –
Post harvest	13.8	39.7	++	6.2	8.1		35.9	17.8	– –

The contrast between increasing mechanization of corn in the fall–winter season and the partial mechanization or rise in animal traction in the spring–summer season, on the one hand, and the abandonment of mechanization and the increased use of manual labor for other crops, on the other, indicates a growing and rapid technological differentiation between crops and producers.

Tables 8.3 and 8.4 analyze the mechanization differentials between large and small farms in the spring–summer season and the changes they have experienced over time. In table 8.3, where corn is analyzed, it can be seen that the larger farms are systematically more mechanized in all tasks. For plowing, 48 percent of the large farms used machinery in 1994, compared to 34 percent of the small farms. For sowing, 28 percent of large farms and 15 percent of small farms used machinery. In contrast, small farms systematically make more use of animal traction; for plowing, 45 percent of small farms used animal traction, compared to 18 percent of large producers. The smallest producers also use more manual labor for weeding and harvesting, but these tasks are highly manual on all farms. Overall, there is a strong technological differentiation between farm sizes.

Table 8.3
Mechanization in spring-summer corn cultivation by farm size, 1990 and 1994
(Percentage using each technology)

Type of task	Manual			Animal			Machinery		
	< 5 ha NRE	≥ 5 ha NRE	Test	< 5 ha NRE	≥ 5 ha NRE	Test	< 5 ha NRE	≥ 5 ha NRE	Test
Plowing									
1990	15.6	37.7	++	52.8	14.6	– –	31.6	47.3	++
1994	20.2	33.2	+	44.7	18.3	– –	34.2	47.5	++
Test	++			– –					
Sowing									
1990	56.3	54.9		32.1	17.5	– –	11.5	27.3	++
1994	45.9	52.6		39.0	19.5	– –	15.1	27.9	++
Test	– –			++					
Weeding									
1990	55.9	57.6		34.1	23.3	– –	8.5	17.9	++
1994	67.0	61.6	– –	25.8	17.9		5.6	18.2	++
Test	++			– –			– –		
Applying fertilizers and agrochemicals									
1990	68.2	74.9	++	0.9	1.5		0.8	3.6	++
1994	60.6	66.9	+	5.1	1.5	–	1.8	4.1	++
Test		– –		++					
Harvest									
1990	91.7	85.4	–	2.0	3.1		1.9	5.3	++
1994	88.1	82.3	– –	2.8	1.6		2.8	12.0	++
Test								++	
Post harvest									
1990	30.4	31.4		13.7	9.5		10.9	19.6	++
1994	45.8	41.2		10.4	7.7		5.2	11.9	++
Test	++	++		– –			– –	– –	

Between 1990 and 1994, this technological dualism deepened. For large farms, there was no change in mechanization except for an increase in harvesting. In contrast, the increases in the use of manual labor (for plowing and weeding) and animal labor (for sowing and applying fertilizers and agrochemicals) took place exclusively on small farms.

In conclusion, there was a strong bias in mechanization favoring larger farms. This partly reflects the differential cost of labor between small and large farms, which favors the former, but it also reflects the bias in access to credit against small farmers. The fall in mechanization is more marked for small farms than for large farms. For small producers, the use of human labor, and in certain cases the use of animal traction, increased. Altogether, the period 1990–94 was a serious setback for the progress of mechanization in Mexican agriculture. It also led to the recomposition of a traditional peasant economy on smaller farms, with increasing use of animal traction and manual labor.

Table 8.4
Machinery and equipment: use and access, 1990 and 1994

	1990	1994	% change 1990-94	Test
Ejidatarios using each type of machinery and equipment (%)				
Tractor	45.2	43.7	-3.3	–
Threshing machine	9.8	8.7	-11.2	– –
Harvester	1.9	2.7	42.1	
Truck	8.8	8.9	1.1	
Pickup truck	19.7	20.5	4.1	
Fumigator	3.3	2.1	-36.4	– –
Chainsaw	1.8	2.1	16.7	+
Others	8.6	7.0	-18.6	
Access to technology through each source (%)				
Individual ownership	37.5	41.5	10.7	++
Collective ownership	13.8	18.9	37.0	++
Rental	73.8	63.7	-13.7	– –

Use of and Access to Machinery and Equipment

In general, there was either no change or a decline in the use of machinery and equipment between 1990 and 1994. As can be seen in table 8.4, the most important category of machinery is tractors; 45 percent of ejidatarios were using tractors in 1990. In 1994 this number fell to 44 percent, a small but significant decline. The use of threshing machines and fumigators also decreased. In terms of forms of access, rentals are dominant, but they declined sharply between 1990 and 1994. Access through collective organizations and through individual

Table 8.5
Forms of access to machinery and equipment, 1990 and 1994

% by type of machinery or equipment	1990	1994	Test
Tractor			
Individual ownership	22.8	16.4	– –
Collective ownership	13.9	19.6	++
Rental	59.7	62.4	
Threshing machine			
Individual ownership	3.1	7.1	+
Collective ownership	6.6	3.4	
Rental	89.6	89.5	
Harvester			
Individual ownership	8.5	5.4	
Collective ownership	8.7	9.6	
Rental	82.8	81.2	
Truck			
Individual ownership	19.8	19.5	
Collective ownership	4.5	8.8	
Rental	70.5	70.2	
Pickup truck			
Individual ownership	38.4	67.5	++
Collective ownership	1.0	2.5	
Rental	50.6	28.9	– –

ownership increased strongly. This underscores the importance of producers' organizations for ejidatarios as a means of access to machinery.

In table 8.5, the sources of access are detailed by type of machinery and equipment. For tractors, individual ownership decreased and access through collective ownership rose. For pickup trucks, individual ownership—which rose strongly—is dominant, in part due to the legalization of foreign vehicles during the period under study.

9

Livestock

Cattle Raising

Between 1990 and 1994, the number of ejidatarios owning cattle increased from 44.1 percent to 44.6 percent (table 9.1). The average number of cattle per ejidatario rose from 10.9 to 13.1, which implies that the total number of animals increased by 20 percent during the period. This indicates a rapid expansion of cattle-raising activity, which is associated with the profitability crisis in crops, the extensification of agriculture, and the use of animals as a source of security and savings, in particular for the capitalization of remittances.[1]

Other animal species experienced a different pattern. There was no change in the percentage of ejidatarios who own other animals, except in the case of pigs. The fall in the number of pigs corresponds to a process of concentration in animal ownership. The number of pigs per person rose by 17 percent at the same time that the number of people who own pigs fell by 16 percent. These two processes partially compensate for each other so that the total stock of pigs fell by only 1.6 percent. This process of concentration in animal ownership is also observed in poultry.

The 1994 survey gives information about the degree of market participation in each animal activity. It reveals a dualism in the levels of activity between those who sell animals and all others. The proportion of ejidatarios who own each type of animal and sell part of their production was the following: cattle, 54.2 percent; pigs, 27.5 percent; poultry, 8.4 percent; goats, 38.3 percent; sheep, 40.3 percent; and horses, 6.1 percent. The average number of animals owned by those

---

[1] The link between migration and investment of remittances in livestock has been documented in Zacatecas by Goldring (1992) and in Michoacán by Fletcher and Taylor (1992).

who sell part of their production was higher than the average number for all farmers who own these animal species. Thus, in the case of cattle, those who sell had 19 animals, compared to an overall average of 13. This relationship was the following for other species: 8/5 for pigs, 41/18 for poultry, 42/23 for goats, 16/11 for sheep, and 4/3 for horses.

Table 9.1
Stocks and sales of animals, 1990 and 1994

	1990	1994	Test
Number of cases	1615	1543	
Cattle			
Percentage of ejidatarios who own	41.1	44.6	++
Of those who own: number of animals	10.9	13.1	
Of those who own: percentage who sell		54.2	
Of those who sell: number of animals owned		18.8	
Of those who sell: number of animals sold		5.4	
Pigs			
Percentage of ejidatarios who own	47.4	39.7	– –
Of those who own: number of animals	4.0	4.7	++
Of those who own: percentage who sell		27.5	
Of those who sell: number of animals owned		7.5	
Of those who sell: number of animals sold		4.1	
Poultry			
Percentage of ejidatarios who own	60.4	57.1	
Of those who own: number of animals	16.3	18.3	++
Of those who own: percentage who sell		8.4	
Of those who sell: number of animals owned		41.4	
Of those who sell: number of animals sold		12.2	
Goats			
Percentage of ejidatarios who own	11.8	10.8	
Of those who own: number of animals	20.9	23.1	
Of those who own: percentage who sell		38.3	
Of those who sell: number of animals owned		42.3	
Of those who sell: number of animals sold		14.2	
Sheep			
Percentage of ejidatarios who own	9.1	8.6	
Of those who own: number of animals	11.6	10.9	
Of those who own: percentage who sell		40.3	
Of those who sell: number of animals owned		15.6	
Of those who sell: number of animals sold		5.6	
Horses			
Percentage of ejidatarios who own	19.1	22.6	
Of those who own: number of animals	4.0	2.6	
Of those who own: percentage who sell		6.1	
Of those who sell: number of animals owned		4.0	
Of those who sell: number of animals sold		1.4	

Note: Blanks indicate information not available.

In table 9.2, the change in the percentage of ejidatarios who own the different animal species is analyzed by farm size. It can be seen that the ownership of cattle was highly concentrated among large farmers: in 1994, 56 percent of larger producers had cattle, compared to 38 percent of the smaller producers. There was also a concentration on large versus small farms of poultry ownership (63 vs. 55 percent), sheep (10 vs. 8 percent), and horses (31 vs. 18 percent). However, it is notable that animal ownership is much less concentrated than land ownership. On average, ejidatarios of the class above 5 ha NRE have 14.6 ha NRE, compared to 2.3 in the class below 5 ha NRE. Thus the ratio of land ownership for large farmers compared to small farmers is 6.3. The ratios for animal ownership are much lower: 3.5 for cattle, 2.2 for sheep, 1.8 for poultry, 1.6 for horses, and 1.6 for pigs. The ratio for goats is 0.4; they are the small producers' animal. This higher equality in animal ownership illustrates the fact that animals are usually a substitute for land, a substitution that is facilitated by access to common-property pastures. This allows those producers who own less land to partially compensate for unequal land distribution through the pasturing of animals in collective pastures and forests, provided they are able to capitalize in animals, which is not always the case for many of the poor ejidatarios.

The increase in cattle raising that took place between 1990 and 1994 was exclusively concentrated among large producers. The number of large producers who own animals increased from 46 to 56 percent between those two years. For small producers, there was no change during the same period. It is interesting, however, that the number of cattle among those ejidatarios who own cattle did not change between 1990 and 1994. This means that the increase in cattle has been unequally distributed between small and large producers, but it was very diffused and egalitarian among large farmers. Those who have acquired cattle have on average eighteen head, which does not differ significantly from the number of cattle per ejidatario in 1990.

Since cattle are the principal form of savings for peasants, the unequal increase in cattle raising is an unequivocal symptom of deepening differentiation between large and small producers. It is a direct indicator of what is happening with the distribution of income within the ejido sector—namely, an increasing concentration of assets toward those households with more land. Although animal ownership fulfills an equalizing function as a substitute to land ownership, it is increasingly becoming complementary to land ownership.

Table 9.2
Stocks of animals by farm size, 1990 and 1994

	% of ejidatarios who own each animal species			Among owners of each animal species, number of animals owned		
	< 5 ha NRE	≥ 5 ha NRE	Test	< 5 ha NRE	≥ 5 ha NRE	Test
Cattle						
1990	37.3	45.9	++	6.4	15.5	++
1994	37.5	56.1	++	7.7	17.8	++
Test		++				
Pigs						
1990	48.1	47.9		3.5	4.8	++
1994	37.2	45.2		4.1	5.4	++
Test	− −			++		
Poultry						
1990	62.7	59.7		12.8	21.0	++
1994	54.5	62.8	++	14.7	22.7	++
Test					+	
Goats						
1990	15.0	8.0	− −	19.9	23.2	
1994	11.4	10.1		30.5	12.8	
Test	− −	+				
Sheep						
1990	9.0	9.2	+	10.1	13.1	
1994	7.9	9.7	++	7.5	13.5	
Test						
Horses						
1990	15.9	23.9	++	5.5	2.7	
1994	17.5	30.6	++	2.7	2.4	
Test		+				

Table 9.3
Benefits derived from common land, 1990 and 1994

	1990	1994	Test
Number of cases	1615	1543	
Ejidatarios who use common land for the following activities (%)			
Collective cultivation	0.7	1.7	++
Grazing animals	25.4	30.2	++
Cutting wood	2.0	9.4	++
Hunting and fishing	0.9	1.7	++
Collecting firewood	18.0	29.3	++
Other (minerals, etc.)	1.4	2.3	++
Ejidatarios who engage in at least one of the activities (%)	33.5	46.6	++

Benefits from Common-Property Resources

A high percentage of ejidatarios have access to common-property lands in the ejido. However, not all of them use this privilege. As can be seen in table 9.3, between 1990 and 1994 the portion of ejidatarios who derived at least one type of benefit from the use of common-property land increased from 33.5 percent to 46.6 percent. This increase in the use of common-property land parallels the increase in cattle raising. It is also the result of liberalization in the direct management of forests by ejidatarios.

The common-property lands that are used for grazing animals benefited 25 percent of ejidatarios in 1990 and 33 percent in 1994, and other benefits that are derived from access to forests have also increased. The number of ejidatarios who were able to collect firewood increased from 18 percent to 29 percent, and those who were able to cut wood increased from 2 percent to 9 percent. Land for common use has thus grown in importance for ejidatarios, and there is an increasing need to regulate the use of these areas, especially due to the strong environmental pressures that such use exerts.

It is also interesting to observe the importance of access to common pastures for the feeding of work animals in 1994. The percentage of ejidatarios who used common pastures for each species of working animal is the following:

Type of Animal	Percentage Who Used Common Pastures
Oxen	80.4
Horses	87.4
Mules	90.4

Access to common-property resources is thus fundamental in enabling ejidatarios to maintain work animals, which is particularly important in a context of decreased mechanization and increased reliance on animal traction.

Backyard Activities

Ejidatarios engage in a number of productive activities in the backyards of their houses. (The average home plot is 0.5 ha [1994 survey].) Backyard activities include agricultural production (such as horticulture and the production of fruits) and animal husbandry, including chicken, pigs, and cattle. Between 1990 and 1994, the portion of ejidatarios who engage in backyard activities increased from 63 percent to 75 percent, as can be noted in table 9.4.

Table 9.4
Backyard activities, 1990 and 1994

	1990	1994	Test
Ejidatarios who engage in backyard activities (% of ejidatarios)			
Number of cases	1615	1542	
Agriculture	7.7	10.8	++
Animal husbandry	41.1	49.4	++
Both	14.4	14.9	
Either	63.2	75.0	--
Objective of agricultural activities (%) [a]			
Number of cases	124	166	
For consumption	90.4	99.0	++
For sale	24.5	5.5	--
For both consumption and sale	14.9	4.5	--
Objective of animal husbandry activities (%) [a]			
Number of cases	664	761	
For consumption	96.5	98.6	++
For sale	19.8	27.0	++
For both consumption and sale	16.3	25.8	++
Objectives of combined agricultural and animal husbandry activities (%) [a]			
Number of cases	232	229	
For consumption	99.5	96.9	--
For consumption only	79.4	74.7	
For sale	20.6	25.5	
For sale only	0.5	3.1	++
For both consumption and sale	20.1	22.3	

[a] % for sale + % for consumption only = 100,
% for consumption + % for sale only = 100.

The majority of families who engaged in only one activity specialized in animal husbandry (49 percent in 1994). Production for family consumption dominated (99 percent of the cases), and only 5.5 percent sold part of their production. Between 1990 and 1994 the percentage of ejidatarios who engaged in these activities for consumption increased, while the percentage selling some of their production declined. Fifteen percent of the households are engaged in both animal husbandry and agricultural activities, again principally for home consumption (97 percent) as opposed to sale (26 percent). Eleven percent of the households engaged only in agricultural activities. Among them, production for consumption has increased, while production for sale has severely decreased.

Like the use of common-property resources, backyard activities are an important element of peasant household livelihood strategies. In times of hardship, these activities acquire greater importance. Between 1990 and 1994, in the context of falling agricultural incomes, the practice of backyard activities became more prevalent. The purpose of these activities is overwhelmingly for family consumption as opposed to sale, and orientation toward family subsistence increased in both animal husbandry and agricultural activities.

10

Credit and Insurance

Credit: Access and Use

In this section, access to credit in 1994 is characterized by contrasting the different sources of credit, the use of credit from these different sources, the kinds of collateral used for each type of credit, the amount of credit supplied, the conditions of payment, and the ejidatarios' perceptions of credit availability. Then the changes between 1990 and 1994 are analyzed with respect to access to credit, amounts received, and use of the credit. There were drastic changes in access to credit for the ejido sector during the 1990–1994 period.

Ejidatarios' Access to Credit in 1994

Between 1990 and 1994, the portion of ejidatarios with access to credit increased from 26 percent to 30.5 percent.[1] (Only the second figure is reported in table 10.1.) As we shall see, this increase in access was due to the emergence of PRONASOL, which made credit available to many ejido families who had never had access to credit before. Although access to credit became more widespread, the amount of credit for those who received it decreased, as did the amount of credit obtained in each transaction.

In table 10.1, the frequency of use of the different sources of credit is recorded for 1994. It can be seen that PRONASOL was the most common source, with 63.1 percent of all transactions, followed by BANRURAL, with 15.0 percent. Commercial banks only provided 5.2 percent of loans to the ejido sector. Through PRONASOL, BANRURAL,

---

[1] The general lack of access to credit for Mexican peasants has been documented by Sanderson (1984) and Hewitt de Alcántara (1976).

Table 10.1
Credit sources, 1994

Credit sources	Number of transactions	Percentage of total transactions	Average value of each loan (pesos)	Percentage of total credit	Average value of each loan (by use)			Percentage of all households who received credit
					Current expenditures (pesos)	Investment (pesos)	Other (pesos)	
Public sources								
BANRURAL	74	15.0	13,708	45.8	12,862	23,230	1,000	4.6
PRONASOL	310	63.1	1,104	15.5	998	7,250	1,046	20.1
Other government agencies	21	2.9	1,365	0.9	1,399	1,121	0	0.9
Formal private sources								
Commercial banks	25	5.2	17,089	19.6	16,081	23,949	0	1.6
Credit unions	2	0.3	12,000	0.9	12,000	0	0	0.1
Savings and credit banks	2	0.4	2,100	0.2	2,100	0	0	0.1
Informal sources								
Friends and/or relatives	25	5.1	5,241	6.0	6,662	600	2,043	1.6
Moneylenders	17	3.5	4,720	3.7	6,090	610	0	1.1
Merchants	1	0.3	832	0.0	1,000	0	200	0.1
Other sources	21	4.3	6,891	7.5	7,207	7,000	100	1.4
Total	498	100		100	4,159	13,485	1,530	30.5

and other government agencies, the public sector was by far the principal source of credit for the ejido, accounting for 81 percent of all transactions. Informal sources (moneylenders, merchants, friends, and relatives) represented 9 percent of the loans. Thus the informal sector was relatively unimportant for production loans; however, it was important for emergency loans, which will be analyzed in the context of insurance.

The average value of credit transactions differed widely across sources. The largest loans were obtained from commercial banks (17,089 pesos on average), from BANRURAL (13,708 pesos), and from credit unions (12,000 pesos). In contrast, loans obtained from PRONASOL were small, with an average of 1,104 pesos per transaction. Moneylenders and friends and relatives—that is, informal sources of credit—reached amounts of 4,720 and 5,241 pesos, respectively, which represent about four times the amount obtained through PRONASOL.

Combining frequency and average size of loan, it can be seen that BANRURAL was the main source of credit for the ejido sector, constituting 45.8 percent of the total lent to the sector, followed by commercial banks, which accounted for 19.6 percent of the total. PRONASOL, even though it accounted for 59.5 percent of all credit transactions, was the source of only 15.5 percent of the total credit to the sector.

Despite the rise in access to credit, there were still many ejidatario households that did not have access to credit. All in all, only 30.5 percent of the households had access to some type of credit. PRONASOL reached 20.1 percent of the ejidatarios and BANRURAL, 4.6 percent. The other sources reached exceedingly low percentages. Therefore, despite PRONASOL's outreach, credit had to be a severely limiting factor for production and for the modernization and diversification of the ejido sector.

The way that obtained credit was used, according to its source, is described in table 10.2. Of the total amount of credit that reached the social sector, 83 percent was used for current production expenditures, 14 percent for investment, and 3 percent for other purposes. Current production expenditures were the motive for 94 percent of all loans, and investment expenditures for only 5 percent. This points to the great lack of credit available to the ejido sector for investment, which explains the general and continuing underinvestment in this sector. Consequently, the ejido sector must depend for its investments on erratic donations of capital goods by the state. Among different sources of credit, only BANRURAL (through 11 percent of its loans), commercial banks (through 13 percent of their loans), and moneylenders (through 17 percent of their loans) had significant numbers of loans for investment (calculated from the data in table 10.2). PRONASOL, on the other hand, supplied credit for current expenditures in 98 percent of its loans; only 2 percent of its loans were for investment. The fall in access to credit through BANRURAL and the increase in access through PRONASOL thus implied a fall in the availability of investment credit to the ejido sector.

Table 10.2
Access and use of credit, 1994

	Use of credit received		
	Current expenditures (%)	Investment (%)	Other (%)
Total credit to the ejido sector	82.6	14.1	3.3

	Sources of credit transactions by use		
Credit sources	Current expenditures (%)	Investment (%)	Other (%)
Public sources			
BANRURAL	14.6	34.0	1.5
PRONASOL	65.8	24.2	20.8
Other government agencies	2.9	7.5	0.0
Formal private sources			
Commercial banks	5.1	14.1	0.0
Credit unions	0.4	0.0	0.0
Credit and savings banks	0.4	0.0	0.0
Informal sources			
Friends and/or relatives	3.6	5.0	62.6
Moneylenders	3.0	11.3	0.0
Merchants	0.2	0.0	3.9
Other sources	4.1	4.0	11.2
Total	100	100	100
Number of cases	437	23	7
Percentage of cases (%)	93.6	4.9	1.5

In table 10.3, the collateral requirements of each credit source are analyzed. We see that land serves as collateral for only 6.4 percent of the loans, principally those made by BANRURAL. This indicates that, despite the current property rights reforms, land is still rarely used as collateral. In contrast, the harvest serves as collateral for 21 percent of all transactions, and animals, houses, and vehicles serve for another 8 percent. These collaterals are used principally by BANRURAL and commercial banks. Loans without collateral requirements are surprisingly important for the ejido sector, accounting for 31 percent of all credit transactions, 80 percent of which originate with PRONASOL and its program of credit without collateral (*crédito a la palabra*). This program is extremely important for the ejido sector since it represents 62 percent of all credit transactions for that sector.

The quality of the different sources of credit is also analyzed in table 10.3 according to the amount of time it took to receive the credit, with timely credit defined as credit received in time for its initially intended use. We see that informal sources have no problems of delay. BANRURAL and commercial banks also performed well, providing 83 percent and 65 percent, respectively, of the credit on time. Although PRONASOL loans have the advantage of not requiring collateral and carrying no interest payments, they arrive on time in less than half the cases (45 percent). This makes the use of PRONASOL credit problematic for production purposes because timely credit is essential for agricultural tasks. Informal-sector loans always arrive on time, which justifies the payment of high interest rates in exchange for reliability of service. The average delay is 1.2 weeks with BANRURAL, 1.6 weeks with commercial banks, and 5.2 weeks with PRONASOL. The time spent on procedures to obtain credit also varies according to the source. Informal credit is more quickly accessible, especially when it is obtained from friends or family. In contrast, public sources, as well as private formal sources, require an average of 5 to 7 weeks of negotiations. Finally, the period established for credit repayment is shorter with PRONASOL and moneylenders (7 and 9 weeks), and it is longer with BANRURAL (12 weeks) and commercial banks (21 weeks). This reflects the differences in the purpose of the credit, with more investment credit lent by BANRURAL and commercial banks.

The ejidatarios who were surveyed and did not have access to credit were also asked the following questions to determine their perceptions about why they did not have access to credit:

- Do you not need credit?
- Do you have overdue loans, making access to new loans impossible?
- Do you perceive that credit is not available to you?

In fact, "not available" and "overdue loans" were confused by respondents because the individual knew that credit would not be available if he or she had an overdue loan. We can nevertheless compare the cases of "does not need credit" and "there is no credit available," whichever was the motive. The 996 ejidatarios who did not have credit and answered this question classified themselves as follows (1994 survey):

Does not need credit	8%
There is no credit available/does not have access to credit	92%

Table 10.3
Types of collateral, 1994

Credit sources	Frequency of transactions (%)	Type of collateral					Quality of credit			
		Land	Animals, house, or vehicle	Harvest	Other	Without collateral	Frequency of timely credit (%)	Delay (weeks)	Time to obtain credit (weeks)	Repayment period (months)
Public sources										
BANRURAL	14.9	69.0	55.4	43.9	7.9	3.3	83.2	1.2	5.6	12.3
PRONASOL	62.2	0.0	11.9	11.9	63.8	84.5	44.5	5.2	6.9	7.2
Other government agencies	4.2	1.6	2.4	2.1	4.7	5.0	81.7	0.9	4.3	7.5
Formal private sources										
Commercial banks	5.0	12.8	24.7	9.7	5.3	2.0	65.2	1.6	7.4	20.7
Credit unions	0.4	0.0	0.0	2.8	0.0	0.0			3.0	7.0
Savings and credit banks	0.4	0.0	0.0	3.1	0.0	0.0				12.0
Informal sources										
Friends and/or relatives	5.0	0.0	0.0	7.7	8.9	2.3	100.0	0.0	0.5	5.3
Moneylenders	3.4	0.0	1.4	7.6	7.4	0.7	100.0	0.1	2.3	9.3
Merchants	0.2	0.0	0.0	0.9	0.5	0.0			1.0	7.0
Other sources	4.2	16.7	4.3	10.3	1.5	2.2	93.0	0.0	2.5	14.6
Number of cases	498	17	22	56	92	86				
Frequency of use as collateral		6.4	7.9	20.5	33.8	31.4				
Average or total	100	100	100	100	100	100	64.6			

Note: Blanks indicate that the number of transactions is too small to calculate the corresponding concept.

This result indicates that a high percentage of ejidatarios who needed credit could not get it. If this is the case, then lack of access to credit is a limiting factor for a large majority of ejidatarios, emphasizing the urgent necessity of reconstructing a network of rural financial institutions accessible to ejidatarios.

Changes in Access to Credit between 1990 and 1994

In table 10.4, the percentages of ejidatarios who had access to credit for current expenditures in 1990 and 1994 are compared according to each source. The following are the statistically significant differences between the years:

- A decline in access to credit through BANRURAL, which fell from 9.7 percent to 4.6 percent of all ejidatarios.
- The great importance of access to credit through PRONASOL, which was null in 1990 and reached 20 percent in 1994.
- The increasing importance of the informal sector (friends and relatives, moneylenders, and merchants), though there were few such transactions.

The fall in access to credit through BANRURAL was more than compensated by PRONASOL in terms of frequency of access to credit. The proportion of ejidatarios with access to some type of credit for current expenditures rose from 14 percent in 1990 to 30 percent in 1994 (table 10.4). Nevertheless, the substitution of PRONASOL for BANRURAL implies that the amount of credit declined, tightening further the credit constraints on ejidatarios. An approximate calculation of the magnitude of the decrease in credit to the sector can be carried out. Assuming that the peso value of credit transactions from each source was equal in 1990 to what it was in 1994, and using the percentages of access observed in table 10.4, the amount of credit received by the sector has fallen by 20 percent in constant 1994 pesos. A triple phenomenon occurred between 1990 and 1994: access to loans increased through PRONASOL, the mass of credit to the sector declined, and access to credit was thus diluted over a larger number of users. Who these recipients were and how they were distributed among large and small producers is what we analyze in the following section.

Table 10.4
Changes in access to credit for current expenditures, 1990 and 1994
(percentage of ejidatarios who have access)

	1990	*1994*	*Test*
Number of cases	1615	1538	
Sources of credit (%)			
Public sources			
BANRURAL	9.7	4.6	– –
PRONASOL	0.0	20.0	++
Formal private sources			
Commercial banks	1.5	1.6	
Informal sources	1.2	2.5	++
Other sources	1.7	2.4	++
Use of credit (%)			
Current expenditures	13.8	30.3	++

Access to Credit by Farm Size

Table 10.5 shows that access to credit for current expenditures is generally biased in favor of larger farmers. For example, in 1994, 10 percent of large farmers had access to BANRURAL, versus 1 percent of small farmers. The only source that was not biased in favor of large farmers was PRONASOL. During the time period studied, access to BANRURAL credit decreased, and it decreased more for small than for large farmers: for the former, access fell by 78 percent, compared to 42 percent for the latter. Smaller farmers lost access to commercial banks. Informal sources were only a partial substitute for the fall in formal credit. Finally, overall access to credit for current expenditures increased for both classes of farmers: by 19 percent for small farmers and by 15 percent for large farmers. However, this increase occurred through very different channels.

Table 10.6 shows that 86 percent of BANRURAL loans and 100 percent of commercial bank loans went to producers with larger farms. Moneylenders also favored larger producers, doubtlessly because they can provide collateral more easily. By contrast, PRONASOL assigned its loans with a bias toward the small farmers.

Analyzing the sources of credit for each group of producers, it can be seen that 82 percent of loans for small producers were from PRONASOL. By contrast, large producers received 45 percent of their loans from PRONASOL, 25 percent from BANRURAL, and 10 percent from commercial banks. Those with larger farms thus have more diversified access to credit.

The amounts of credit obtained in these transactions are very different. Consequently, the distribution of credit amounts from each source is different for each group. For small producers, 54 percent of the credit they received came from PRONASOL. In contrast, large producers received 51 percent from BANRURAL and 23 percent from commercial banks. In spite of the egalitarian access to PRONASOL for small and large producers, when it comes to the amounts received, PRONASOL is the poor people's bank and BANRURAL, the bank for wealthier farmers.

Table 10.5
Access to credit for current expenditures by farm size, 1990 and 1994
(% of ejidatarios who have access)

	< 5 ha NRE	> 5 ha NRE	Test
Sources of credit			
Public sources			
BANRURAL			
1990	4.9	16.5	++
1994	1.1	9.5	++
Test	– –	– –	
PRONASOL			
1990	0.0	0.0	
1994	22.1	18.0	
Test	++	++	
Formal private sources			
Commercial banks			
1990	0.1	3.5	++
1994	0.0	3.8	++
Test	– –		
Informal sources			
1990	0.9	1.7	
1994	1.9	3.5	+
Test	++		
Other sources			
1990	1.6	2.0	
1994	1.6	3.6	++
Test			
Use of credit for current expenditures			
1990	7.5	23.0	++
1994	26.2	37.1	++
% points	18.7	15.1	
Test	++	++	

Table 10.6
Credit sources by farm size, 1994

	Allocation of credit by source (%)			Source of credit by farm size (%)		Average amount of credit by source (pesos)		Amount of credit by farm size (%)	
	≤5 ha NRE	>5 ha NRE	Total	≤5 ha NRE	>5 ha NRE	≤5 ha NRE	>5 ha NRE	≤5 ha NRE	>5 ha NRE
Public sources									
BANRUAL	13.6	86.4	100	4.2	25.0	4143	217	13.1	51.3
PRONASOL	62.9	37.1	100	82.3	45.2	887	1471	54.5	8.9
Other government agencies	63.8	36.2	100	3.9	2.0	1204	1650	3.5	0.5
Formal private sources									
Commercial banks	0.0	100.0	100	0.0	9.9	0	17087	0.0	22.9
Informal sources									
Friends and/or relatives	41.4	58.7	100	4.4	5.8	3459	6497	11.3	5.1
Moneylenders	36.9	63.1	100	2.7	4.3	1910	6364	3.9	3.7
Other sources	23.0	77.1	100	2.5	7.8	4080	7333	13.7	7.7
Total				100	100	1306	7415	100	100

It is, of course, no surprise that large farmers received more credit since they have more land to cultivate. The criterion for an accurate analysis of access to credit by farm size should thus be based on the quantity received per ha NRE. The amount obtained in each transaction for every class of farm is detailed in table 10.7. It can be seen that the amount of credit per hectare received from public and from informal sources favored small producers. This is particularly true for PRONASOL, from which small producers received 398 pesos/ha compared to 115 pesos/ha for large producers. Friends and relatives were also fundamental sources of liquidity for smallholders. Commercial banks, by contrast, were biased in favor of large producers. While the sources of access to credit differ sharply, the total amount received appears to be relatively equal: 595 pesos/ha for large producers and 562 pesos/ha for small producers.

Table 10.7
Distribution of credit in the ejido sector, 1994

	Ejidatarios who receive credit: average amount of credit per ha, by source (pesos/ha NRE)		All ejidatarios: average amount of credit per ha, by source (pesos/ha NRE)	
	≤5 ha NRE	> 5 ha NRE	≤5 ha NRE	> 5 ha NRE
Public sources				
BANRURAL	1,743	1,117	19	106
PRONASOL	398	115	88	21
Other government agencies	526	206	6	2
Formal private sources				
Commercial banks	0	1,454	0	55
Informal sources				
Friends and/or relatives	1,327	387	16	9
Moneylenders	629	493	5	8
Other sources	1,533	667	11	21
Total	562	595	153	222

Yet it should not be forgotten that access to credit is extremely unequal among small and large producers, in favor of the latter. A test of equity in credit allocation requires combining access to credit with the amount obtained per hectare in each transaction. This is what we do in table 10.7. It can be seen that small farmers, including those who do and those who do not receive credit, obtained on average, from all sources, 153 pesos/ha, compared to larger producers, who received 222 pesos/ha. Among specific sources, PRONASOL's bias in favor of small producers was enhanced, with 88 pesos/ha, compared to 21 pesos/ha for large producers, while BANRURAL's bias in favor of large producers deepened, with 106 pesos/ha, compared to 19 pesos/ha for small producers.

Finally, we analyze those farmers in both groups who did not use credit, according to the reasons they gave for not doing so. The following data show that the perception of nonavailability dominated among small farmers, while overdue portfolios were the more limiting factor for large producers (1994 survey).

	< 5 ha NRE	> 5 ha NRE
Declared Motive for Non-use		
Does not need credit	6.2%	9.8%
Perceives Restriction of Access		
Credit not available	83.8%	72.3%
Has overdue loan	10.0%	17.9%
Total	100.0%	100.0%

Insurance: Access and Use

In 1990, agricultural insurance was mandatorily tied to BANRURAL credit through ANAGSA (the National Agriculture and Livestock Insurance Company). By 1994 BANRURAL had changed its credit policy, requiring collateral such as vehicles, houses, and other capital goods instead of insurance, even though it maintained this requirement in certain cases. Moreover, we have seen that the number of BANRURAL loans to the ejido sector decreased considerably. As a consequence, there were few ejidatarios with crop insurance in 1994.

Table 10.8 compares access to harvest insurance in 1990 and 1994. There was a significant fall in the incidence of access, decreasing from 9.8 percent of the households in 1990 to 3.2 percent in 1994. Table 10.9 gives the incidence of the different types of insurance across households in 1994. A total of 11.4 percent of ejidatarios had some type of insurance. Among them, 3.2 percent had crop insurance; 0.2 percent, vehicle insurance; 1.3 percent, life insurance; and 9.1 percent, health insurance. Insurance is obviously a minor instrument among ejidatarios for confronting risk.

Ejidatarios were asked what they did when they had a short-term emergency such as high medical expenses or a medium-term emergency like a bad harvest (table 10.10). For high medical expenses, 8.1 percent of respondents had medical insurance, while 44.2 percent used loans obtained from the informal sector. Formal bank loans are not useful for emergency purposes, primarily because they do not arrive on time, require a long period of transactions, and are directed toward supporting production, not the family. Thirty-one percent of the households used the sale of animals as a source of liquidity for these emergencies. Animals thus serve as an important savings fund for insurance. The use of money savings served as insurance in only 6.7 percent of the cases, which suggests that few ejidatarios have access to financial institutions to save money, a major institutional gap still to be addressed in the Mexican rural sector.

Table 10.8
Change in access to harvest insurance, 1990 and 1994

	Ejidatarios with harvest insurance		
	1990	*1994*	*Test of difference means*
Number of cases with insurance	158	49	
Percentage with insurance	9.8	3.2	--

To face up to medium-term emergencies, such as a bad harvest, only 4.4 percent of ejidatarios had insurance, while 47 percent used informal loans and 29 percent sold animals. Here again, formal sources of insurance are weakly developed, while informal loans and precautionary savings in animals dominate.

Table 10.9
Access to insurance, 1994

Types of insurance	*Number of ejidatarios who have*	*Percentage of ejidatarios who have (%)*
Harvest	49	3.2
Machinery or vehicles	3	0.2
Life and family	20	1.3
Medical	141	9.1
Some kind of insurance	176	11.4

Lack of access to insurance is not compensated by access to formal credit that could be used as an instrument of risk coping. Families have to resort to the informal sector—principally friends, relatives, and moneylenders—or they have to self-insure. The current increase

Table 10.10
Sources of liquidity in case of emergency, 1994

	Types of emergencies			
	Short-term emergencies: high medical expenses		Medium-term emergencies: bad harvest	
	Number of ejidatarios who use	Percentage of ejidatarios who use	Number of ejidatarios who use	Percentage of ejidatarios who use
Assistance from formal sector				
Have insurance	101	8.1	53	4.4
Bank loans	5	0.4	6	0.5
Assistance from informal sector				
Informal loans	552	44.2	563	47.3
Self-insurance				
Use of savings	84	6.7	94	7.9
Sale of animals	392	31.4	45	29.0
Sale of other assets	18	1.4	23	2.0

in cattle raising in the ejido is thus likely to be partially induced by the decline in access to credit and insurance, as ejidatarios are forced to use animals as an inferior and more costly substitute for formal-sector insurance.

11

Organization

The information available about organizations includes the types of organizations to which ejidatarios belong, the purposes for which the producers are organized, the organizational forms through which they try to obtain their objectives, the perceived benefits that each organization provides, and the legal status of the organizations.

It is difficult to make an unambiguous statement about change in the overall degree of organization between 1990 and 1994 because there were different types of organizations included in the two surveys, and neither survey included information about all of the organizations that existed in the corresponding survey year. There were some organizations surveyed in 1994 that did not exist in 1990—the solidarity committees, for example, because PRONASOL'S rural lending programs had not been initiated. Another difficulty is that information about organizations like the ARIC and ejido unions, which do not have individual ejidatarios as members but rather ejidos as a whole, was obtained in 1990 from the survey of individual ejidatarios. This may have underestimated ejidatario participation in 1990 because some ejidatarios could have been misinformed about whether or not their ejido was a member of one of these organizations. In 1994, information about the ARIC and ejido unions was included in the ejido-level survey. Also, the mutual assistance and labor exchange organizations, which were included in detail in 1994, were not singled out in the 1990 survey, where they appear in the category of "other organizations." We must therefore proceed with caution when making a statement about change in the total level of organization during this period.

The types of organizations common to both surveys are credit unions, rural production societies, and cooperative societies. We can make a statement about the change in these forms of organization between 1990 and 1994. The percentages of ejidatarios associated with these bodies are low, and they declined from one period to the next. The qualitatively most important fall in membership, due to the role of the organization, is that of credit unions. Membership in these organizations fell from 4.2 percent in 1990 to 0.7 percent in

Table 11.1
Membership in organizations, 1990 and 1994

	Frequency of membership among households (%)			Frequency of registration within organizations (%)	
	1990	1994	Test	1990	1994
Number of households	1615	1543			
Formal organizations with					
individual participation	8.4	7.6	–		
Credit unions	4.2	0.7	– –	74.4	94.5
Rural production societies	2.9	1.0	– –	72.2	92.1
Cooperative societies	1.1	0.5	– –	83.4	43.0
Agricultural cooperatives	0.4			89.5	
Social solidarity societies		0.6			88.3
Agro-industrial units for women		0.1			67.9
Insurance funds		1.2			100
Savings banks		0.0			100
Local agricultural associations		2.5			99.3
Local livestock associations		1.8			97.0
Formal organization with					
partipation through the ejido [a]	24.0	36.1	n.a.		
ARIC	1.0	4.1	n.a.	100	
Ejido unions	23.4	35.1	n.a.	91.1	
Informal and social organizations	26.7	25.9		70.2	
Solidarity committees		5.0			84.0
Organizations for collective work					
Social tasks organizations		16.9			17.7
Mutual assistance and labor					
exchange organizations		4.2			0.8
Municipal duties organizations					5.9
Other organizations	26.7	10.3		68.6	74.7

[a] For 1990 this information was obtained from the ejidatario survey, for 1994 from the survey to ejidos.
Note: n.a. indicates test of difference not applicable.

1994, as can be seen in table 11.1. This reflects the crisis of the credit sector and the shift in access to credit toward the PRONASOL programs.

We consider first the formal organizations with individual participation that were included in both surveys. In addition to credit unions, rural production societies, and cooperative societies, which are common to both surveys, we had the agricultural cooperatives in 1990, and in 1994 we had the social solidarity societies, Agro-Industrial Units for Women (UAIMs), insurance funds, savings banks, local agricultural associations, and local livestock associations. We see that the number of ejidatarios who belonged to at least one of these organizations decreased slightly, from 8.4 percent to 7.6 percent, between 1990 and 1994.

To characterize participation through the ejido in ARICs and ejido unions, we compare the percentage of ejidatarios who declared they were members of these organizations in 1990 with the percentage of ejidatarios who were members in 1994, determined for the 1994 ejidatarios by the participation of their respective ejidos in these organizations. We observe an increase in participation in these organizations from 23 percent to 35 percent, but, again, this could be due to an underestimation in 1990. Ejido unions are the most important form of organization: 35 percent of ejidatarios were members of this type of organization in 1994.

Participation in informal organizations and organizations for social mobilization has stayed the same or increased. This is partly due to PRONASOL's promotion of solidarity committees. The informal nature of the mutual assistance and labor exchange organizations and of the municipal duties organizations is seen in the low percentage of these organizations that were officially registered (0.8 percent and 5.9 percent, respectively). Nevertheless, we prefer to conclude that these data cannot be used to obtain a definitive characterization of global change in the degree of organization of ejidatarios during the period observed.

Among the organizations surveyed, the objectives sought through organization have changed, as can be seen in table 11.2. In the 1990 survey, objectives focused on obtaining credit (67.9 percent of organized ejidatarios); acquiring inputs (38.6 percent) and infrastructure (24.0 percent); obtaining capital goods such as equipment, machinery, and installations (17.9 percent); and marketing agricultural products (14.1 percent). In 1994, the data indicate that objectives focused on agricultural production (35.4 percent) and on the development of infrastructure (34.8 percent), especially roads (33.7 percent). Within these large objectives are subsumed goals related to credit and the acquisition of agricultural inputs.

Other important objectives of organization in 1990 were pressuring the government to answer demands for land (10.1 percent of organized peasants) and the regularization of land tenure (10.9 percent). It is important to mention that in 1990 requests for land were channeled principally through ejido unions, which gave these organizations the role of political representation for groups of ejidatarios who were seeking access to land. By 1994, after the reform of Article 27, there was no longer any possibility of demanding access to land. Ejido unions changed their objectives and became important institutions in support of production. Also, the objective of regularizing land tenure fell from 10.9 percent to 0.8 percent because specialized government programs, such as PROCEDE, had been created for this purpose.

Table 11.2
Objectives of organizing
(percentage of organized farmers who seek each objective)

	1990	1994	Test
Number of cases	902	624	
Demand land	10.1		
Regularize land tenure	10.9	0.8	– –
Assist production			
Agriculture		35.4	
Aquaculture		1.7	
Infrastructure	24.0	34.8	++
Roads		33.7	
Bridges		10.9	
Dams		1.9	
Obtain credit	67.9	10.9	– –
Bank credit		10.6	
Credit from mutual savings		0.4	
Obtain public resources		6.4	
Obtain private economic resources		1.8	
Acquisition of inputs	38.6	7.0	– –
Aquisition of capital goods	17.9	6.3	– –
Equipment		2.5	
Machinery		3.3	
Installations		1.8	
Marketing of agricultural products	14.1	6.1	– –
Other objectives	8.3	44.7	++
Benefits obtained from organization			
Economic		83.8	
Social		24.9	
Economic and social		9.1	

Note: blanks indicate information not available.

With respect to the legal status of formal organizations (credit unions, rural production societies, and cooperative societies), in 1990 all organizations had a high percentage of registration. This percentage was even higher in 1994.

Finally, in 1994 the majority (83.8 percent) of organized producers obtained purely economic benefits through their organizations (table 11.2). This is in contrast to the 24.9 percent who sought purely social benefits and the 9.1 percent who derived both economic and social benefits.

The objectives of belonging to each type of organization, as they were perceived by members, are analyzed in table 11.3. In 1990, the ejido unions, which grouped the largest number of members among formal organizations, had a wide range of objectives, including access to bank credit, acquisition of inputs, infrastructure, capital goods, and marketing. The other organizations had much more specialized objectives: credit unions sought access to credit, and cooperative societies sought access to inputs and to credit. In 1994, the solidarity committees were principally for access to inputs (70.1 percent) and infrastructure (9.3 percent). Organizations for collective work provided access to infrastructure (48.3 percent), particularly through municipal duties for roads and bridges, and the acquisition of inputs (15.0 percent).

In table 11.4, the declared economic, social, and political benefits of each type of organization are analyzed. In the opinion of those surveyed, there was no organization that sought purely political benefits. It was economic benefits that dominated among formal and informal organizations. Collective work organizations provided the most social benefits, particularly municipal duties organizations (43.7 percent) and mutual assistance organizations (26.1 percent). In the case of municipal duties organizations, social benefits arise because these organizations are used to build local social infrastructure. The other collective work organizations are inserted in a network of social relationships through which other benefits are gained, such as mutual insurance and community activities. The collective work organizations that had the highest relative percentages of economic benefits were labor exchange (95 percent) and social tasks (76 percent) organizations.

We conclude by observing that ejidatarios are not strongly organized, with only about a third belonging to organizations through the ejido, a quarter belonging to informal and social organizations, and 7 percent belonging to formal organizations with individual participation. In these formal organizations, the objective of accessing land has shifted to supporting production. The declared benefits of membership in organizations are overwhelmingly economic. As ejidatarios

Table 11.3
The organizations' objectives by type of organization, 1990 and 1994

Objectives	Ejido unions 1990	Credit unions		Rural production societies Cooperative societies		Solidarity committees 1994	Organizations for collective work 1994
		1990	1994	1990	1994		
Number of cases	712	82	14	87	27	89	522
Regularize land tenure	4.4	1.2	0.0	3.3	0.0	0.0	0.5
Infrastructure	16.3	1.5	0.0	7.2	0.0	9.3	48.3
Obtain bank credit	31.4	73.2	18.1	55.1	20.0	2.1	0.0
Acquisition of inputs [a]	24.0	9.3	64.5	19.0	40.7	70.1	15.0
Acquisition of capital goods	11.8	8.4	0.0	7.9	12.3	2.4	1.4
Marketing	11.8	6.3	6.7	7.5	1.4	0.7	0.1
Others	0.3	0	10.8	0.0	25.8	15.4	34.6
Total	100	100	100	100	100	100	100

[a] In 1994, organizations for production and for acquisition of private and public resources are included.

Table 11.4
Declared benefits by organization, 1994

Organization	Benefit (%)	
	Economic	*Social*
Credit unions	80.8	19.2
Rural production societies	95.3	4.7
Cooperative societies	94.9	5.2
Social solidarity societies	71.4	28.6
Agro-industrial units for women	100	0
Insurance funds	100	0
Solidarity committees	94.9	5.1
Savings banks	100	0
Local agricultural associations	79.2	20.8
Local livestock associations	64.8	35.3
Collective work organizations		
Social tasks organizations	75.9	24.1
Mutual assistance organizations	73.9	26.1
Labor exchange organizations	94.5	5.5
Municipal duties organizations	56.3	43.7
Other	84.6	14.5

become more exposed to the rigors of competitive markets and less sheltered by government through the ejido itself, these organizations in support of production and competitiveness will have to assume an increasingly important role if ejidatarios are to successfully modernize and diversify their production.

12

The Availability and Use of Corn by Household Type

The Importance of Corn for Ejido Families

The 1994 survey included a quantification of the annual balance of availability and use of corn by corn-producing families. On the side of availability, sources were the following:

- corn stocks before the spring–summer harvest,
- production obtained in the spring–summer season,
- production obtained in the fall–winter season,
- corn purchased before the next spring–summer harvest, and
- corn received through other sources, such as gifts, payments in kind, etc.

On the side of use, destinations were the following:

- sales,
- use for human consumption,
- use for animal consumption,
- use for seed, and
- other uses.

Furthermore, information was obtained about the prices received or paid in each transaction. The objective of this information is to characterize the position of different families with respect to the market, contrasting those who only sell, those who only buy, those who buy and sell, and those who neither buy nor sell. Self-sufficient households are not directly affected by variations in the corn price, such as changes anticipated as a consequence of NAFTA or of exchange rate devaluation. A distinction is made between those who have a significant number of animals and those who do not. Some producers who do not sell corn are important users of corn for animal consumption if they have many head of livestock. We thus distinguish between those farmers who have fewer than six head of cattle and those who have six or more. This allows further differentiation among those who only buy and among those who neither sell nor buy corn, according to their level of cattle ownership.

Of all the ejidatarios surveyed, 75 percent, or 1,158 households, were corn producers (table 12.1). The balance of availability and use of corn has been constructed for these producers. Among them, the large majority (94 percent) cultivated in the spring–summer season, obtaining an average total production of 4.0 tons. Twenty-five percent cultivated in the fall–winter season, obtaining a higher average production (5.3 tons). This is due to differences in technology and irrigation use between the two seasons, as we have seen in chapter 7; producers in the fall–winter season tend to use more advanced technology and irrigation. Seventy-five percent of the producers planted only in the spring–summer season and 6 percent only in the fall-winter season, while 19 percent cultivated in both seasons. The great majority of households consequently obtain the corn they need for the year from only one harvest, and they have to store or buy corn to regulate its availability during the year.

Although almost half (49 percent) of the producers had stocks from the previous harvest when the spring–summer harvest began, these stocks averaged 331 kg, which represents on average three months of corn consumption.[1] Few people received corn through payments in kind or donations (6 percent), although for those who receive them these payments and gifts are important in relation to family consumption (they measured 480 kg).

Uses of Corn

The vast majority of producers (90 percent) declared that they used corn for human consumption (table 12.1). Animal consumption is also important since 74 percent of producers used corn for this purpose. Also, 74 percent kept corn for seeds. In terms of quantity of grain, similar amounts were used to feed animals and to feed the family: on average, 1.2 tons for animal consumption and 1.4 tons for human con-

---

[1] Based on data collected by Donald Rose (Rose 1992) for families of the Valle de Solís in the state of México, it is estimated that for a family with two adults and four children, annual needs for corn consumption are 1.3 tons, without including losses.

sumption. With respect to seeds, the quantity used was small, an average of 113 kg. Almost one-third of the producers (32 percent) used part of the corn for other purposes, such as the holding of stocks until the next harvest or to make payments in kind. In terms of grain, this last objective accounted for about 1 ton of use.

Table 12.1
Characterization of corn producers by annual corn balance, 1994

	Percentage of producers (%)	Average quantity per producer in each category (tons)	Average quantity per household (tons)
Number of cases	1158	Variable	1158
Availability of corn			
Corn production season:			
Spring-summer	93.9	4.0	3.7
Spring-summer only	74.6		
Fall-winter	25.4	5.3	1.4
Fall-winter only	6.1		
Both seasons	19.3		
Have initial corn stocks	49.0	0.4	0.3
Buy corn	40.4	0.6	0.2
Have access to corn			
through other sources [a]	6.4	0.4	0.0
Total availability			5.6
Use of corn			
Human consumption	90.4	1.4	1.2
Animal consumption	73.9	1.2	0.9
Sell corn	41.4	7.5	3.1
Use corn for seeds	74.0	0.1	0.1
Have other uses for corn			
(stocks, payments in kind)	32.3	1.0	0.3
Total use			5.6

Relationship with the market		Availability and total use
Only buy (and do not sell)	27.3	2.1
Neither buy nor sell	31.3	2.1
Buy and sell	13.1	12.5
Only sell (and do not buy)	28.3	9.2

[a] Gifts, payments in kind, etc.

Commercialization

It is interesting to observe that the proportions of producers who sell and of those who buy corn were similar, at 41.4 percent and 40.4 percent, respectively (table 12.1). However, the average amount sold was 7.5 tons, while the average amount purchased was 0.6 tons. This last result likely underestimates corn purchases because the survey did not explicitly ask about buying dough for tortillas.

Disaggregating the percentages of people who buy and sell shows that 28.3 percent of producers only sold, 27.3 percent only bought, and 13.1 percent engaged in both transaction types. This leaves 31.3 percent of producers who neither bought nor sold corn and were thus self-sufficient with respect to their corn needs.

Sources of Availability and Destinations of Use

The sources of annual corn availability for corn-producing households (measured in tons per year) were distributed as follows:

Stocks of corn before the spring–summer harvest	5.4%
Production obtained in the spring–summer season	66.1%
Production obtained in the fall–winter season	25.0%
Purchases made before the next spring–summer harvest	3.6%
Volume received from other sources, such as donations, payments in kind, etc.	0.5%
Total availability	5.6 tons

The largest portion of available corn thus comes from spring–summer production, with a smaller part from fall–winter production. A total of 90.5 percent of total availability came from home production. The contributions made by the carryover of stocks, the purchase of grain, and acquisition from other sources were small, adding up to a total of 9.5 percent. The destinations of this annual availability were the following:

Sales (marketed surplus)	55.4 %
Use for human consumption	21.4%

Use for animal consumption	16.1%
Use as seed	1.8%
Other uses	5.4%
Total use	5.6 tons

In the ejido sector the marketed surplus of corn is 61 percent of production, while 39 percent is retained for home and other uses.

Transaction Costs and Market Participation

Producers Who Sell and Do Not Buy

For farmers who sell and do not buy (28.3 percent of producers), around 40 percent of the sales were made at the farm gate, and the rest (60 percent) were made away from the plot (table 12.2). The average sale price was 696 pesos per ton of corn (table 12.3). On average, a higher price was received away from the plot (707 pesos away, compared to 679 pesos at the plot) since sale at the plot does not include transportation costs. Furthermore, there are economies of scale for sales away from the plot: the average amount sold away from the plot was 7.54 tons, while the amount sold at the farm gate was 4.60 tons. Sales away from the plot are much more important, representing 77 percent of total sales for these farmers. Even though only 19 percent of the transactions of these sellers were with CONASUPO, these transactions were much larger than those with other buyers (table 12.3). As a consequence, CONASUPO received 52 percent of the sales made by this group. The average amount sold to CONASUPO was 15.4 tons, at a price of 728 pesos per ton, which was inferior to the price for direct sales to consumers (761 pesos per ton). Furthermore, this price included transportation costs, which have to be subtracted from the price to make it comparable to the private sales price or to the direct sales price to consumers. Although the price received from CONASUPO is adjusted for the quality of corn, this price varies little from one farmer to the next. This is seen by the standard deviation of the CONASUPO price (59) compared to the sales price to a consumer (258).

More than half of the transactions made by producers who only sell (61 percent) were with private merchants, accounting for 41 percent of the volume of sales. Generally, prices offered by private merchants are low (671 pesos per ton in 1994), which partly reflects the lack of competitiveness among local merchants and partly the implicit transportation cost for sales to merchants who pick up the product at the farm gate.

Direct sales to consumers are the most favorable for producers, but there is not much local demand. The price received was 761 pesos per ton; however, transactions were only 1.70 tons on average, compared to 4.77 tons for sales to merchants and 15.43 tons for sales to CONASUPO. These direct sales represented only 3.7 percent of the total sales of these farmers.

Table 12.2
Places where corn is bought and sold, 1994

	Class of producers	
	Only sell	Sell and buy
Percentage of producers (%)	28.3	13.1
Sale at the farm gate (%)	40.2	57.3
Price received (pesos)	679	654
Quantity sold per transaction (tons)	4.60	4.22
Sale away from the plot (%)	60.0	42.7
Price received (pesos)	707	692
Quantity sold per transaction (tons)	7.54	17.2
	Only buy	Sell and buy
Percentage of producers	27.3	13.1
Purchase in the locality (%)	72.7	70.0
Price paid (pesos)	915	910
Quantity bought per transaction (tons)	0.63	0.61
Purchase outside the locality (%)	27.3	30.0
Price paid (pesos)	894	951
Quantity bought per transaction (tons)	0.61	0.24

The balance of the transactions of these producers is summarized in table 12.4. They had an average production of 9.2 tons and a total availability of 9.6 tons. They used 6.7 tons of corn for sale, 1.3 tons for human consumption, 1.0 tons for animal consumption, and 0.67 tons for seeds and stocks.

Producers Who Buy and Do Not Sell

For producers who buy and do not sell (27.3 percent of producers), the average purchase price was 909 pesos, which was 31 percent higher than the price received by those who sell, establishing a large

Table 12.3
Price bands and corn transactions, 1994

Only buy: 27.3% of producers			
		Purchases	
Sources	Price (price/ton)	Volume (%)	Transactions (%)
Merchant	960	31.0	30.3
Producer	948	31.5	33.5
CONASUPO	831	35.3	33.4
Others	799	2.2	2.8
Average price	909		

Only sell: 28.3% of producers			
		Sales	
Destination	Price (price/ton)	Volume (%)	Transactions (%)
Consumer	761	3.7	17.7
CONASUPO	728	51.6	19.0
Merchant	671	40.9	61.1
Others	581	3.7	2.2
Average price	696		

Buy and sell: 13.1% of producers			
		Purchases	
Sources	Price (price/ton)	Volume (%)	Transactions (%)
Merchant	945	47.4	53.7
Producer	934	33.3	26.8
CONASUPO	794	18.8	19.6
Others	800	0.4	0.4
Average price	922		

		Sales	
Destination	Price (price/ton)	Volume (%)	Transactions (%)
Consumer	593	1.3	12.2
CONASUPO	733	76.7	29.5
Merchant	656	21.7	56.6
Others	655	0.2	2.2
Average price	670		

Table 12.4
Corn balance of ejido families who produce corn, 1994
(in tons per year)

	Only buy (27.3% of producers)		Neither buy nor sell (31.3% of producers)		Only sell (28.3% of producers)	Buy and sell (13.1% of producers)
	Have fewer than 6 cattle: (22.0%)	Have 6 or more cattle (5.3%)	Have fewer than 6 cattle: (23.8%)	Have 6 or more cattle (7.5%)		
Availability						
Production	1.12	2.12	1.75	3.04	9.22	11.30
Purchases	0.61	0.65	0.00	0.00	0.00	0.50
Reserves	0.15	0.12	0.25	0.59	0.35	0.21
Other sources [a]	0.07	0.01	0.03	0.06	0.01	0.04
Total availability	2.0	2.9	2.0	3.7	9.6	12.1
Use						
Human consumption	1.25	0.93	1.07	1.09	1.34	1.41
Animal consumption	0.54	1.72	0.63	2.23	0.95	0.72
Sales	0.00	0.00	0.00	0.00	6.66	9.42
Seeds	0.04	0.08	0.06	0.09	0.14	0.08
Other uses [b]	0.13	0.12	0.27	0.28	0.53	0.44
Total use	2.0	2.9	2.0	3.7	9.6	12.1

[a] Other sources include donations and payments in kind.
[b] Other uses include principally stocks and also donations and payments in kind.

price band between sale and purchase. Most of these producers make their purchases of corn in the locality where they live (72.7 percent in 1994), and the rest (27.3 percent) make their purchases outside of the village (table 12.2). The average amounts purchased were 630 kg for local and 610 kg for outside transactions. This preference for purchases within the same locality can be explained by the lower prices and much lower transactions costs.

With respect to sources for purchase, there are no large differences between the percentages obtained from official sources (35.3 percent), individual producers (31.5 percent), and merchants (31.0 percent), as seen in table 12.3. The official source, CONASUPO stores, was clearly preferred because it offered the lowest price: 831 pesos per ton. However, for many buyers high transaction costs were incurred getting to these stores. The price paid for purchases from individual producers was 948 pesos per ton, while from merchants it was 960 pesos.

To analyze the corn balance of producers who only buy, a distinction is made between those who have less than six head of cattle and those who have six or more (table 12.4). There is a clear difference between the two groups. Those who have fewer animals represented 22.0 percent of the total number of producers. They produced 1.12 tons of corn, bought 0.61 tons, and derived 0.22 tons from reserves and other sources, for a total availability of 2.0 tons. They used 1.25 tons for human consumption, 0.54 tons for animal consumption, and 0.17 tons for seeds and stocks. Those who have more animals represented only 5.3 percent of producers and had much higher corn production and use. They produced 2.12 tons, bought 0.65 tons, and derived 0.13 tons from reserves and other sources, reaching a total availability of 2.9 tons. They used 0.93 tons for human consumption, 1.72 tons for animal consumption, and 0.20 tons for seeds and stocks.

Producers Who Buy and Sell

We have seen that 13.1 percent of corn producers sell and buy during the year. In general, these are poorer families who need liquidity and therefore sell part of the harvest. They later buy the deficits needed to feed the family and the animals. This group also includes larger producers who are well located with respect to storage facilities and CONASUPO stores. These transactions imply the cost of a price margin, but this margin is below the cost of storage (including the opportunity costs of the liquidity immobilized) because the nominal transaction cost with CONASUPO is 8 percent (table 12.3), which is inferior to the opportunity cost of capital (a real 10 percent with 10 percent inflation). Those who engage in this transaction of purchase and sale with CONASUPO would be those who have easy access to CONASUPO storage facilities for sales and to CONASUPO stores for purchases. For producers who buy and sell, the average sales price was 670 pesos per ton, and the purchase price was 922 pesos. These prices created a 38 percent margin between purchase and sale price, which was wider than the 31 percent price band between prices received by pure sellers and prices paid by buyers. This reflects a difference in the synchronization of purchases and sales, with a larger time interval between sales and purchases for seller/buyers and hence higher storage costs to be paid in the transaction.

Among producers who sell and buy corn, 43 percent sold away from the plot, while 57 percent sold at the farm gate (table 12.2). For those who only sell corn, 40 percent sold at the farm gate and 60 percent sold away from the plot. This suggests that the producers who only sell are better organized to commercialize their corn.

Regarding the destinations of sales, producers who buy and sell channeled a higher percentage of their sales (77 percent) via CONASUPO than pure sellers (52 percent) (table 12.3). As to the origin of purchases, pure buyers used CONASUPO in 35 percent of their purchases, while those who sell and buy only made 18 percent of their purchases from this source. CONASUPO was clearly the most advantageous trading partner for those who buy and sell because it offered both the highest price for sales (733 pesos per ton) and the lowest price for purchases (794 pesos per ton) among alternative sources and destinations. Sales to CONASUPO were much larger than sales to individual consumers. This indicates that some ejidatarios with large production use this system of sales to CONASUPO both to benefit from high price support and later to satisfy their corn necessities by buying from CONASUPO at subsidized prices. This privilege, however, only applies to a minority of households with easy access to CONASUPO's storage facilities and consumer stores.

Producers Who Neither Buy Nor Sell

The group of households who are self-sufficient in corn was large, representing 31.3 percent of corn-producing ejidatarios. Their average availability of corn was 2.41 tons, of which they produced 2.06 tons. The rest stemmed from reserves, payments in kind, and gifts. They used 1.08 tons for human consumption, 1.01 tons for animal consumption, and the rest for seeds and stocks.

In this group, it is important to separate out those who have significant numbers of animals, again using a threshold of six head of cattle. Those who have few animals represented 23.8 percent of the producers. They produced 1.75 tons of corn and obtained 0.28 tons

from reserves and other sources. They used 1.07 tons for human consumption and 0.63 tons for animal consumption. For seeds and other
uses they needed 0.33 tons. Their total availability and use was only
2.0 tons, identical to pure buyers with few animals.

Figure 12.1
Price bands on the corn market

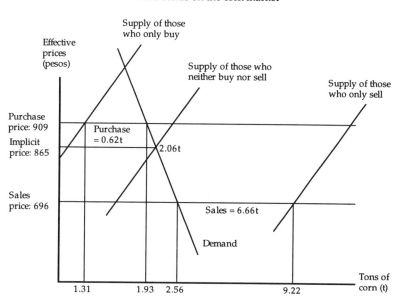

Accounting for 7.5 percent of the producers, those who have six or
more head of cattle had a much higher level of economic activity,
even though they do not buy or sell corn. They produced 3.04 tons of
corn and had a total availability of 3.7 tons. They used 1.09 tons for
human consumption, 2.23 for animal consumption, and 0.37 for seeds
and other uses, making the total use of corn 3.7 tons.

In figure 12.1, the average price band between those who only buy
and those who only sell is represented. It can be seen that the average
self-sufficient farmer had an implicit price for corn that was around
865 pesos per ton. This is why this farmer neither sells (he would
have received a lower price, 696 pesos) nor buys (he would have paid
a higher price, 909 pesos). He is thus voluntarily not participating in
the market. With the implementation of NAFTA, if the purchase price
does not fall below 865 pesos per ton, he will remain self-sufficient

and therefore be protected from the negative impact of trade liberalization on the price of corn.[2] If the price falls below 865 pesos/ton, then households will become net buyers of corn, benefiting from the lower price to acquire part of their food needs.

Producer Traits by Relationship to the Corn Market

Table 12.5 gives a list of characteristics of the six types of corn-producing households, defined according to their relationship with the corn market and their use of corn for animal consumption. It shows that those who only buy corn and have few animals were those with the least land (4.1 ha NRE). They had only 1.7 ha of rainfed corn and 0.2 ha of irrigated corn, and more than a third of their rainfed corn was intercropped. Fundamentally, they are the smallest farmers: 46 percent were in the category of farms below 2 ha NRE. In contrast, buyers of corn who own animals had more than twice as much land (10.3 ha NRE) and an average of twenty-one head of cattle. Generally, they are producers with more than 2 ha NRE, a well-developed livestock economy, but strong peasant characteristics (intercropped corn).

Those who are in a situation of corn self-sufficiency and own few animals had a little more land and cultivated a little more corn than those who buy and have equally few animals. Their farms had an average size of 4.7 ha NRE, and they cultivated 2.1 ha of rainfed corn. While their farms are marginally larger than those of buyers, they still mainly belong to the lowest two classes of farms: 71 percent of them were under 5 ha NRE. In contrast, ejidatarios who are self-sufficient with animals had an average of 13.6 ha NRE and twenty-one head of cattle. Seventy-three percent of them belonged to the farm class above 5 ha NRE. They are farmers with an important animal economy who do not use the corn market because they produce their animal feed themselves.

Producers who only sell corn had 9.1 ha NRE, and 51 percent were in farms below 5 ha NRE. Finally, those who buy and sell resemble those who only sell. Their market integration strategy seems to be dictated more by privileged access to CONASUPO stores than by differential producer characteristics.

The household characteristics of the six classes are not very different. The differential position of corn-producing households with re-

---

[2]For a development of this point, see de Janvry, Sadoulet, and Gordillo de Anda 1995.

spect to the corn price bands thus stems from their condition as producers and not from differences in their family structure or from their structure of income external to the farm.

Table 12.5
Characteristics of corn-producing households according to their relationship with the corn market, 1994

	Only buy		Neither buy nor sell		Only sell	Sell and buy
	< 6 cattle	≥ 6 cattle	< 6 cattle	≥ 6 cattle		
Corn producers (%)	22.0	5.3	23.7	7.5	28.3	13.1
Characteristics of the farm						
Agriculture						
Farm area (ha NRE)	4.1	10.3	4.7	13.6	9.1	7.0
Rainfed area (ha)	3.3	7.7	3.9	7.4	6.0	4.5
Irrigated area (ha)	0.4	0.3	0.3	1.1	1.0	1.1
Natural pasture area (ha)	1.4	5.4	1.8	8.0	3.5	2.4
Forest area (ha)	0.5	0.0	0.3	0.2	0.4	0.0
Rainfed corn area (ha)	1.7	2.6	2.1	4.4	3.8	3.8
Irrigated corn area (ha)	0.2	0.4	0.1	0.4	0.7	0.8
Intercropped rainfed corn area (ha)	0.6	0.9	0.4	0.3	0.5	0.2
Intercropped irrigated corn area (ha)	0.0	0.0	0.0	0.0	0.0	0.0
Livestock						
Number of cattle	0.7	21.4	0.6	21.1	6.4	4.3
Number of pigs	1.5	3.7	1.8	2.8	2.2	2.2
Percentage of producers in each farm class						
< 2 (ha NRE)	45.7	21.1	33.3	4.1	12.4	13.1
2–5	30.9	24.7	38.1	22.4	38.9	40.5
5–10	10.2	29.7	15.9	30.3	17.4	13.0
≥ 10	12.3	24.6	11.3	42.4	30.6	27.1
Household characteristics						
Family size	5.1	5.4	5.1	5.1	5.3	4.9
Number of adults	3.5	3.7	3.4	3.8	3.4	3.5
Age of head of household	50.4	52.0	48.8	53.6	48.2	51.0
Number of wage earners	0.4	0.3	0.4	0.4	0.3	0.4
Number of migrants	0.4	0.4	0.6	0.5	0.4	0.6

13

Ejidatarios with an Entrepreneurial Character

The data have demonstrated the emergence of a peasant economy based on production systems with typical peasant features, particularly the displacement of crops in pure stands by intercropping and the reliance on manual and animal-powered technology. Other important characteristics of this peasant economy are extensive participation in the labor market, migration, the diversification of activities away from agriculture, the increase in cattle raising by the most successful households, and a high level of self-sufficiency in basic foods. The emergence of a peasant economy is the product of the liberalization of ejidatarios from state controls.

Liberalization also induced the emergence of a small group of entrepreneurial households whose presence reveals an accelerating process of social differentiation within the ejido. The emergence of this group, and the consequent social differentiation, was strongly constrained in 1994 by the unfavorable institutional and economic context. This context was characterized by appreciation of the real exchange rate, severely restricted access to credit, high interest rates, the systematic elimination of subsidies before the initiation of PROCAMPO, and the dismantling of many public institutions that serviced the ejido with credit, marketing, technical assistance, access to modern inputs, and so on. These institutions have been very partially replaced by the private sector, producers' organizations, and the ejido organization itself. Within this unfavorable context, the success of these Schumpeterian entrepreneurs' initiatives is compromised as they are forced to concentrate their energies on limiting their technological and economic downfall and on avoiding being drawn into the general fall of the ejido sector, extensively documented in the preceding chapters.

In analyzing technological change between 1990 and 1994, we have noted that producers of monocropped corn in the fall–winter season had a differential technological behavior. Also, in the analysis of changes in cropping patterns, we have seen that the production of fruits and vegetables increased among a small number of farmers. There was an increase in cattle raising as well, which was confined to producers with large farms. Finally, migration is a restricted but important source of income and accumulation, in particular for those ejidatarios with less access to land, for whom migration provides one of the few opportunities for capitalization. In this part of the study, we use these four manifestations of entrepreneurial behavior to analyze who these households are and what factors explain their differential success.

Producers of Fall–Winter Monocropped Corn

The characteristics of these producers are identified in table 13.1. Analyzing first the contrast between these producers and the rest of the ejidatarios in 1994, it is seen that they are located principally in the Gulf and South Pacific. They have larger farms (10.1 ha NRE vs. 6.8 ha NRE) and more irrigated land (0.98 ha vs. 0.92 ha). Forty-five percent are in the > 10 ha NRE class of farms, compared to 19 percent for the other ejidatarios. They plant more corn, both rainfed and irrigated, but they plant less intercropped rainfed corn, which we have used as the principal indicator of a traditional peasant economy. They use more improved seeds (50 percent vs. 13 percent), chemical products (74 percent vs. 25 percent), and fertilizers (79 percent vs. 47 percent) than the rest of the ejidatarios. They reach much higher yields under irrigation (3.8 tons/ha vs. 1.6 tons/ha). Their family characteristics indicate that they are younger and have fewer household members participating in the labor market and migration. This is undoubtedly associated with the larger farm size, but it also suggests that the modernization of agricultural activities decreases as dedication to agriculture falls. Their corn balance indicates that they have a higher production of corn and use more corn for animal consumption. They have less access to credit through PRONASOL but more through commercial banks.

The last columns of table 13.1 provide a comparative analysis of the changes between 1990 and 1994 for these entrepreneurial producers and for the other ejidatarios. First, it can be seen that the portion of ejidatarios who are members of this category of entrepreneurs increased between 1990 and 1994 from 13.9 percent to 16.6 percent, confirming the acceleration of a process of differentiation based on the reduction of state controls. Expansion in the number of these producers occurred principally in the North Pacific. Among these more dynamic producers there were no changes in land distribution. In contrast, among the other ejidatarios, the incidence of very small farms between 0 and 2 ha NRE decreased, while that of farms between 2 and 10 ha NRE increased. This concentration of small-farm land toward family plots between 2 and 10 ha NRE is induced by migration and the abandonment of land by the smallest farmers when modernization options are least present. Modernization thus acts as an alternative to abandoning the land or migrating. It is also among these more modern producers that there was a conversion of natural pastures and fallow land to the production of irrigated corn. Their irrigated area increased by 66 percent, indicating the fundamental importance of irrigation in support of modernization. During the four years surveyed, when there were no new investments in large irrigation projects, this expansion in the ejido was the result of small projects promoted by FIRCO and CNA, and above all by sustained efforts to rehabilitate existing facilities. For the other ejidatarios, as well as for these modernizers, the use of technology (chemical products and technical assistance) fell strongly between 1990 and 1994. However, the modernizers' distinguishing technological achievement was the adoption of improved seeds in corn cultivation in the fall–winter and spring–summer seasons. This technological diffusion was a consequence of the increased efforts of the Ministry of Agriculture to promote the diffusion of improved seeds. What these observations suggest is that the success of this diffusion effort was confined to a small group of ejidatarios with differential entrepreneurial characteristics.

Fruit and Vegetable Producers

With Mexico's entry into NAFTA and expectations of a fall in the prices of corn and beans, the main crops that will acquire comparative advantages are fruits and vegetables, which are intensive in unskilled labor. In table 13.2, the characteristics of fruit and vegetable producers are analyzed in contrast to those of all other ejidatarios. It can be seen that, similarly to the increase in entrepreneurial corn cultivation in the fall–winter cycle, the portion of families who produce fruits and vegetables increased, rising from 14.1 percent in 1990 to 17.3 percent in 1994. This also indicates that the differentiation process, based on opportunities offered by market liberalization and the relaxation of state control, has accelerated, even though the economic and institutional context has been adverse. There is a high concentration of fruit and vegetable producers in the Gulf. These producers had more irrigated area than other ejidatarios (1.3 ha vs. 0.9 ha), which indicates the importance of access to irrigation for these activities. Fewer of

Table 13.1
Differential characteristics of monocropped corn producers in the fall-winter season, 1990 and 1994

		1990 producers			1994 producers			Test: 1994 vs 1990	
		All other ejidatarios	Monocropped corn, fall-winter	Test	All other ejidatarios	Monocropped corn, fall-winter	Test	All other ejidatarios	Monocropped corn, fall-winter
Number of cases	#	1391	224		1287	256			+
Percentage of cases	%	86.1	13.9		83.4	16.6			
Geographic region									
North	%	25.8	6.7	– –	27.3	6.6	– –		
North Pacific	%	10.5	2.2	– –	9.3	9.6	– –		++
Center	%	36.7	5.0	– –	37.5	8.0	– –		
Gulf	%	11.7	65.3	++	10.8	54.1	++		–
South Pacific	%	15.2	20.7		15.2	21.6	++		– –
Land									
Total area used	NRE	6.91	10.31	++	6.81	10.07	++		
Rainfed area	ha	4.07	4.15	++	4.94	5.15	++	++	
Irrigated area	ha	1.01	0.59	– –	0.92	0.98	++		++
Natural pastures area	ha	2.92	8.11	++	2.21	6.09	++		– –
Farm class									
≤ 2 ha	%	33.9	11.2	– –	28.9	6.7	– –	– –	
2–10 ha	%	46.4	39.9		52.5	48.7		++	
> 10 ha	%	19.7	49.0	++	18.6	44.6	++		
Land use									
Rainfed monocropped corn area	ha	1.89	3.94	++	2.05	4.36	++	+	
Irrigated monocropped corn area	ha	0.19	0.54	++	0.29	0.93	++	++	
Rainfed intercropped corn area	ha	0.30	0.03	– –	0.50	0.07	– –		
Irrigated intercropped corn area	ha	0.01	0.00		0.02	0.00			
Producers of fruits and vegetables	%	11.8	28.0	++	14.9	29.0	++	++	+
Irrigated corn technology									
Improved seeds	%	22.6	30.1		13.2	49.7	++	– –	
Chemical products	%	50.9	74.0	++	24.5	73.9	++	– –	
Fertilizers	%	73.7	56.0		47.2	78.5	++	– –	++
Technical assistance	%	72.0	63.8		4.2	34.6	++		– –

Rainfed corn technology									
Improved seeds	%	8.7	1.5	--	7.7	--	7.4	++	+
Chemical products	%	37.3	80.9	++	35.1	++	67.6	--	--
Fertilizers	%	59.9	51.5	++	54.3	--	36.6	--	--
Technical assistance	%	54.4	66.7	++	4.2	++	5.7	--	--
Corn technology, fall-winter									
Improved seeds	%		4.6		n.a.		15.5		++
Chemical products	%		77.4		n.a.		67.0		--
Fertilizers	%		50.2		n.a.		45.2		
Technical assistance	%		66.1		n.a.		10.1		--
Corn technology, spring-summer									
Improved seeds	%	10.4	3.9	++	8.4	++	10.0	++	--
Chemical products	%	39.0	84.9		33.6	--	67.8		--
Fertilizers	%	61.6	51.7		53.2	--	41.3	--	
Technical assistance	%	56.5	64.3		4.2		4.2		--
Yield									
Irrigated corn	t/ha	2.11	1.90	++	1.57	++	3.83	++	--
Rainfed corn	t/ha	1.13	1.37		1.08		1.19		
Family characteristics									
Education		1.35	1.30		1.41		1.41		++
Family size	#	5.4	6.3	++	5.1		5.1	--	--
Number of adults	#	3.7	3.8		3.5		3.2	--	--
Age of head of household	Years	49.1	48.1		50.3	--	46.7	--	++
Number of wage earners	#	0.45	0.21	--	0.44		0.25	--	--
Number of migrants	#				0.54		0.29	--	--
Corn balance									
Production	tons				4.74		6.61	++	++
Animal consumption	tons				0.80		1.25	++	++
Credit sources (% receiving from)									
BANRURAL	%				4.3		5.9	--	--
PRONASOL	%				23.1		4.7	--	--
Commercial banks	%				1.1		3.8	++	++

Table 13.2
Differential characteristics of fruit and vegetable producers, 1990 and 1994

		1990 producers			1994 producers			Test: 1994 vs 1990	
		All other ejidatarios	Fruits and vegetables	Test	All other ejidatarios	Fruits and vegetables	Test	All other ejidatarios	Fruits and vegetables
Number of cases	#	1387	228		1276	267			
Percentage of cases	%	85.9	14.1		82.7	17.3			++
Geographic region									
North	%	24.3	16.5	– –	24.6	20.3	– –		
North Pacific	%	9.8	6.4		9.6	8.1			
Center	%	32.7	30.2		34.3	24.1	– –		
Gulf	%	16.6	34.4	++	14.5	35.1	++		
South Pacific	%	16.5	12.4		17.0	12.5			
Land									
Total area used	NRE	7.20	8.51		7.08	8.67	++		
Rainfed area	ha	4.02	4.42		4.95	5.10	++	++	
Irrigated area	ha	0.89	1.30	++	0.85	1.31	+		
Natural pastures area	ha	3.54	4.22		2.69	3.68	++		
Monocropped corn producers, fall-winter	%	11.6	27.6	++	14.3	28.0	++	+	
Farm class									
≤ 2 ha	%	33.5	13.8	– –	27.7	13.2	– –	– –	
2–10 ha	%	44.8	49.3		50.7	57.3		++	
> 10 ha	%	21.7	36.9	++	21.5	29.4	++	++	

Use of land

Rainfed monocropped corn area	ha	2.24	1.80		2.44	2.43		++
Irrigated monocropped corn area	ha	0.26	0.15		0.43	0.23	++	++
Rainfed intercropped corn area	ha	0.29	0.08	--	0.47	0.22	--	++
Irrigated intercropped corn area	ha	0.01	0.05	++	0.02	0.02		
Rainfed fruits and vegetables area	ha		2.26			2.00		
Irrigated fruits and vegetables area	ha		0.95			0.61	--	--

Family

Education		1.32	1.43	++	1.40	1.46	++	++
Size of family	#	5.53	5.69		5.06	5.17		--
Number of adults	#	3.64	3.90	+	3.48	3.37	--	--
Age of head of family	Yrs	48.6	51.0		49.7	49.7		
Number of wage earners	#	0.43	0.35	++	0.43	0.34	++	++
Number of migrants	#				0.52	0.39	--	

Credit sources

% who received credit from								
BANRURAL	%		3.9			7.7	++	
PRONASOL	%		21.2			14.5	--	
Commercial banks	%		1.6			1.6		

them belonged to the smallest farm class (0 to 2 ha NRE), and more of
them were found in the largest farm class. They had a higher educational level and received more credit from BANRURAL. Their entrepreneurial capacity and access to significant amounts of credit are essential to the production of fruits and vegetables, just as they are for the
modernization of corn cultivation.

With respect to changes between 1990 and 1994, there was no land
concentration away from the smallest farms toward the medium-
sized farms, unlike those who do not cultivate fruits and vegetables.
As in corn modernization, participation in fruit and vegetable cultivation thus appears as a substitute to migration.

It is evident that this analysis of entrepreneurial behavior in the
ejido, and identification of the conditions for modernization and diversification, requires more attention, especially through detailed case
studies. However, the above analysis reveals the acceleration of these
two processes and a deepening social differentiation resulting from
the new opportunities offered by the reforms. The success of these
two processes is associated with a large number of conditions internal
and external to the ejido household. This means that there are numerous ways to give incentives for these transformations. They include
reorganizing access to credit, improving educational levels of decision
makers, and facilitating access to technical assistance for the adoption
of modern technology. Some of these instruments work through the
promotion of organizations and institutional reconstruction. They
should occupy an important place in a rural development program to
assist the transformation of the ejido.

The Increase in Cattle Raising

The growth of cattle raising responds to two rationales. One is
through entrepreneurial activity, principally by ejidatarios with larger
farms and pastures. The other is through capitalization that substitutes cattle for the use of the financial system, particularly by small
farmers who participate in migration and receive remittances. We will
analyze these two entrepreneurial strategies.

In table 13.3, the characteristics of ejidatarios who have farms
above 10 ha NRE are analyzed, contrasting ejidatarios with five or
more and those with fewer than five head of cattle. It can be seen that
the number of ejidatarios with five or more cattle increased by 26 percent between 1990 and 1994, from 39.2 percent to 49.3 percent. This
indicates an important growth of participation in cattle raising during
these four years. These ejidatarios were more frequently represented
in the Gulf, South Pacific, and Center regions. They had more rainfed

land and more pastures. They had less irrigated land and were less frequently producers of monocropped corn in the fall–winter season, indicating that cattle-raising is an entrepreneurial activity that differs from the modernization of corn. However, their entrepreneurial character is observed in the technology they applied to corn: they increased the use of improved seeds, fertilizers, and chemical products—a marked contrast to the technological backsliding of other ejidatarios with the same land area. They had more access to common-property land, which is important for grazing livestock. They had more access to credit from private and public sources. Their family characteristics and activities do not distinguish them from those who have fewer animals. It can be concluded, therefore, that there is an entrepreneurial class in the ejido whose strategy of accumulation is commercial cattle raising. This group has expanded rapidly during the last four years. Key to their success are the larger size of their farms and their access to credit and modern technological options.

The Migration–Subsistence Corn Strategy

We have seen that an important economic strategy among the smallest ejidatarios is a combination of wage labor, migration, and corn production for family consumption. For those who are successful, the strategy also includes accumulation of savings through cattle raising, supported by access to common lands in the ejido. To see the role of migration in this strategy (table 13.4), the differential characteristics of small ejidatarios (below 2 ha NRE) are analyzed, comparing those households with migrants to those without migrants.

As we saw in the analysis of migration to the United States in chapter 5, families with migrants were more frequently represented in the Center and North regions. They were not among the producers of corn in the fall–winter season. However, they displayed more entrepreneurship not only in migratory activity but also in agriculture, having more access to public credit, producing more fruits and vegetables, and having a slightly higher orientation toward corn sales. But 71 percent of them did not sell corn, being either purely self-sufficient (33 percent) or net buyers of corn (38 percent). Their family characteristics did not differentiate them, which suggests that the determinant in success of migration is more regional, through the accumulation of migration capital consisting of knowledge of family and community members who have established bases in the U.S. labor market. The success of migration is confirmed by the increase in animal ownership: on average, the smallest farmers who have migrants in the family have 11 percent more cattle and 44 percent more pigs.

Table 13.3
Differential characteristics of cattle owners with farms larger than 10 ha NRE, 1990 and 1994

	1990			1994			Test: 1994 vs 1990	
	Fewer than 5 cattle	5 or more cattle	Test	Fewer than 5 cattle	5 or more cattle	Test	Fewer than 5 cattle	5 or more cattle
Number of observations	233	151		179	174			
Percentage of cases	60.8	39.2		50.7	49.3			++
Distribution by geographic region (%)								
North	23.5	14.5	-	22.9	16.3			
North Pacific	24.4	10.4	- -	18.9	13.5	++		
Center	10.1	18.1	+	9.9	20.9	-		
Gulf	33.4	38.6		36.6	25.5	++		
South Pacific	8.6	18.5	++	11.7	23.8	++		
Land (ha NRE)	17.94	23.64	+	17.01	23.74	++		++
Rainfed (ha)	6.90	7.45		7.69	12.21	++		
Irrigated (ha)	2.89	1.54	- -	3.33	1.95	- -		
Pasture (ha)	9.84	19.39	++	7.08	14.00	++	- -	
Forest (ha)	1.46	0.27	- -	1.52	0.57	++		
Ejido's area (ha NRE [a] by ejidatario)	22.95	27.00		16.91	23.56	++	- -	
Distribution by class (%)								
≤10 ha NRE	29.2	18.6	-	36.0	15.0	- -		
10–30 ha NRE	49.5	60.7	+	54.9	64.6			
> 30 ha NRE	21.3	20.7		9.1	20.4	++		
Monocropped corn producers, fall-winter (%)	21.7	39.2	++	37.1	27.7		++	-
Producers of fruits and vegetables	18.4	27.0		23.0	21.3			
Corn crop (ha)								
Rainfed, monocropped	3.05	3.59	-	4.19	4.14			
Irrigated, monocropped	0.72	0.32		1.54	0.78	- -	++	
Rainfed, intercropped	0.19	0.11		0.27	0.38			++

	0.00	0.05		0.04	0.01		
Irrigated, intercropped	0.00	0.05	++	0.04	0.01		
Balance of corn							
% of those who buy				23.8	12.1	– –	
% who neither sell nor buy				23.2	30.3		
% of those who sell				32.1	46.7	++	
% of those who buy and sell				20.9	10.9	–	
Animals (number)							
Cattle	0.5	23.6	++	0.5	24.4	++	
Pigs	2.2	3.5	++	2.1	2.7		
Credit sources: % who receive							
Public				23.8	35.1	++	
Formal private				1.9	6.4		
Other				7.4	6.4		
Technology (%)							
Improved seed	36.8	25.1	– –	28.2	38.1		++
Fertilizers	57.3	48.8		38.0	57.1	++	– –
Chemical products	68.1	61.7		56.7	74.4	++	– –
Technical assistance	74.6	67.5		17.7	14.1		– –
Family							
Size of family	5.72	6.00		5.27	5.24		–
Number of adults	3.71	4.03		3.48	3.73		– –
Age of head of family	48.3	48.2		47.3	50.0	+	
Educational capital	1.41	1.36		1.50	1.51	++	++
Employment: number of adults who							
Work at home	1.45	1.45		1.30	1.41	++	– –
Earn wages	0.37	0.17	– –	0.38	0.31		– –
Migrated				0.43	0.35	+	+

[a] Total area adjusted by the regional coefficient of rainfed corn.

Table 13.4
Characteristics of the population with farms under 2 ha NRE and migrants, 1994

	Without migrants	With migrants	Test
Number of observations	218	171	
Percentage of cases	56.0	44.0	
Distribution by geographic region (%)			
North	17.7	20.8	
North Pacific	8.3	5.8	
Center	44.3	52.3	
Gulf	5.4	4.4	
South Pacific	24.3	16.8	
Land (ha NRE)	0.96	1.14	++
Rainfed (ha)	1.23	1.50	++
Irrigated (ha)	0.10	0.10	
Ejido's area (ha NRE by ejidatario [a])	22.90	22.18	
Distribution by class (%)			
≤ 10 ha NRE	50.6	51.2	
10–30 ha NRE	25.3	22.7	
> 30 ha NRE	24.1	26.2	
Producers of monocropped corn, fall-winter (%)	6.0	2.4	
Producers of fruits and vegetables (%)	7.7	10.8	
Corn crops (ha)			
Rainfed, monocropped	0.70	0.79	
Irrigated, monocropped	0.08	0.03	–
Rainfed, intercropPed	0.26	0.34	
Irrigated, intercropped	0.00	0.01	
Balance of corn			
% of those who buy	47.6	38.1	
% who neither buy nor sell	32.9	32.6	
% of those who sell	12.2	16.5	
% of those who buy and sell	7.3	12.8	
Animals (number)			
Cattle	1.9	2.1	
Pigs	0.9	1.3	
Credit sources: % who receive			
Public	16.3	18.7	
Other	0.7	1.8	
Technology (%)			
Improved seed	4.2	4.7	
Fertilizers	50.2	55.6	
Chemical products	24.8	16.9	
Technical assistance	2.3	1.7	
Family			
Size of family	4.69	5.00	
Number of adults	3.09	3.19	
Age of head of family	50.0	47.6	
Education capital	1.32	1.40	++
Employment: number of adults who			
Work at home	1.26	1.31	
Earn wages	0.34	0.40	
Migrated	0.00	1.11	++

[a] Total area adjusted by the regional coeffecient of rainfed corn.

Conclusion

We have identified four entrepreneurial strategies in the ejido that are symptoms of the beginning of a differentiation process. The analysis suggests that there exist many means of differentiation: modernization of traditional crops, diversification toward crops that acquire comparative advantage, accumulation of capital through cattle raising for those who have more land, and, for a few with little land, success in migration through the complex nexus of subsistence corn, migration, and cattle raising. With improved agricultural profitability for the ejido and reconstruction of the network of institutions and organizations that support ejido producers, this process of differentiation could accelerate. Who will benefit from the new opportunities will depend on the relative competitiveness of members of the ejido, which, in turn, depends on differential access to the determinants of success identified in this chapter: access to credit through BANRURAL and commercial banks, access to irrigation, access to pastures and common grazing lands, higher educational levels, access to technologies (improved seeds), and access to migration capital.

14

The Ejido and Its Forms of Organization

Structural Characteristics and Organization

The 1990 and 1994 surveys include the same 276 cases (255 ejidos and 21 indigenous communities). In 1994, the ejidatario-level survey was complemented by an ejido-level survey wherein questions were asked of the ejido leadership. Data from this latter survey are analyzed in this chapter. The characterization of the ejidos includes the following: structural characteristics, internal decision-making mechanisms, rules managing access to common-property land and the role of this land for cattle raising by individual ejidatarios, sources and uses of collective income, and the quality of infrastructure and levels of social welfare in these ejidos. To contrast different ejidos, the following three alternative typologies are used:

Typologies	Percent of Ejidos and Communities
Geographic Zone	
North	25.2
North Pacific	10.3
Center	33.2
Gulf	20.6
South Pacific	10.7
Ethnic Composition	
Mestizo-majority ejido	82.3
Indigenous-majority ejido	11.4
Indigenous community	6.4
Date of Land Endowment	
<1940	52.5
1940–1970	26.3
>1970	21.3

In table 14.1, the structural characteristics of these ejidos and communities are observed. On average, ejidos had ninety-five ejidatarios, eighty-three of whom had rights to a plot of land, but they also included a large number of settlers (*avecindados*), an average of eighty-five per ejido. These settlers live in the ejido but do not have rights to a plot of land. This large number of settlers, who cannot legally acquire land already allocated to a member, reflects the increasing demographic pressures within the ejido. The presence of settlers is much lower in the indigenous communities, which have the right to give land access to new families. However, in these communities the land becomes increasingly atomized in response to demographic growth.

Common-access land represented 68 percent of the ejidos' total land area, while individual plots accounted for 28 percent and the area for human settlement, 4 percent. Of these common-access lands, 67 percent were pastures and 24 percent, forests. The share of common land in the total land area has been about constant through the different historical periods of land grants. It is larger in the indigenous communities (85 percent) than in the ejidos because, as we saw in chapter 4, individual land in the communities becomes common-access area when it is not cultivated.

The geographic distribution of the different types of ejidos locates the ejidos with mestizo dominance in the North and North Pacific, the ejidos with indigenous dominance in the Gulf, and the indigenous communities in the South Pacific.[1]

The regional distribution of ejido formation by time periods recounts the history of the Mexican land reform. Until the 1940s, land grants were principally in the Center and North. During the period from 1940 to 1970, land endowments were equally distributed throughout the country. After 1970, during the period that started with the presidency of Luis Echeverría (1970–1976), many new ejidos were organized in the Gulf and the North Pacific, compensating for the initial delay in implementing land reform in these regions.

In table 14.2, the internal organization of the ejido is analyzed. It is observed that 39 percent of the ejidos declared that they have unresolved legal problems regarding the borders of their territory. These conflicts seem to be more intense in the South Pacific, in the indigenous communities, and among the older ejidos. Conflict regarding the definition of common-access areas were almost exclusively with persons foreign to the ejido. Only 55 percent of the ejidos had internal

---

[1]The importance of indigenous communities relative to ejidos in Oaxaca is analyzed in detail by Dennis (1976).

rules, and 29 percent had rules that were up to date according to the agrarian law. These rules pertained to agricultural activity in 36 percent of the cases. For those who have common pastures, official rules regulated access to these pastures in only 22 percent of the cases. In general, the organizational structure of the ejido is weak, particularly among the oldest ejidos.

The data also reveal that the frequency of summons to assemblies and ejidatarios' participation in those assemblies is modest: 52 percent of the ejidos had a monthly assembly; 66 percent of the ejidatarios attended assemblies, but only 38 percent of them participated actively. Finally, 32 percent of ejidos belonged to an ejido union and 2.8 percent to an ARIC. In general, the organizational weakness of the ejido, both internally and in terms of membership to peak organizations, is a potentially serious barrier to the ejido's adaptation to the new market rules and institutional context.

Management of common-access pastures is an important aspect of the ejido's organization. The rules for the management of these pastures are analyzed in table 14.3. Their objective is to avoid the overgrazing typically associated with common-access resources (nonexcludable) and individual (rival) appropriation of benefits. Only 33 percent of the ejidos had the capacity to prevent use of these pastures by outsiders. Controlling access is therefore a very important problem for the rational management of common pastures by the ejido. Without this, grazing land becomes open-access land instead of a common-property resource, and overgrazing inevitably follows (Bromley 1991). This problem seems to be most serious in the South Pacific, the indigenous-majority ejidos, and the more recently constituted ejidos. Fifty-three percent of the ejidos with common pastures had rules for the management of pastures that were either part of the general set of rules of the ejido (22 percent of the cases) or a special set of rules for pastures (15 percent of the cases). In 32 percent of the cases, these rules imposed a limit to the number of cattle that each ejidatario could have on the common-access pastures. There were also obligations to participate in the maintenance of pastures (29 percent of the cases). In 81 percent of the cases, the representative of the ejido's executive committee declared that the rules had been obeyed by almost all the ejidatarios.

Looking for differences in the ejido typologies, it can be observed that the ejidos most organized for the management of pastures are in the North, Gulf, and North Pacific. Also, ejidos with a mestizo majority are generally better organized than the indigenous-majority ejidos and the indigenous communities.

Table 14.1
Structural characteristics of the ejidos, 1994

	All ejidos	Geographic zone					Ethnic composition			Date of land endowment		
		North	North Pacific	Center	Gulf	South Pacific	Mestizo majority ejido	Indigenous majority ejido	Indigenous community	≤1940	1940–1970	>1970
Number of observations	276	70	28	92	57	30	227	31	18	145	73	59
Percentage of cases	100	25.2	10.3	33.2	20.6	10.7	82.3	11.4	6.4	52.5	26.3	21.3
Population per ejido												
Ejidos with settlers (%)	75.0	66.9	65.4	72.4	95.0	73.2	76.7	74.1	54.7	76.7	72.0	80.9
Ejidatarios with a plot of land (%)	94.0	96.0	97.3	95.8	86.0	96.0	95.3	89.5	85.6	93.8	96.3	91.3
Number of ejidatarios	95	86	105	91	77	158	91	99	147	101	88	77
Number of settlers	85	42	182	120	45	65	88	100	22	122	40	43
Number of ejidatarios with plots	83	76	94	79	63	139	79	85	131	89	74	71
Land per ejidatario (ha)												
Total area	38.8	66.5	65.3	20.0	12.6	32.0	39.5	30.3	45.9	31.7	54.8	34.0
Common-access area	26.5	52.4	53.7	11.9	8.3	19.8	26.9	16.7	39.1	20.8	40.7	19.4
Pastures	17.8	35.4	49.3	8.0	1.5	8.0	20.1	2.1	16.5	15.8	28.6	11.3
Forests	6.4	12.6	4.0	2.6	5.9	6.7	4.9	11.9	15.7	3.7	9.1	6.7
Parceled area	10.9	12.5	11.0	7.3	15.3	9.6	11.0	12.4	6.4	9.1	12.8	13.6
Rainfed	8.5	11.3	4.5	5.3	12.6	7.7	8.3	11.1	6.2	7.1	9.3	11.2
Irrigated	1.1	1.1	5.1	0.7	0.4	0.3	1.3	0.5	0.0	1.2	1.0	1.1

Common pastures												
Ejidos with common pastures (%)	52.6	73.0	67.9	51.0	24.0	49.8	53.7	40.3	60.3	61.8	47.0	40.8
Adjusted area (ha NRE)	13.1	24.3	36.5	6.3	1.4	8.2	14.4	2.2	16.8	11.0	20.8	8.6
Geographic zone (%)												
North	25.2	100					28.9	10.7	3.8	29.9	24.7	14.9
North Pacific	10.3		100				11.6	1.8	9.4	6.6	12.9	17.8
Center	33.2			100			35.5	22.5	22.5	42.5	20.0	18.7
Gulf	20.6				100		16.3	49.8	23.8	13.3	27.3	38.6
South Pacific	10.7					100	7.8	15.2	40.4	7.7	15.1	10.0
Ethnic composition (%)												
Mestizo majority ejido	82.3	94.2	92.2	88.0	65.2	59.7	100			89.3	81.7	69.9
Indigenous majority ejido	11.4	4.8	2.0	7.7	27.5	16.2		100		7.6	10.8	23.5
Indigenous community	6.4	1.0	5.8	4.3	7.4	24.2			100	3.1	7.4	6.6
Date of land endowment (%)												
≤1940	52.5	61.8	32.5	70.7	31.2	40.0	56.3	33.8	32.5	100		
1940–1970	26.3	25.6	31.9	16.6	32.0	39.1	25.8	24.0	39.3		100	
>1970	21.3	12.5	35.6	12.6	36.7	20.9	17.9	42.1	28.3			100

Table 14.2
The ejido as a form of organization

	All ejidos	Geographic zone					Ethnic composition			Date of land endowment		
		North	North Pacific	Center	Gulf	South Pacific	Mestizo majority ejido	Indigenous majority ejido	Indigenous community	≤1940	1940–1970	>1970
Legal problems with respect to borders (%)												
Of the ejido	38.9	47.8	42.6	30.8	26.4	63.4	40.1	26.7	44.6	40.0	40.9	29.9
Of common land	24.0	35.1	20.5	22.4	7.0	38.6	25.1	6.0	41.3	25.9	22.5	11.7
With outsiders	95.3	97.3	100.0	100.0	n.a.	94.8	96.7	n.a.	100.0	92.9	100.0	89.4
Between members of ejido	4.7	2.7	0.0	0.0	n.a.	5.2	3.3	n.a.	0.0	7.1	0.0	10.6
Rules (%)												
Has internal rules	54.7	50.8	48.2	47.9	68.4	65.1	53.7	61.4	55.6	48.6	64.5	60.9
If not, why:												
Because of ignorance	18.5	11.6	8.3	33.6	8.0	4.8	17.4	28.6	17.3	22.2	14.7	8.9
Because of lack of advice	24.4	20.0	11.9	14.0	57.1	47.6	23.3	34.4	22.6	23.5	12.3	34.1
Not agreed upon in assembly	30.2	48.3	64.7	14.7	15.7	17.6	33.4	11.5	16.1	30.3	48.3	22.7
Other motives	18.5	14.3	15.1	28.0	4.0	18.1	17.4	16.3	36.3	20.0	10.5	20.4
Up to date according to agrarian law	28.9	19.9	28.1	21.5	45.0	42.5	29.2	31.2	20.3	25.3	31.2	41.7
Include agricultural activities	36.4	44.7	29.5	29.9	34.9	46.5	37.2	30.8	35.1	37.0	40.4	31.9
Include pastures (among ejidos with pastures)	21.9	36.5	23.9	13.5	4.1	12.1	24.7	9.8	4.1	22.1	22.7	23.1

Assemblies (%)

Frequency of assembly											
Monthly	52.1	71.6	46.1	45.6	45.7	43.3	54.3	47.4	32.3	52.3	61.6	41.5
Quarterly	8.8	6.3	10.2	13.7	26.9	10.5	13.1	12.4	24.1	16.4	13.3	5.9
Half-yearly	5.1	0.0	7.5	6.9	6.5	6.4	4.3	13.6	0.0	3.4	7.4	6.5
Other frequency	28.9	22.1	34.7	33.8	20.8	39.8	28.0	26.6	43.7	27.9	17.7	45.2
Participation of ejidatarios											
Attend (%)	65.5	64.2	58.7	60.3	78.4	67.3	64.2	73.4	68.7	61.2	70.8	72.0
Participate actively (%)	37.5	36.8	22.4	35.5	48.2	39.3	37.3	40.8	33.7	33.9	42.8	42.6
Determine agreements (%)	53.0	46.1	47.6	50.8	62.5	63.2	50.6	63.8	63.0	48.1	55.0	65.1
Of those who attend (%)	81.8	73.6	83.5	84.2	78.8	98.0	80.2	87.4	92.4	81.9	75.9	90.4
Organization: % belonging to											
An ARIC	2.8	1.2	8.3	1.6	0.9	8.3	3.0	3.4	0.0	3.5	2.6	2.5
An ejido union	31.8	35.9	25.1	27.9	30.5	42.8	30.7	49.9	13.7	34.7	27.7	34.3
Another form of peak organization	13.0	14.0	26.4	8.4	9.6	16.7	13.2	8.2	18.3	12.0	12.9	19.2

Note: n.a. indicates not applicable due to insufficient number of observations.

Table 14.3
Rules for pasture management in ejidos with common-access pastures

	All ejidos	Geographic zone					Ethnic composition			Date of land endowment		
		North	North Pacific	Center	Gulf	South Pacific	Mestizo majority ejido	Indigenous majority ejido	Indigenous community	≤1940	1940–1970	>1970
Number of observations	135	47	18	43	13	14	113	12	10	82	31	22
Ejidatarios in the category (%)	70.9	74.9	64.0	51.0	22.7	52.6	52.9	43.1	64.7	62.2	43.9	42.0
Ejidos with common pastures (%)	100	35.0	13.3	32.2	9.4	10.1	84.0	8.7	7.3	60.6	23.1	16.2
Animals												
Number of animals/ha	0.3	0.3	0.2	0.4	0.1	0.2	0.3	0.2	0.1	0.3	0.2	0.3
Number of animals/ejidatario	10.3	15.8	12.3	6.0	2.3	6.5	11.2	3.2	7.6	10.2	12.5	6.4
Pasture management (% of ejidos)												
Can prevent use by outsiders	32.8	42.6	25.6	30.8	39.7	8.3	33.4	27.7	31.3	33.5	44.0	19.7
Do not have weed problems	67.6	75.0	31.5	74.0	76.9	62.0	65.2	80.2	68.7	63.3	63.3	65.4
No erosion furrows have appeared	67.7	50.4	75.4	69.1	100.0	83.3	64.6	79.4	78.4	71.8	47.1	76.3
There are improvements [a]	61.8	80.0	54.2	42.2	67.7	66.1	63.6	32.4	76.1	59.8	78.4	42.0
Rules for the management of pastures												
Have rules (%)	52.7	78.1	54.8	27.4	57.5	37.7	59.2	37.4	53.3	50.1	65.3	40.1
Pasture rules part of general rules	21.9	36.5	23.9	13.5	4.1	12.1	24.7	9.8	4.1	22.1	22.7	23.1
Pasture rules separate	14.7	22.5	10.3	16.9	0.0	0.0	15.9	11.3	4.1	12.3	12.1	25.4

Specific rules (%)												
Limited number of cattle	32.2	49.0	46.9	13.8	19.0	25.6	32.6	27.2	33.5	27.3	51.6	21.0
Use of the land (rotation, use of parcels, use of forests)	10.6	12.4	10.9	13.6	0.0	4.3	10.2	16.6	8.3	8.1	11.6	14.8
Maintenance obligations	28.8	50.4	18.7	13.8	39.7	4.3	30.4	17.0	23.9	27.9	38.1	18.6
Rules are obeyed												
Number of observations	35	19	6	7	2	1	30	3	2	17	7	7
By almost all ejidatarios (%)	80.8	95.3	46.1	59.3	n.a.	n.a.	78.7	n.a.	n.a.	73.6	100.0	91.7
By more than half the ejidatarios (%)	32.4	34.3	10.8	45.1	n.a.	n.a.	37.1	n.a.	n.a.	37.8	36.2	20.2
Many do not obey (%)	15.4	9.5	43.1	13.1	n.a.	n.a.	18.4	n.a.	n.a.	14.1	25.2	0.0

Note: n.a. indicates not applicable due to insufficient number of observations.
[a] Includes cattle pens, fences, pumps, weed control, etc.

Access to Common Land for Cattle Raising

One of the distinctive features of the ejido relative to private-sector farms is the access their members have to common areas. These lands vary from zero in certain ejidos, where all the land has been parceled, to common-access lands that are several times the size of the parceled area. Where common-access land exists, those with small farms can increase the quantity of their cattle holdings by using common land to compensate for lack of individual land. Ejidatarios with more capital, usually those endowed with larger individual land plots, are able to accumulate herds by using common lands, particularly if there are clear rules about grazing. These lands thus serve at the same time to increase the animal stocks of those who have less land and as a source of differentiation for those who have more capacity to accumulate capital.

In table 14.4, cattle ownership is analyzed in relation to the size of the individual plot and total ejido area per ejidatario.[2] First, doing a structural analysis in 1994, it can be seen that the percentage of ejidatarios who have cattle increases with the size of the individual land plots, as well as with the per-member area of the ejido. This relationship was maintained for the number of cattle by individual plot size. It increased from 0.7 to 6.8 between the lowest class and the highest class of individual plot sizes in ejidos with less than 10 ha NRE' per ejidatario. It rose from 0.7 to 3.6 when the size of the ejido per member increased from less than 10 ha NRE' to more than 30 ha NRE'. This implies, for those with small farms, that the number of animals can be multiplied by 5.1 thanks to greater access to common lands. Those who have larger individual farms benefit relatively less, though absolutely more. Access to common land permitted them to multiply the number of animals by 3.1, which was relatively less than those with smaller individual plots. Yet it meant an absolute increase of 14.6 head of cattle (from 6.8 to 21.4), compared to 2.9 for those with smaller farms (from 0.7 to 3.6).

Another way of measuring the differential role of access to common land for different individual farm sizes is to calculate what the number of animals per hectare of individual land would be if the total herd were assigned to the individual plot. It can be seen that it would be 1.2 head of cattle per hectare on farms below 2 ha NRE, compared to 0.3 on farms of more than 10 ha NRE. Access to common lands and the differential intensity of land use thus create an inverse relationship between the number of cattle and individual farm size. However, those who

---

[2] The total area of the ejido is used because of the prevalence of the system of *año-y-vez*, where private land is opened to collective grazing after the corn harvest. With this system, the totality of the area, parceled and in common, is available to all members to graze cattle. The area of the ejido is adjusted for quality using the regional coefficient of rainfed corn yield. The hectares that have been adjusted are denominated NRE'.

have more individual land are in a better position to capitalize in cattle and can take advantage of common-access land more easily than can smaller farmers. On small farms, the number of animals increased from 1.2 to 2.3 when the common area increased, which represents a rise of 92 percent. In contrast, on larger farms above 10 ha NRE, the number of animals increased from 0.3 to 0.8, or by 166 percent. We can conclude that access to common grazing lands differentially helps more small than large farmers relax their land constraint, thus helping reduce poverty. However, large farmers are better able to capitalize and take advantage of greater access to common grazing land, thus deepening the process of social differentiation within the ejido.

What was the impact of access to common land on the growth of cattle raising between 1990 and 1994? Generally, significant increases in the number of animals were confined to ejidatarios with individual plots above 5 ha NRE and who are located in ejidos of more than 10 ha NRE per ejidatario. But the impact of access to common land is most evident among farmers with the least amount of land. For these farmers who belonged to ejidos with the most total land per ejidatario, there was a significant increase in the number of cattle. But for farmers who were members of ejidos with the least amount of land per ejidatario, there was a general process of decapitalization of cattle during these four years of economic hardship.

Sources of Income and Social Welfare

The ejido is also a source of income that serves to improve the welfare of its members. In table 14.5, it can be seen that 40 percent of the ejidos declared that they generated some collective income. Among ejidos that have collective income, 33.4 percent derived income from the exploitation of common-access land. For these activities, the most frequent source of income was the renting of land for cattle grazing (49.3 percent of the cases). Grazing lands were rented principally to outsiders.

Another frequent source of income is access to public funds, which were received by 57 percent of the ejidos with collective incomes. The most frequent source of these transfers was municipal (state government) funds (in 53 percent of the cases), followed by nonreimbursable federal funds (in 13 percent of the cases), and FIFONAFE transfers.[3]

---

[3] FIFONAFE was a trust fund with two main revenue sources: the expropriation of ejido lands in periurban zones, and the sale of rights to exploit forests owned by ejidatarios. The mechanism was as follows: the government collected money obtained from those operations, opened an account for the ejido, and returned the money to the ejido only if it presented a productive project authorized by trust fund staff members. Administrative costs were to come from sales of government-owned lands, but in fact much of the these costs were covered by the returns on the ejidos' money entrusted to the fund. With the recent property rights reforms, FIFONAFE is expected to disappear.

Table 14.4

Importance of common-access land for cattle raising, 1990 and 1994

	1990					1994					Difference between 1990–1994 (%)					
	Ejido size (ha NRE'/per ejidatario) [a]					Ejido size (ha NRE'/per ejidatario)					Ejido size (ha NRE'/per ejidatario)					
	≤10	10–30	Test	>30	Test	≤10	10–30	Test	>30	Test	≤10	Test	10–30	Test	>30	Test
Ejidatarios with cattle by individual plot size (%)																
<2 ha NRE	27.0	35.0		29.5		21.9	34.4	+	34.9		-18.9		-1.7		18.3	
2–5 ha NRE	36.7	53.4	++	54.4		35.1	45.6		52.2		-4.4		-14.6		-4.0	
5–10 ha NRE	37.8	35.1	++	56.9	++	44.1	55.3	++	69.5	++	16.7		57.5	++	22.1	
≥10 ha NRE	30.1	61.7	++	46.5	−−	37.9	63.6	++	75.4	++	25.9		3.1		62.2	++
All	32.4	48.6	++	44.1		33.0	52.5	++	52.7	++	1.9		8.0		19.5	++
Number of cattle by individual plot size																
<2 ha NRE	1.2	2.3	+	1.5		0.7	2.8	++	3.6		-41.7		21.7		140.0	++
2–5 ha NRE	1.8	4.3	++	5.9		2.5	3.2	++	5.9	++	38.9		-25.6		0.0	
5–10 ha NRE	2.7	2.7		10.7	++	4.3	7.4	++	12.9	++	59.3	+	174.1	++	20.6	
≥10 ha NRE	4.8	9.3	++	15.7	++	6.8	12.4	++	21.4	++	41.7		33.3		36.3	
All	2.2	5.2	++	7.3	++	2.9	7.4	++	8.5	++	31.8		42.3	++	16.4	++
Number of cattle per ha of individual plot																
<2 ha NRE	0.8	1.4	++	1.5		1.2	2.0	++	2.3		50.0		42.9		53.3	
2–5 ha NRE	0.6	1.3	++	1.7		0.8	1.0		1.8		33.3		-23.1		5.9	
5–10 ha NRE	0.4	0.4		1.5	++	0.6	1.0	++	1.7	+	42.9		150.0	++	13.3	
≥10 ha NRE	0.3	0.6	++	0.5		0.3	0.7	++	0.8	++	5.3		21.3	+	60.0	
All	0.6	0.9	++	1.3		0.8	1.0	++	1.7	++	33.3	++	11.1		30.8	+

[a] NRE' = total area of the ejido adjusted by the regional coefficient of rainfed corn.

These resources were used principally for the introduction or improvement of public services (52 percent of the cases). They also served for social services (23 percent) and productive activities or projects (17 percent).

The level of satisfaction of basic needs is analyzed in table 14.6. These include electricity, potable water, drainage, means of communication, and availability of public services. What is remarkable in this

Table 14.5
Sources and use of collective income of the ejidos

	N	%
Ejidos with collective income	276	40.2
Among those who have income: sources of income		
Exploitation of common-access land	99	33.4
Agriculture	33	6.3
Renting of fallow land for grazing	33	49.3
Urban development	33	0.9
Aquaculture	33	7.6
Forest exploitation	33	9.9
Other income	33	21.5
Nonrenewable natural resources	99	13.0
Tourism	99	2.0
Remittances	99	2.6
Public funds	99	57.3
Donations	99	6.4
Of those who rent fallow land		
Rent to members of the ejido	16	6.5
Rent to settlers (avecindados)	16	0.0
Rent to outsiders	16	56.6
Among those who receive public funds: sources of the funds		
Municipal funds (state governments)	57	52.9
Nonreimbursable federal funds	57	13.2
Nonreimbursable state funds	57	4.0
FIFONAFE transfers [a]	57	8.1
Other sources	57	18.3
Use of collective income		
Productive activities or projects	75	16.7
Introduction or improvement of public services	75	52.1
Social services	75	22.7
Reserve funds	75	11.8
Payment of debt	75	9.2
Other	75	44.7

[a] FIFONAFE: see text.

Table 14.6
Indicators of social welfare at the ejido level

	All ejidos	Geographic zone					Ethnic composition			Date of land endowment		
		North	North Pacific	Center	Gulf	South Pacific	Mestizo majority ejido	Indigenous majority ejido	Indigenous community	≤1940	1940–1970	>1970
Percentage of cases	100	25.2	10.3	33.2	20.6	10.7	82.3	11.4	6.4	52.5	26.3	21.3
Have electric light (%)	81.4	68.9	90.6	85.2	77.3	97.8	81.9	84.0	69.5	85.8	79.5	75.1
% of houses with light	71.9	64.0	91.9	73.3	60.5	86.7	73.8	66.7	53.0	75.2	69.3	69.3
Have running water (%)	40.5	40.5	18.3	37.8	57.9	37.1	37.9	51.5	55.2	32.3	46.5	51.7
% of houses with water	51.9	51.6	81.0	54.4	32.6	53.8	55.0	36.2	39.5	59.5	45.0	42.8
Have drainage	79.8	90.4	78.8	78.7	65.0	88.0	79.0	82.8	84.7	79.8	83.8	74.1
% of houses with drainage	12.4	4.4	16.8	15.6	16.1	9.9	13.3	10.6	3.6	12.3	12.4	12.4
Have the following means of communication (%)												
Dirt road	22.2	25.2	19.5	26.0	19.6	11.9	22.6	22.9	17.8	30.8	16.3	13.8
Paved road	75.2	70.9	82.0	71.7	79.6	82.0	74.9	68.1	93.3	70.0	79.3	81.9
Phone	51.6	54.0	40.1	53.3	57.8	40.2	48.6	57.5	79.6	44.5	62.1	55.9
Mail	17.3	15.4	31.6	18.3	6.2	26.6	17.7	14.1	18.4	16.3	24.9	10.4
Telegraph	95.8	97.4	93.8	96.4	95.1	93.8	95.5	97.7	96.7	97.2	92.2	97.9
CB radio	94.1	95.3	87.9	94.3	95.5	94.3	94.4	93.3	91.7	96.4	93.8	88.7
Radio	77.5	73.8	77.2	77.4	81.6	79.5	77.2	76.6	83.4	79.1	75.3	71.3
Have the following public services (%)												
School	4.4	7.5	6.2	5.0	0.0	2.2	5.4	0.0	0.0	5.4	6.5	0.0
Health center	63.5	70.0	66.5	68.8	51.1	52.8	65.0	56.0	58.5	60.0	67.9	64.0
CONASUPO store	51.2	45.6	29.6	63.8	49.4	49.4	51.7	38.6	66.9	53.3	51.9	49.4
Street lighting	38.9	47.1	11.3	42.1	48.3	18.3	37.2	52.0	38.2	32.7	44.4	49.8
Transportation	36.7	41.0	28.8	37.2	34.6	37.1	34.6	48.5	42.8	35.3	42.9	28.2
Sports field	27.0	31.8	32.7	31.3	17.9	14.6	27.6	20.5	31.6	30.8	19.6	34.6

table is that it does not reveal systematic biases in the availability of these services, neither between geographic regions nor between different types of ejidos, whether by ethnicity or by date of land endowment. In general, the availability of infrastructure such as electricity, drainage, paved roads, telegraph, CB radio, and radio was reasonably high at the ejido level. Services such as telephone, health center, and CONASUPO store cover approximately half the ejidos. However, services were low at the household level, with running water reaching only 52 percent of houses and sewerage available to only 12 percent. Overall it can be said that the conditions of social infrastructure and basic services are relatively acceptable at the ejido level, partly because of the state's special attention to the social sector, but lacking at the ejidatario level.

Inequality in the Ejido Sector

The typology of ejidatarios that has been used in this study is by individual plot size, measured in hectares NRE. However, we have not analyzed the sources of inequality between plots—whether it is

Table 14.7

Inequality in the distribution of individual land plots within and between ejidos, 1994 ejidatario survey

	Average plot size (ha NRE)	*Coefficient of variation (% of plot size)*	*Sources of variation (% of total variation)*	
			between ejidos	*within ejido*
All ejidos	10.0	92.9	67.6	32.4
Geographic zone				
North	8.5	104.2	72.6	27.4
North Pacific	8.0	82.8	48.8	51.2
Center	6.6	102.8	71.6	28.4
Gulf	9.3	68.8	61.3	38.7
South Pacific	8.0	90.8	59.7	40.3
Ethnic composition				
Mestizo majority	8.9	86.1	70.1	29.9
Indigenous majority	7.3	116.6	40.1	59.9
Indigenous community	2.5	129.4	33.8	66.2
Date of land endowment				
≤ 1940	7.4	88.4	73.0	27.0
1940–1970	9.0	90.9	66.2	33.8
> 1970	8.8	80.7	62.8	37.2

Table 14.8
Inequality in the distribution of individual land plots within ejidos, 1994 ejido survey

	Plot size [a]				Inequality indicators [b]			% of ejidos by inequality level (indicator I2)		
	Avg. (ha)	Min. (ha)	Max. (ha)	I1=avg./min.	I2=max./min.		I2 ≤ 3	3 < I2 ≤ 7	I2 > 7
All ejidos	12.1	7.3	19.1	4.3	6.9		54.2	24.2	21.6
Geographic zone									
North	13.1	10.3	21.6	3.1	6.5		54.2	29.0	16.8
North Pacific	11.7	6.1	24.3	3.8	7.6		66.0	15.4	18.6
Center	8.6	3.2	13.5	5.6	7.3		45.3	27.2	27.5
Gulf	18.3	12.2	19.5	3.0	2.8		75.7	17.2	7.1
South Pacific	10.8	4.1	25.1	6.1	13.0		32.4	24.1	43.5
Ethnic composition									
Mestizo majority	12.2	7.1	18.7	4.2	6.5		53.3	25.2	21.6
Indigenous majority	14.4	9.8	18.5	3.1	6.8		69.1	23.1	7.8
Indigenous community	7.6	2.1	26.8	9.4	13.5		39.7	11.2	49.1
Date of land endowment									
≤ 1940	10.2	5.2	14.8	4.8	6.1		51.4	27.9	20.7
1940–1970	14.0	7.7	20.6	3.9	6.2		56.8	23.4	19.9
> 1970	15.3	13.4	28.2	2.5	6.2		66.2	21.3	12.6

[a] Mean calculated among all ejidos in each category.
[b] Mean or ratio calculated within each ejido.

caused by differences within the ejido or by differences between ejidos. This is done in table 14.7, using the data from the survey of ejidatarios, and then in table 14.8, using the survey of ejidos.

According to table 14.7, the average plot size is 10 ha NRE. Because of reasons that we have already discussed, individual plots were smaller in the indigenous communities (2.5 ha NRE) and their size was much more variable, as the coefficient of variation of plot size evidences. The plots were also somewhat smaller in older ejidos. The principal result is that two-thirds of the inequality between land plots, measured by the variance, was caused by differences between ejidos, and only one-third was due to differences among ejidatarios within the same ejido. The ejidos with the smallest internal inequality compared to external inequality were those in the Center and the North, those with a mestizo majority, and those with the oldest endowments. In contrast, it was the indigenous communities that had the highest internal inequality. In this case two-thirds of total inequality was internal to the community, and only one-third external. The communities thus has the dual characteristic of consisting of very small farms with large internal differences.

Inequality between plots can also be analyzed using the survey of ejidos. There is no exhaustive characterization of the distribution of land plots in the survey of ejidatarios since it only characterizes the landholdings of the randomly chosen families. In contrast, in the survey of ejidos, the sizes of the smallest, the largest, and the average land plot of the ejido were recorded. In this case these sizes were in hectares, with an average of 12.1 hectares (table 14.8), and not in ha NRE as calculated from the survey of ejidatarios, where the average was 10.0 ha NRE (table 14.7). The average value in the ejido survey for the smallest plot was 7.2 ha; for the largest it was 19.1 ha. Again, in the indigenous communities the minimum parcel was much smaller (2.1 ha).

The two inequality indicators used here are the ratio of the average plot to the smallest plot in the ejido (indicator I1) and the ratio of the largest plot to the smallest plot in the ejido (indicator I2): both indicators increase with inequality. In general, indicator I1 reveals that the ejido is a very egalitarian institution, with the average plot being only 4.3 times larger than the smallest plot in 1994. (Inequality was higher in the South Pacific and Center and in the indigenous communities.) Indicator I2 indicates the same tendency. Analyzing the distribution of ejidos by the level of indicator I2 indicates that 54 percent of the ejidos had an I2 below 3. In other words, in half of the ejidos the range of inequality between the largest and smallest land plot was only 3 to 1, which is remarkably equal. In the South Pacific region and the indigenous communities, less equality was observed, with a lower frequency of I2 ≤ 3 and a higher frequency of I2 > 7.

We conclude by observing that inequality in land endowments is an important contributor to social differentiation in the ejido, with implications for income inequality, as will be analyzed in the following chapter. But the largest part of this social heterogeneity comes from differences between ejidos rather than differences within ejidos. Only in the ejido with indigenous majority, and most particularly in the indigenous community, is internal inequality more important than external inequality in explaining total inequality. This implies that targeting the poor among ejidatarios can largely be done by focusing on ejidos with smaller land endowments and on the ethnic community.

15

Income and Poverty

Measurement of Income

In any survey, measuring household income is difficult. This is especially true in the case of agricultural producers because quantification of production costs requires a large amount of information. Furthermore, information about income is always a sensitive issue, especially when it is connected to remittances received from migrants. The enumerators are reluctant to pressure those surveyed to reveal this information, and the persons questioned have little incentive to provide this information truthfully. As a consequence, the income derived from migration tends to be systematically underestimated. In this situation, either the remittances can be used as they have been declared (which is what is done with most household survey data) or one can seek ways to predict normal levels of remittances based on extraneous information. In this study we have chosen the second option by using information derived from specialized remittances surveys to predict remittances according to the characteristics of the migrant, of the household to which he or she belongs, and of the migration experience.

Sources of income for ejido households include agriculture, livestock activities, the sale of labor in agricultural and nonagricultural activities, self-employment in microenterprises, and migration to the rest of Mexico and to the United States. In this section, we will briefly explain how each of these sources of income was measured.

Agricultural incomes are measured as the gross value of total production (sold and used by the household) net of nonlabor input costs and the cost of hired labor. This defines household income as the return to all factors that the family owns, including family labor. Data from a separate survey were used to measure agricultural production costs. These data came from a joint project of Mexico's Ministry of

Agriculture and the Economics Center at the Colegio de Postgraduados in Chapingo (Matus 1994). The raw data include information for
each crop surveyed within each state of the Mexican republic. The
crops included in the survey vary by state. For each crop surveyed,
average per-hectare costs for inputs (fertilizer, labor, tractors, irrigation, credit, insurance, and so on) were given. For some crops, costs
were further disaggregated by type of technology (irrigation, high-
yield seeds, fertilizer use, or mechanization) and/or by region or
municipality.

We matched the input cost data with production and technology
information provided in the 1994 ejido household survey. This
matching was done on a state-by-state, crop-by-crop basis, arranging
the cost categories to match the technology categories of the survey
according to the following classifications: rainfed/irrigated, tradi-
tional/high-yield seeds, fertilizer/no fertilizer, and mechanized/
animal/manual power. The first three were considered to be the core
technologies. The matching was disaggregated as much as possible
for each crop. For some crops, regional, municipal, or irrigation-
district cost figures were given, and if possible these figures were
matched to the same level of disaggregation in the household survey.
Where it was not possible to bring over the level of disaggregation,
state averages were used by the most disaggregated level of technology possible. In all cases, cost data aggregation was weighted by area
planted.

These data were then matched to the technology characteristics of
the production of each producer's crops. For each crop, a producer
was given a base technology category, from which cost figures would
be applied under certain conditions. For example, although the production cost data had figures for fertilizer or insecticides, these were
applied to a producer only if the producer indicated that he/she used
such an input.

Credit and labor costs were treated in a different fashion. Credit
costs were taken directly from the household survey and applied as a
global cost to the producer's overall agricultural portfolio. In the case
of labor, the share of paid labor was obtained for each household
from the 1994 household survey. This share was then multiplied by
the labor cost figures from the production cost data to give the labor
costs per crop. The figure was then also adjusted by the share of land
harvested over land planted, in order to avoid including harvest labor
costs for area that was not harvested.

All applicable costs were then summed up to a per-hectare figure,
by producer and by crop, and then multiplied by the number of hectares planted of that particular crop in order to obtain a total cost figure for each crop. This was subtracted from gross agricultural income
to obtain net agricultural income.

For income from animals, the 1994 ejido survey includes data about the number of animals and sales. To complete the information in cases where there was information about the number of animals but not about sales, the value of sales was predicted based on the estimated relationship between sales and herd size. The prices declared were used when sales were observed. When sales were predicted, or when there was no information about the value of sales, the median observed price was used. Estimates of the nonlabor costs in animal production were derived from detailed case studies of ejidos with livestock (García-Barrios et al. 1995). A cost figure per animal (for livestock and pigs) was derived and then applied directly to the reported number of animals in the survey. These costs assumed that owners had access to pastures.

The incomes earned by household members in activities external to the farm—including income from wages, microenterprises, payments in kind, and other sources—were measured directly in the survey. Around two hundred observations, where activities external to the farm were reported but without a corresponding declaration of income, were eliminated. The income derived from migration and remittances was predicted based on detailed surveys of remittances conducted by the Colegio de la Frontera Norte (Corona Vázquez 1994; Bustamante 1994). From the 1994 ejido survey, it is known whether the household head and each family member who reside in the ejido have migrated, where and when they migrated, and whether they found a job. This allows identification of household members who are actively involved in migration as seasonal migrants. Information about migration was also obtained for the children of the household head and his/her spouse even if they did not live in the ejido. Thus other family members were included in the survey, even though they might have been living in other places such as the United States, migrating seasonally to the United States from other residences, or residing in other parts of Mexico. For each of these family members, gender, age, employment status, and whether he or she sends remittances were recorded in the survey.

For migrants to the United States, the observations on remittances collected by the Colegio de la Frontera Norte were used to construct a conditional remittances function. The share of migrants who send remittances and the average amount of remittances by those who remit depend on employment status, place of residence, gender, and age, as described in table 15.1. The average level of remittances for those who send money was U.S.$4,385 per year. For a man it was $4,386 and for a woman, $4,310. It also varied with age, from $6,476 sent by those below 24 years of age to $2,360 by those above 45 years. Employment status is also recorded in the survey. As seen in table 15.1, the portion of migrants who send remittances among those who worked in the United States varies by place of residence, with 66 percent for residents of Mexico and 36 percent for residents of the United States. If it is known that the person was unemployed in the place to which he or she migrated, the remittance was zero. This was the case for housewives who visited family members in the United States. In cases where it was not known whether a person was employed, the average probability of sending money by all migrants in the applicable age/gender category was used. For all migrants, these average percentages were 51 percent for residents in Mexico and 31 percent for residents in the United States. The percentages are adjusted by gender and age of the migrant in table 15.1.

Table 15.1
Estimated remittances of migrants in the United States
(data obtained between March 1993 and March 1994)

| Migrant characteristics | % of migrants who sent money | | | | Remittances: average sent (dollars per year) |
| | All migrants | | Migrants who worked in the US | | |
	Residents of Mexico	Residents of the US	Residents of Mexico	Residents of the US	
All	0.51	0.31	0.66	0.36	4,385
By gender					
Man	0.54	0.33	0.67	0.37	4,386
Woman	0.11	0.17	0.40	0.28	4,310
By age					
12–24	0.45	0.25	0.64	0.33	6,476
25–34	0.56	0.35	0.68	0.38	5,166
35–44					1,776
≥ 45	0.48	0.25	0.65	0.31	2,360

Source: Corona Vázquez 1994.

The data derived from case studies of remittances were used for those migrating within Mexico (Fletcher and Taylor 1992). The amount they send is about half the amount sent by migrants to the United States, and this fraction was used to measure remittances. A comparable figure was obtained from the 1992 National Household Income and Expenditure Survey conducted by INEGI (Deininger and Heinegg 1995a).

In figure 15.1 and table 15.2, a comparison is made between income levels obtained by INEGI in the 1992 National Household Income and Expenditure Survey and the data obtained in the ejido study. The incomes measured by INEGI are those of households in localities with less than 2,500 inhabitants, classified by income deciles. They have been adjusted to pesos of the first semester of 1994 to be comparable with the incomes measured in the ejido survey, and the correspondence is quite close. The five classes of farms used for the typology of ejidatarios correspond to the following INEGI income deciles:

0 to 2 ha NRE	between deciles 4 and 5
2 to 5 ha NRE	between deciles 5 and 6
5 to 10 ha NRE	between deciles 7 and 8
10 to 18 ha NRE	between deciles 7 and 8
above 18 ha NRE	between deciles 9 and 10

The ejido survey does not include landless households, which are the poorest in the rural areas, whereas they are represented in the INEGI survey. This explains why the lowest class of farms is above the lowest four deciles. In addition, compared to the levels derived from national accounting, the INEGI survey underestimates income levels by as much as 45 percent (Lustig 1993). This could explain why the highest class of ejidatarios is close to the most well-off decile observed in the INEGI survey.

Figure 15.1
Comparison of rural incomes, INEGI-92 and ejido survey

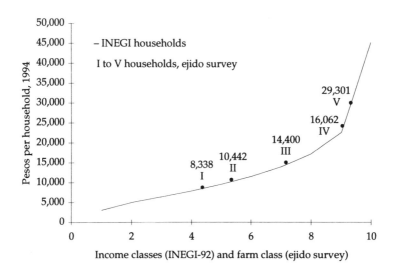

Source: INEGI, *Encuesta nacional de ingresos y gastos de los hogares,* 1992.
Note: Data for households in localities under 2,500 inhabitants.

Table 15.2
Comparison of rural incomes according to the INEGI-1992 survey
and the 1994 ejido survey
(in pesos, first semester of 1994)

INEGI-1992 Households in towns under 2,500 inhabitants	Number of households (%)	Annual household income (pesos)
All households	100	14,267
Deciles		
1	10	3,042
2	10	4,986
3	10	6,448
4	10	7,876
5	10	9,574
6	10	11,539
7	10	13,942
8	10	17,268
9	10	22,633
10	10	45,327
1994 ejido survey		
All households	100	13,090
Property classes		
I. < 2 ha NRE	21.4	8,338
II. 2–5 ha NRE	34.4	10,442
III. 5–10 ha NRE	20.1	14,400
IV. 10–18 ha NRE	17.0	16,062
V. ≥ 18 ha NRE	7.1	29,301

Levels and Sources of Income by Farm Size

The role that access to land plays in determining the total level of
family income can be observed in table 15.3 and figure 15.2. Total income increases regularly with farm size, reaching a level more than
three times higher on the largest farms than on the smallest farms.
Income derived from agriculture increases most with farm size; it is
almost twelve times higher on large farms than on small farms, and
the income derived from livestock activities is nine times higher on
large farms. Off-farm income, derived from the labor market and microenterprises, is more egalitarian, increasing only by two between
small and large farmers. Finally, migration contributes equal amounts
of income across farm sizes. Wages, income from microenterprises,

Table 15.3
Household income levels in 1994 pesos, by farm size

	All	<2	2–5	5–10	10–18	≥18
			Farm size (ha NRE)			
Number of cases	1,342	287	462	270	228	95
Total income	13,090	8,338	10,442	14,400	16,062	29,301
Agriculture	3,519	850	1,991	3,852	6,820	10,063
Livestock	1,817	657	1,213	1,880	2,610	6,129
Wages and microenterprises	4,867	3,898	4,591	5,474	3,942	9,599
Migration to Mexico and the US	2,519	2,709	2,234	2,826	2,334	2,916
Other	368	224	413	368	356	594
Agricultural income						
Corn and beans	1,210	448	1,056	1,576	2,645	-238
Other crops	2,309	402	935	2,276	4,175	10,301
Livestock income						
Cattle	1,011	277	568	1,244	1,326	3,945
Other animals	806	380	645	636	1,284	2,184
Income external to the farm						
Wages	4,148	3,254	4,168	4,477	3,768	6,698
Microenterprise income	719	644	423	997	174	2,901
Migration income						
Household member residing in the ejido						
1. Family residing						
in the ejido in Mexico	861	1,263	858	656	685	685
2. Family residing						
in the ejido in the US	305	186	327	576	132	201
Household member not residing in the ejido						
3. Family not residing						
in the ejido in Mexico	170	130	166	209	241	24
4. Family not residing						
in the ejido in the US	1,183	1,130	884	1,385	1,276	2,006
Migrant remittances: 3+4	1,353	1,260	1,050	1,594	1,517	2,030
Income from the US: 2+4	1,488	1,316	1,211	1,961	1,408	2,207

and remittances from migrants thus help reduce the income inequality implied by unequal distribution of the land, resulting in a comparatively egalitarian distribution of income across farm classes.

As a portion of total income, the contribution of agriculture and livestock increases from 18.1 percent to 55.2 percent when farm size increases from the smallest to the largest class (table 15.4 and figure 15.3). In agriculture, other crops gradually overwhelm corn and beans as farm size increases. For those who had small amounts of land, off-farm activities contribute more to total income than do on-farm activities. For the smallest farms, 81.9 percent of total income comes

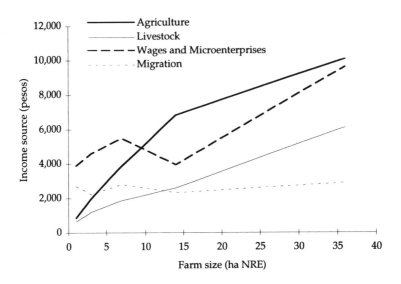

Figure 15.2
Income levels by source and farm size

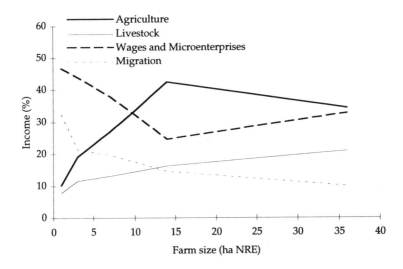

Figure 15.3
Sources of income by farm size

from off-farm activities, including 46.7 percent from wages and microenterprises. For the largest farmers, these off-farm activities represent 44.8 percent of their income, 32.8 percent from wages and microenterprises—still a remarkably high percentage. Migration is vital for small farmers since they derive 32.5 percent of their income from this source. Households in all farm classes thus rely very heavily on off-farm income, and this dependency increases as farm size falls. Dominance of income derived from outside the farm continues up to the third category of farm size (5–10 ha). Clearly, then, permanence of small farms in the ejido depends on the continuing possibility of access to other sources of income, most particularly an active labor market and migration opportunities.

Table 15.4
Sources of household income by farm size
(As a percentage of the total)

		Farm size (ha NRE)				
	All	*< 2*	*2–5*	*5–10*	*10–18*	*≥ 18*
Total income	100	100	100	100	100	100
Agriculture	26.9	10.2	19.1	26.8	42.5	34.3
Livestock	13.9	7.9	11.6	13.1	16.2	20.9
Wages and microenterprises	37.2	46.7	44.0	38.0	24.5	32.8
Migration to Mexico and the US	19.2	32.5	21.4	19.6	14.5	10.0
Other	2.8	2.7	4.0	2.6	2.2	2.0
Agricultural income						
Corn and beans	9.2	5.4	10.1	10.9	16.5	-0.8
Other crops	17.6	4.8	9.0	15.8	26.0	78.7
Livestock income						
Cattle	7.7	3.3	5.4	8.6	8.3	13.5
Other animals	6.2	4.6	6.2	4.4	8.0	7.5
Off-farm income						
Wages	31.7	39.0	39.9	31.1	23.5	22.9
Microenterprise income	5.5	7.7	4.1	6.9	1.1	9.9
Migration income						
Household member residing in the ejido						
1. Family residing in the ejido in Mexico	6.6	15.1	8.2	4.6	4.3	2.3
2. Family residing in the ejido in the US	2.3	2.2	3.1	4.0	0.8	0.7
Household member not residing in the ejido						
3. Family not residing in the ejido in Mexico	1.3	1.6	1.6	1.5	1.5	0.1
4. Family not residing in the ejido in the US	9.0	13.6	8.5	9.6	7.9	6.8
Migrant remittances: 3+4	10.3	15.1	10.1	11.1	9.4	6.9
Income from the US: 2+4	11.4	15.8	11.6	13.6	8.8	7.5

Levels and Sources of Income by Income Quintiles

To understand the determinants of the income levels achieved, it helps to rank households by income level and analyze how sources of income vary by income quintiles. The data in table 15.5 and figure 15.4 show that income derived from agriculture and wages are the two main sources of income for both the lowest and the highest income quintiles. Thus agriculture, and not just off-farm income, is key for the poor. And wage income, not just agricultural income, is key for the rich. Livestock is also very important for the poor since they derive 27 percent of their income from this activity. It is the only source of income that acts as an equalizer. Migration plays a major role for the middle income groups, but it is less important for both poor and rich. This shows that it is neither the poorest nor the richest who migrate most, an observation similar to that made regarding educational levels, where it is neither the least nor the most educated who migrate most. It also shows that migration is not able to erase extreme poverty and that it is not the source of the highest incomes in the social sector. Income from microenterprises is not a source of income differentiation, remaining relatively constant as a share of total income across income quintiles. Altogether, off-farm income is most important for the middle income quintiles, while on-farm income is most important for the poorest and richest households.

Households in indigenous communities are disproportionately represented in the lowest income quintile: the share of indigenous community members falls from 15.2 percent in the lowest income quintile to 4.4 percent in the highest. By regions, households in the North and North Pacific are disproportionately represented in the highest income quintile, while households in the Gulf and South Pacific are most represented in the lowest quintile. The Center has households in all income quintiles, indicating a more equal pattern of income distribution than in the other regions. The age of the household head is higher in the highest income quintile, showing that income improves through the life cycle. Finally, households in the highest income quintile have more of all income-generating assets: they have higher land assets (quality-adjusted hectares), higher labor market assets (number of working adults and educational levels), and higher migration assets. This indicates that all three types of capital afford an escape from poverty, either in combination or as substitutes for one another. Success stories about emerging from poverty can thus be quite heterogeneous, and they do not depend exclusively on access to agricultural assets.

Table 15.5
Sources of household income by income level

	Income quintile				
	1	2	3	4	5
Income levels by source (pesos)					
All sources	-853	3167	7315	14178	41596
Agriculture	-1673	844	1232	2762	14407
Livestock	438	862	1071	2013	4693
Wages	180	775	2323	4562	12890
Microenterprises	32	171	299	451	2638
Migration	103	296	2123	3813	6263
Other incomes	67	219	267	577	706
Income composition (% of total income)					
All sources		100	100	100	100
Agriculture		26.6	16.8	19.5	34.6
Livestock		27.2	14.6	14.2	11.3
Wages		24.5	31.8	32.2	31.0
Microenterprises		5.4	4.1	3.2	6.3
Migration		9.3	29.0	26.9	15.1
Other incomes		6.9	3.7	4.1	1.7
% of households with majority of income from nonfarm sources	57.8	38.6	71.1	71.2	62.0
% of households belonging to indigenous communities	15.2	15.0	10.6	3.8	4.4
% distribution of households in each quintile by region					
North	19.1	21.6	22.3	28.2	28.0
North Pacific	2.6	5.7	4.2	9.4	19.9
Center	31.4	25.5	34.3	35.3	32.0
Gulf	26.8	26.5	22.0	15.2	6.1
South Pacific	20.2	20.7	17.3	11.9	14.0
Age of household head	49.6	44.6	49.4	50.0	52.7
% of households with					
high agricultural assets [a]	41.2	48.7	41.6	53.2	70.3
high labor market assets [b]	21.7	17.5	20.7	27.7	47.3
high migration assets [c]	29.5	32.2	55.9	62.4	62.2

[a] High agricultural assets is more than 4 ha of rainfed equivalent.
[b] High labor force (education) assets is more than 6 unskilled equivalent adult.
[c] Migration asset = permanent migrants from extended family and from household + (seasonal migrants from household – 1).

Figure 15.4
Income levels by income quintiles

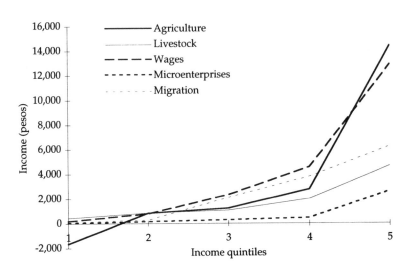

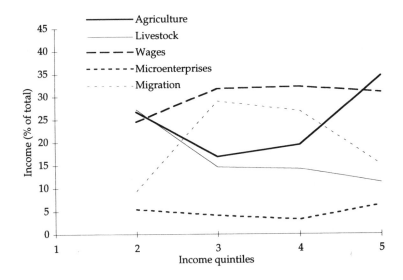

Transitory and Permanent Poverty

The income data we have are for realized incomes in 1994. Because Mexican agriculture and animal husbandry are importantly based on rainfed lands with high climatic fluctuations, it is not surprising that a significant share of farm households have negative agricultural and livestock incomes in one particular year. In table 15.5, we see that agricultural and total incomes are negative for the first income quintile. We analyze the incidence of negative agricultural and livestock incomes (farm income) in table 15.6. For the whole sector, 22.7 percent of the households had a negative farm income in 1994. The profitability crisis that prevailed in 1994 contributed to increasing these numbers because it enhanced the likelihood of achieving negative incomes as yields fluctuated with weather risks.

By region, the North is the area with the greatest exposure to farm income risk, with 29.3 percent of the households having negative farm income, followed by the Center with 24.2 percent and the North Pacific with 21.6 percent. These areas were affected by drought in 1994. The Gulf and South Pacific are more sheltered from climatic fluctuations, with 18.7 percent and 15.5 percent, respectively, of the households having negative farm income.

Table 15.6
Risk and transitory poverty, 1994

	% of households with negative agricultural and livestock income
All households	22.7
Geographic region	
North	29.3
North Pacific	21.6
Center	24.2
Gulf	18.7
South Pacific	15.5
Farm size (ha NRE)	
≤ 2	24.5
2–5	24.2
5–10	24.2
10–18	14.3
> 18	25.8
Income quintile	
1	49.7
2	18.9
3	17.4
4	18.3
5	9.2

By farm size, there is no particular bias in the exposure to farm income risks. There are sharp contrasts by income quintiles, with the percentage of negative incomes falling from 49.7 percent in the lowest quintile to 9.2 percent in the highest. This shows that transitory poverty is a very important component of poverty as measured by annual income in a context where farm income is exposed to climatic risks and a global profitability crisis in agriculture reduces security margins for positive incomes.

Decomposition by geographic region, farm size, and income quintiles can also be used to compare the percentage of households that depend on nonfarm activities for a majority of their income. In table 15.7, we see that households in the North and Center are more dependent on off-farm sources of income, while households in the Gulf, North Pacific, and South Pacific are more agrarian. Small farms (0–5 ha NRE) and large farms are less agrarian than middle-sized

Table 15.7
Dependency on nonfarm sources of income, 1994

	% of households with more than 50% of income from non-farm activities
All households	60.1
Geographic region	
North	72.7
North Pacific	54.3
Center	66.5
Gulf	43.9
South Pacific	51.7
Farm size (ha NRE)	
≤ 2	72.0
2–5	62.2
5–10	57.0
10–18	44.2
> 18	61.3
Income quintile	
1	57.8
2	38.6
3	71.1
4	71.2
5	62.0
Ethnicity	
Indigenous community	63.4
Ejidos	58.6

farms. The middle income quintiles are also composed of households that are more dependent on off-farm incomes. Finally, members of indigenous communities are more dependent on off-farm sources of income (63.4 percent) than are households in ejidos (58.6 percent), indicating the formers' weak access to land following generations of population pressure on the resources controlled by the communities. Ethnicity thus increases the pressure to participate in the labor market and in migration.

Characteristics of the Poor

To differentiate the poor from other households, we use a poverty line of 6,700 pesos per household and an extreme poverty line of 3,819 pesos, which correspond to the poverty lines used by CEPAL (1989). Under this definition, the overall incidence of poverty, measured by the headcount ratio, is 47.3 percent.[1] This is similar to the 46 percent headcount ratio estimated by ECLAC (1994) for the rural sector in 1992. This compares to an urban headcount ratio of 24.6 percent, showing that the rural sector is an important reservoir of national poverty: with 26 percent of the national population, it harbors approximately 40 percent of national poverty. In the social sector, the extreme poverty headcount ratio (including transitory poverty) is 33.8 percent, while it is close to zero in the urban sector.

In table 15.8, the incidence of poverty is disaggregated by the variables that are hypothesized to be the main determinants of poverty: geographical region, farm size, ethnicity, human capital assets, and migration assets. Assets are defined as follows:

- Agricultural assets: land in usufruct measured in ha NRE.
- Labor force assets: number of unskilled equivalent adults (UEA) in the household. For each adult in the household, UEA is defined as: 1.06^i for $i \leq 6$, $1.06^6 \, 1.12^{i-6}$ for $6 < i \leq 12$, and $1.06^6 \, 1.12^7$ for $i > 12$, where i is the number of years of schooling, a scale based on the role of education in labor market earnings estimated by Schultz (1993).
- Migration assets: the sum of permanent migrants from the extended family (brothers and sisters of the head of household), members of the household who have migrated in the past, either seasonally or permanently, and members of the household who are currently engaged in migration less one.

---

[1] The headcount ratio is $P_0 = q/n$, where q is the number of households below poverty line and n is the population size. Multiplied by 100, the headcount ratio thus gives the percentage of households in the category analyzed who are below poverty line.

Table 15.8
Incidence of poverty and income structure of the poor and nonpoor, 1994

	Share of total number of households (%)	Extreme poverty [a]			Poverty [b]		
		Headcount ratio (%)	Share of extreme poverty (%)	Share of extreme poverty/share of population	Headcount ratio (%)	Share of poverty (%)	Share of poverty/share of population
Total population	100	33.8	100	1	47.3	100	1
Geographic region							
North	23.8	28.0	19.7	0.8	41.3	20.8	0.9
North Pacific	8.4	19.2	4.8	0.6	21.9	3.9	0.5
Center	31.7	28.6	26.8	0.8	42.9	28.7	0.9
Gulf	19.3	48.8	27.9	1.4	64.8	26.4	1.4
South Pacific	16.8	42.0	20.9	1.2	56.7	20.1	1.2
Farm size (ha NRE)							
≤2	21.2	41.0	25.6	1.2	56.4	25.2	1.2
2–5	34.6	35.1	35.9	1.0	50.6	37.0	1.1
5–10	20.1	30.8	18.3	0.9	41.0	17.4	0.9
10–18	17.0	32.7	16.5	1.0	45.2	16.3	1.0
>18	7.1	17.6	3.7	0.5	27.0	4.1	0.6
Indigenous community	9.8	54.9	15.9	1.6	71.2	14.8	1.5
Ejidos	90.2	31.5	84.1	0.9	44.7	85.2	0.9
Labor market asset							
1–2.6	22.0	47.4	30.9	1.4	64.7	30.1	1.4
2.6–4.2	26.1	35.5	27.4	1.1	52.3	28.9	1.1
4.2–6.3	27.6	28.6	23.3	0.8	40.8	23.8	0.9
more than 6.3	24.3	25.6	18.4	0.8	33.4	17.1	0.7
Migration asset							
0	51.6	45.1	68.8	1.3	59.8	65.2	1.3
1–2	33.4	23.7	23.4	0.7	36.9	26.1	0.8
2–11	15.1	17.6	7.8	0.5	27.6	8.8	0.6

[a] Using an extreme poverty line of 3,819 pesos per household.
[b] Using a poverty line of 6,700 pesos per household.

By region, the incidence of poverty is highest in the Gulf (64.8 percent) and the South Pacific (56.7 percent).[2] By farm size, the incidence of poverty declines from 56.4 percent on farms less than 2 ha NRE to 41 percent on farms between 5 and 10 ha NRE and to 27 percent on farms larger than 18 ha NRE. In the range of farms between 0 and 18 ha NRE, access to land is, however, not a highly powerful determinant of poverty reduction, suggesting that other important sources of income are at play. It is only when farm size exceeds 18 ha NRE that poverty falls sharply. Extreme poverty, by contrast, declines steadily as farm size increases, indicating that access to land is important to reduce this form of poverty, which virtually disappears (3.7 percent) on the largest farms.

The third important determinant of poverty identified in table 15.8 is ethnicity. The indigenous community included 14.8 percent of the social sector's rural poor though it included only 11.9 percent of the total number of households. Among members of indigenous communities, 71.2 percent were poor, compared to 44.7 percent in the ejidos. Ethnicity is thus an overwhelming determinant of poverty, as had been observed in other analyses of rural poverty, for instance by COPLAMAR (1982), Cortés and Rubalcava (1992), and Deininger and Heinegg (1995b). This key role of ethnicity in explaining poverty is starkly illustrated by the contrast in poverty profiles between indigenous community and ejido households in figure 15.5.

The labor-market-assets position of households, which characterizes both the number of working-age adults available to the household and the level of education of these adults, is the fourth important determinant of poverty. Across the four levels of these assets, each of which included approximately a quartile of the households, poverty falls from 30.1 percent in the lowest assets group to 17.1 percent in the highest assets group. Improving the ability of households to participate in the labor market is thus important in reducing poverty. Finally, migration assets, which measure the extensiveness of the kinship migration network to which a household belongs, is also a very powerful instrument for escaping from poverty. Those with zero migration capital have a poverty headcount ratio of 65.2 percent, compared to 26.1 percent for those with one or two migrants in the extended family, and 8.8 percent for those with two to eleven migrants.

Ethnicity appears repeatedly as a strong determinant of poverty. However, this may be due to a spurious correlation between ethnicity and the other determinants of poverty—namely, region, farm size, labor market assets, and migration assets. It may indeed be that ethnic populations appear poor because they possess more of these other

---

[2] The long history of the concentration of marginality in these regions had been documented by COPLAMAR in 1982.

attributes that determine poverty, leaving no explanatory power to ethnicity once these other determinants of poverty have been controlled for. We explore this possibility in the following two tables.

Figure 15.5
Poverty profiles for ejido and indigenous community households

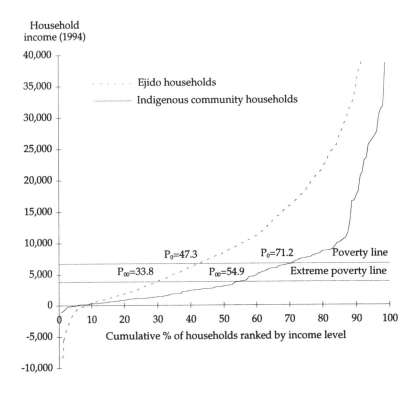

P_0 = headcount ratio with poverty line equal to 6,700 pesos.
P_{00} = headcount ratio with extreme poverty line equal to 3,819 pesos.

In table 15.9, we separate the role of ethnicity within each of the determinants of poverty to see if there is any role left for ethnicity. The results are striking. Even while controlling for these determinants one at a time, there remains a very powerful role for ethnicity. For instance, in the South Pacific the incidence of poverty is 48.5 percent among households in ejidos and 69.6 percent among households in indigenous communities. Controlling for farm size, poverty is 48.5

percent in the 0–2 ha NRE class in ejidos and 77.8 percent in indigenous communities. At all educational levels, indigenous populations are poorer than the others. And migration assets similarly allow a higher share of the nonindigenous population to escape from poverty compared to indigenous populations.

Poverty differences attributed to ethnicity could still come from spurious correlations because all the other determinants of poverty need to be controlled simultaneously, not one at a time as in table 15.9. To verify this, we estimate a probit equation on the probability of being poor, introducing in the equation all the determinants of poverty in addition to ethnicity. A positive regression coefficient for ethnicity would indicate that ethnicity still plays a direct role in explaining differentially higher poverty, even when controlling for the regional, farm class, labor market, and migration asset positions of households. In addition, the instruments for escaping from poverty—farm size, labor market assets, and migration networks—may be more or less effective when controlled by indigenous or nonindigenous households. The tests of these propositions are given in table 15.10.

In terms of region, results show that, compared to the South Pacific, the probability of being poor is significantly lower in the North Pacific and higher in the Gulf. Both larger farm size and higher labor market assets lower the probability of being poor. Migration assets also reduce the incidence of poverty in two ways: one is through membership to a migration network; the other is the size of the migration network. Given control over these determinants of poverty, ethnicity still plays a very important role in explaining poverty. Hence, households in indigenous communities are not poor merely because they have less land, lower education, and weaker migration networks. Controlling for these determinants of poverty, ethnicity is an additional powerful determinant of poverty. On the positive side, from a policy standpoint, interaction variables between assets and ethnicity show that labor market assets (education) and membership to migration networks not only have a direct effect in reducing poverty but, in addition, are more effective in reducing poverty when applied to indigenous populations. This suggests (1) that because indigenous populations are at low levels of education and initiation of migration, these two instruments have a stronger poverty reduction effect among indigenous populations than for the overall set of social sector households, and (2) that a higher poverty reduction effect is obtained by targeting educational programs and migration assistance for households in indigenous communities. This is not the case for farm size and size of migration networks (in other words, what matters is initiating the migratory process, not the magnitude of the networks), which have no differential poverty reduction capabilities for indigenous populations compared to the overall social sector population.

Table 15.9

Incidence of poverty in indigenous communities and ejidos

	Extreme poverty [a] Headcount ratio				Poverty [b] Headcount ratio			
	All households (%)	Ejidos	Indigenous communities	Chi-square [c]	All households (%)	Ejidos	Indigenous communities	Chi-square [c]
Total population	33.8	31.5	54.9	**	47.3	44.7	71.2	**
Geographic region								
South Pacific	42.0	36.1	51.5	**	56.7	48.5	69.6	**
Farm class (ha NRE)								
≤2	41.0	33.0	62.5	**	56.4	48.5	77.8	**
2–5	35.1	34.1	48.3	*	50.6	49.1	70.1	**
Labor market asset								
1–2.6	47.4	43.5	74.7	**	64.7	60.2	96.5	**
2.6–4.2	35.5	34.2	45.5	**	52.3	50.3	67.9	**
4.2–6.3	28.6	26.5	51.0	**	40.8	38.9	61.9	**
more than 6.3	25.6	24.3	45.0	**	33.4	32.3	48.4	**
Migration asset								
0	45.1	41.7	77.3	**	59.8	56.5	91.1	**
1–2	23.7	22.5	33.3	*	36.9	35.2	51.1	**

[a] Using an extreme poverty line of 3,819 pesos per household.
[b] Using a poverty line of 6,700 pesos per household.
[c] Test of difference of headcount ratios between indigenous communities and ejidos.
** Significant at the 95% confidence level.
* Significant at the 90% confidence level.

Table 15.10
Probability of being poor

	Coefficient	P-value [a]	Significance test
Geographic region (relative to South Pacific)			
North	- 0.025	15.5	
North Pacific	- 0.865	100.0	**
Center	- 0.097	56.8	
Gulf	0.333	98.9	**
Farm size (ha NRE)	- 0.011	99.4	**
Labor market assets			
(number of adults and educational level)	- 0.075	100.0	**
Migration asset (kin migration network)			
Membership to a migration network	- 0.411	100.0	**
Migration network size (number of people)	- 0.105	99.6	
Ethnicity			
Member of an indigenous community	1.943	100.0	**
Interactions with ethnicity			
Farm size * ethnicity	- 0.073	76.5	
Labor market assets * ethnicity	- 0.156	97.3	**
Migration network * ethnicity	- 0.670	92.5	**
Size of migration network * ethnicity	0.01	10.0	
Intercept	0.662	99.9	**
Goodness-of-fit	*Poor*	*Nonpoor*	
% correctly predicted	64.5	72.1	

[a] Probability of being significantly different from zero.
** Significant at the 95% level.

We calculate in table 15.11 how much the poverty headcount ratio would be reduced by transferring one additional unit of asset to either the indigenous or the nonindigenous population. This gives guidelines for the targeting of poverty interventions. Transferring one additional NRE hectare of land to the average indigenous and non-indigenous household decreases P_0 by 3.8 percent among the former compared to 0.9 percent among the latter. A similar differential payoff is observed for education: transfer of one additional unit of labor market capital decreases P_0 by 10.1 percent among indigenous households, compared to 6.5 percent among the other households. Finally, gaining membership to a migration network—that is, initiating migration—reduces P_0 more extensively among indigenous than nonindigenous households. However, this is not the case for the size of the network. In this case, the effect of migration deepening is more effective in reducing poverty among the nonindigenous populations. We can speculate that nonindigenous migrants have a greater ability to succeed in migration, possibly because it is easier for them to become inserted in the U.S. labor market than it is for ethnic populations. These results show that there is merit in targeting to indigenous households the limited resources available to provide access to land and education, and to support the initiation of migration among these households (as seen strictly from the angle of their welfare).

In table 15.12, we see that the poor achieved income levels that were only 8.1 percent of the incomes of the nonpoor. The greatest income gap is in agriculture due to the incidence of transitory poverty coming from crop failures among the poor. Income that the poor de-

Table 15.11
Poverty reduction effects of access to assets

	Households		
	All	In ejidos	In indigenous communities
Poverty: headcount ratio (%)	47.3	44.7	71.2
Land assets			
Average farm size (ha NRE)	7.6	8.1	2.5
Marginal effect on P_0 of gaining access to one additional ha NRE	-0.8	-0.4	-2.7
% reduction in P_0 due to gaining access to one additional ha NRE	-1.7	-0.9	-3.8
Labor market assets (number of adults and education)			
Average labor market assets endowment	4.8	4.9	4.1
Marginal effect on P_0 of gaining access to one additional unit of labor market assets	-3.7	-2.9	-7.2
% reduction in P_0 due to gaining access to one additional unit of labor market assets	-7.8	-6.5	-10.1
Migration assets (number of kin migrants)			
% of households with access to a migration network	49	49	53
Effect on P_0 of gaining access to a migration network	-23.3	-20.2	-33.1
% reduction in P_0 due to gaining access to a migration network	-49.3	-45.2	-46.5
Average size of migration asset endowment (number of kin migrants)	1.09	1.09	1.12
Marginal effect on P_0 of one additional unit of migration asset	-4.1	-4.1	-2.8
% reduction in P_0 due to gaining access to one more migrant	-8.7	-9.2	-3.9

rive from wage labor, self-employment in microenterprises, and migrant remittances was only about 10 percent of the income derived by the nonpoor. This suggests that the poor are households with low income from all sources. Being poor in rural Mexico thus results from a failure to derive sufficient income from any of these sources. On the positive side, this also implies that the poor can escape poverty through a number of alternative routes, including agriculture, livestock, the labor market, self-employment in microenterprises, and migration. When seen from the contrast between poor and nonpoor, income levels are thus highly unequal, with the poorest 47 percent achieving on average an income level that is only 8 percent of the income level achieved by the richest 53 percent.

Table 15.12
Differential income structure of poor and nonpoor of the ejido sector, 1994

Poor and nonpoor income shares	Poor [a]	Nonpoor	% difference in income level poor/nonpoor
Sources of income (pesos)			
Agriculture	-218	6,873	n.a.
Livestock	655	2,859	22.9
Wage labor	617	7,317	8.4
Microenterprise income	133	1,245	10.7
Migrant remittances	534	4,300	12.4
Other incomes	157	556	28.2
Total income	1,878	23,151	8.1
Sources of income (% of total)			
Agriculture	-11.6	29.7	
Livestock	34.9	12.3	
Wage labor	32.9	31.6	
Microenterprise income	7.1	5.4	
Migrant remittances	28.4	18.6	
Other incomes	8.4	2.4	
Total income	100.0	100.0	

Note: n.a. indicates not applicable.
[a] Using a poverty line of 6,700 pesos per household.

The differential characteristics of poor and nonpoor households are analyzed in table 15.13. Endowments in agricultural assets are systematically higher among the nonpoor. Cultivated land in ha NRE was 40 percent higher among the nonpoor compared to the poor, and the difference was even greater for irrigated land, which was three times larger among the nonpoor. Differential access to quality land is

Table 15.13
Differential characteristics of the poor and the nonpoor of the ejido sector

Poor and nonpoor characteristics	Poor [a]	Nonpoor	% difference nonpoor/poor	Poor and nonpoor characteristics	Poor [a]	Nonpoor	% difference nonpoor/poor
Agricultural assets				Behavioral patterns			
Land				Land use (ha)			
Total area used (ha NRE)	6.40	8.95	40	Monocropped corn, rainfed	2.58	2.65	3
Rainfed area (ha)	4.96	5.42	9	Monocropped corn, irrigated	0.19	0.61	221
Irrigated area (ha)	0.46	1.34	191	Intercropped corn, rainfed	0.44	0.46	5
Natural pasture area (ha)	2.85	3.42	20	Intercropped corn, irrigated	0.01	0.02	100
Area of the ejido				Technology: % who use			
(ha NRE per ejidatario[b])	21.8	22.9	5	Improved seeds	11.1	25.8	132
Animals (#)				Fertilizers	49.5	61.1	23
Cattle	3.42	9.09	166	Chemical products	44.3	49.6	12
Pigs and goats	5.46	9.30	70	Corn balance			
Agricultural assets: % who own				% who buy	29.5	24.8	-16
A tractor	5.2	8.8	69	% who neither sell nor buy	33.7	27.7	-18
Means of transportation	9.3	20.6	122	% who sell	25.0	33.7	35
Human capital assets				% who sell and buy	11.8	13.8	17
Family (#)				Labor balance			
Family size	4.98	5.17	4	% who sell	13.6	30.1	121
Number of adults	3.11	3.68	18	% who neither sell nor hire	51.8	29.4	-43
Age of household head	47.4	50.9	7	% who hire	27.5	24.7	-10
Number of skilled workers	0.42	0.79	88	% who sell and hire	7.1	15.8	123
Migration assets	0.67	1.42	112	Family labor allocation: # of adults who work			
Institutional assets				In agriculture at home	1.46	1.51	3
Access to credit: % receiving credit from				In non-agriculture at home	0.01	0.06	500
Public sources	21.0	25.8	23	For a wage in agriculture	0.05	0.20	300
Private sources	0.7	3.2	357	Work for a wage in non-agriculture	0.05	0.37	640
Other sources	3.2	5.8	81	Migrate seasonally to the US	0.36	0.90	150
Access to technical assistance	6.1	11.1	82				

[a] Using a poverty line equal to 6,700 pesos per household.
[b] Defined in the text.

thus important in explaining poverty. Cattle ownership is nearly three times higher among the nonpoor. By contrast, small animals (pigs and goats) are more accessible to the poor, with a differential in ownership of less than two. Tractor ownership is 69 percent more frequent among the nonpoor and ownership of means of transportation, 122 percent more frequent. Human capital assets also differ. While family size is about the same, the families of the poor have fewer adults, and the family head is younger. This indicates that labor availability is a factor that helps alleviate poverty. The lower age of household heads among the poor suggests that vertical mobility is occurring as assets are accumulated during the life cycle. The educational level of the poor, who have only half the number of skilled adults present, is clearly inferior. And migration assets, measured by the number of individuals in the extended family system who have migrated, are also less than half the amount of the nonpoor. Institutional assets, characterized by access to credit and particularly access to credit from formal private sources, are systematically lower among the poor. Public credit, which is dominated by the credit without collateral delivered by PRONASOL, is relatively more equally distributed among poor and nonpoor. However, access to technical assistance is highly biased against the poor, indicating that better targeting of government services is required to improve the level of productivity of the poor in using the limited resources that they currently control. The poor also cultivate less monocropped irrigated corn. And they make less use of improved seeds, fertilizers, and chemical products.

The balance of corn availability and use reveals that the poor are more dependent on corn purchases and are also more frequently self-sufficient in corn than the nonpoor. In contrast, it is the nonpoor who most frequently sell corn. In the labor market, the poor are more frequently self-sufficient, making use of family labor without hiring or selling labor. The nonpoor, by contrast, are more frequently sellers of labor since wage earnings are an effective way out of poverty. Surprisingly, the poor hire more labor than the nonpoor. This is a consequence of crop failures among households who have incurred the cost of hired labor, throwing them into poverty as measured by their income achieved that particular year. The number of adults who participate in the labor market and in activities outside the farm is much lower among the poor, as is the number of migrants. Participation in these activities, which are fundamental for escaping from poverty, is hampered by the lack of the human capital assets needed for success in the labor market and in migration.

Asset Entitlements and Poverty

We have seen that characterizing poverty among farming households using income data from a year when there is substantial instability in agricultural production ends up placing among the poor a number of households affected by crop failures. For this year, they appear among the poor even though they may not have been poor in a year of average yields, and hence may not be poor over the long term. Since chronic poverty is the consequence of low entitlements in productive assets, another possibility for identifying the poor is to categorize households by asset endowments—that is, by their potential to generate income, as opposed to their actual income, which is affected by stochastic weather factors. This is done in table 15.14, where households are categorized by their current control over the three types of assets that are the main determinants of time allocation strategies and levels of income achieved. To define categories of households we use the following thresholds in the three categories of assets:

- Agricultural assets, with a threshold of 4 ha NRE for high assets.
- Labor force assets, with a threshold of 6 UEA for high assets.
- Migration assets, with a threshold of greater than zero for high assets.

In table 15.14, households are classified in eight groups according to their endowments in these assets, ranging from those that are below the threshold for all three assets (group 1), to those with one asset above the threshold (groups 2, 3, and 4), two assets above the threshold (groups 5, 6, and 7), and all three assets above the threshold (group 8). Ownership of these assets represents the *potential* that households have in designing income-earning strategies that capitalize on these assets, not the actual income strategies; and it represents the *potential* they have in reaching higher income levels as asset ownership increases, not the actual income levels achieved. If the typology has predictive power, these potentials should materialize in contrasted income-earning strategies that specifically correspond to asset ownership. In addition, income levels should rise as asset endowments place households above the threshold in a larger number of asset categories. These expected regularities provide us with a test of the validity of the proposed assets approach to the characterization of household behavior.

The income data for the eight groups of households in table 15.14 show that assets do indeed matter: households with zero assets achieve 21 percent of the income achieved by those with all three assets, while those with one asset achieve between 41 and 48 percent, and those with two assets, between 68 and 93 percent of that level. The poverty headcount ratio also falls as the number of assets owned increases, from 75 percent with zero assets to between 56 and 40 percent with one, between 37 and 17 percent with two, and 19 percent with three. Extreme poverty also falls with asset endowment. It is interesting to note that the poverty gap is systematically higher among households with high agricultural asset endowments.[3] This is because of the high incidence of crop failure in rainfed agriculture, which creates the largest losses among large farmers with greater exposure to risk because they have higher cash expenditures on production inputs.

The predictive power of asset endowments on income and poverty is very strong. Those with no assets (group 1) are poor and derive 47 percent of their income from the labor market. When migration assets are the only entitlement (group 2), remittances account for 45 percent of total income. When land is the only asset (group 3), crops and livestock generate 73 percent of total income. And when labor force assets are the only entitlement (group 4), wages account for 58 percent of total income. As the number of assets controlled by the household increases, income portfolios become more diversified. In the end, households endowed with all three assets (group 8) generate 32 percent of their income from crops and livestock, 36 percent from wage labor, and 23 percent from remittances.

The regional distribution of asset endowments reveals that households in the Center and South Pacific are more frequently in the zero assets category and in the category with only migration assets (compared to the percentage distribution of all households across regions). Regarding the indigenous community, table 15.14 shows that it is overrepresented in the categories of zero assets, migration assets only, and labor plus migration assets. Lack of access to land is thus the overwhelming determinant of poverty among members of the indigenous community.

Elimination of poverty would require a welfare budget able to bring all households in poverty to the poverty line. Assuming perfect targeting, the last line in table 15.14 shows that 30 percent of this budget would be spent on the 19.5 percent of households dispossessed of all assets.

---

[3] The poverty gap is $z - y_i$, where z is the poverty line and y_i the income level of household i in poverty. It measures the deficit in pesos to bring household i to poverty line. The sum of these deficits over households in poverty is the welfare budget necessary to bring all poor households to poverty line, assuming that there is perfect targeting on the poor.

Table 15.14
Typology of households by asset ownership

	Household classes								
	Zero assets	One asset			Two assets			Three assets	
Agricultural assets [a]	low	low	high	low	low	high	high	high	
Labor market assets [b]	low	low	low	high	high	low	high	high	
Migration assets [c]	none	yes	none	none	yes	yes	none	yes	All
	-1-	-2-	-3-	-4-	-5-	-6-	-7-	-8-	households
Number of cases	259	249	250	88	61	222	95	118	1342
Households (%)	19.5	17.1	18.4	5.9	4.6	17.7	7.2	9.6	100
Regions (%)									
North	18.9	24.6	11.4	29.3	27.6	34.8	13.7	40.8	23.8
North Pacific	3.4	2.2	18.6	4.7	4.5	6.0	21.9	9.0	8.4
Center	38.8	46.4	14.0	39.7	50.8	29.2	11.1	27.7	31.7
Gulf	17.9	7.5	41.2	12.8	4.3	17.7	33.5	5.4	19.3
South Pacific	21.1	19.3	14.7	13.7	12.8	12.4	19.8	17.0	16.8
Indigenous communities									
(% ejidos in class)	18.4	17.4	3.1	9.4	14.3	3.7	2.8	4.4	9.8
Sources of income by activity (%)									
Crops	27.8	13.6	49.3	8.5	6.4	30.1	38.7	17.4	26.9
Livestock	9.4	7.3	23.3	22.6	9.4	11.3	14.8	14.4	13.9
Self-employment in non-ag.	8.7	3.6	1.8	8.7	3.5	7.6	4.1	7.7	5.5
Wage labor	47.3	27.5	22.5	58.0	49.3	15.9	41.1	35.5	31.7
Remittances	2.5	45.2	0.6	0.0	31.1	29.9	0.0	23.2	19.2
Other sources	4.3	2.8	2.5	2.2	0.3	5.1	1.3	1.9	2.8
Total income (pesos)	4,973	10,586	11,512	9,932	19,745	16,582	22,620	24,255	13,090
Poverty (headcount ratio in %) [d]	74.8	40.2	56.1	55.1	17.3	37.2	32.4	23.8	47.3
Extreme poverty (headcount ratio in %) [e]	59.0	23.0	40.7	41.1	10.1	25.0	22.6	19.4	33.8
Poverty gap (pesos)	3,530	1,426	3,012	2,679	676	1,653	1,996	1,732	2,281
% welfare budget for poverty elimination	29.9	11.6	24.6	7.7	1.3	12.0	6.2	6.7	100

[a] High agricultural assets is more than 4 ha of rainfed equivalent.

[b] High labor force (education) assets is more than 6 unskilled equivalent adult.

[c] Migration asset = permanent migrants from extended family and from household + (seasonal migrants from household − 1).

[d] With a poverty line of 6,700 pesos.

[e] With an extreme poverty line of 3,819 pesos.

Conclusion

The principal conclusion of this analysis of income and poverty in the ejido sector is that poverty is extensive, deep in the sense of extreme poverty, and at the same time highly heterogeneous. Overall, 47 percent of the households are in poverty and 34 percent in extreme poverty. Poverty consists of both transitory and chronic poverty. It varies by region, farm size, human capital and migration asset endowments, and ethnicity. It is highest in the Gulf (65 percent poverty incidence) and the South Pacific (57 percent, with Chiapas excluded), among those with small plots of land (56 percent on farms less than 2 ha NRE), in indigenous communities (71 percent), among those with low labor market assets (65 percent), and among those with no migration capital (60 percent).

Cultivation of very small plots of land, when households have no other assets, is still an important factor for remaining in poverty in the ejido, calling attention to the still unresolved problem of sufficient access to land for a large share of social sector households. More important than land area is access to irrigated land, except in the Gulf, where irrigation is not critical. Hence public investment in irrigation and the rehabilitation of irrigation systems is an important instrument for reducing poverty. Inferior access to public institutions and services is also a feature of poverty in the social sector: poor households have less access to technology, technical assistance, and credit, despite the valuable achievements of PRONASOL. A larger area of common-property land in the ejido is an inadequate compensatory factor, partly because the poor do not have the ability to capitalize in cattle and take advantage of access to common pastures. The poor have an economy that is more agricultural in character, consisting of inter-cropped rainfed corn, traditional technology, and orientation toward family consumption. It is thus important that technical assistance be designed specifically for these production systems and be modernized while accounting for the rural poor's extensive participation in off-farm activities. Participation in the labor market and migration are fundamental for escaping from poverty, especially for those who have little access to land. For this to happen, education and migration assets are key. Finally, ethnicity is a fundamental feature of rural poverty, and especially of extreme poverty. Here ethnicity combines low access to land, low educational achievements, and generally low migration assets, in addition to potential discrimination in accessing markets and institutions. This dominant role of ethnicity in identifying extreme poverty suggests that a good indicator for the targeting of poverty interventions is the ethnic community as a cluster of poor households.

16

Summary and Conclusions

We began this study with a historical perspective, recalling that the ejido had been organized as an institution with the multiple aims of organizing production among smallholders, achieving political control over the peasantry, and representing peasants in their relations with the state. By 1992, when Article 27 of the 1917 Constitution was reformed, the ejido was a complex institution, constituted by a peasant economy repressed through a set of state controls and obligations tied to the organization of production. It was characterized by strong state intervention in the internal life of the ejido, including its decision-making mechanisms, conditions for access to public resources, and the management of rural welfare. And the ejido's corporatist, communitarian, and representative functions were strongly codified by the state.

Regulation of the forms of production included prohibitions against employing wage labor, renting and selling land, and being absent for more than two years without losing land rights. The state intervened directly, imposing conditions on the channeling of public resources: credit was given to the ejido as a whole, with restrictions on the selection of crops, a prohibition against intercropping, and few technological options because of the small amount of credit and the delivery of credit in kind. Access to water required irrigation permits that carried conditions about land use. Insurance was mandatory for access to official credit. And production was done under contracts with CONASUPO and specialized parastatal enterprises. These controls were at the same time associated with a large variety of subsidies, which partially compensated for the loss of opportunities that these controls implied but which also served as instruments of political control. To obtain these subsidies, access to the state and effective political representation were fundamental. Inevitably, this dependency on compensatory institutional rents delivered by the state reinforced the government's control over ejidatarios. This tenuous balance between controls and subsidies thus became the fundamental determinant of the political and economic status of the ejido.

As we have seen, this system of controls and subsidies eroded slowly. After a long and successful initial phase (see Lamartine Yates 1981), the ejido sector entered a severe crisis; production was stagnant and the economic condition of ejido households increasingly lagged behind that of the rest of the population. It is this very decay of the ejido system in a global context of political and economic liberalization that induced the profound reforms initiated under President Salinas. These reforms included a redefinition of the relations between the state and the members of the ejido sector, a change in the public institutions serving the sector, a reform of the legal framework that regulates access to land, and a modification in the instruments of agricultural policy. The changes observed in the ejido sector between 1990 and 1994, which are the subject of this book, therefore reflect:

- The impact of macroeconomic policies, characterized by an effective control of inflation but also by a serious profitability crisis in agriculture linked to decreasing global growth rates, an increasing appreciation of the real exchange rate, a fall in the real support price of the main staple crops, high interest rates, and the loss of subsidies to the sector.

- An institutional vacuum created by a decline in the state's role in agriculture, leading to the privatization, scaling down, or liquidation of many of the public institutions supporting the sector and only a very partial reconstruction of alternative institutions to support the ejido sector. In general, this reduced availability and raised the cost of access to credit, insurance, markets, modern inputs, seeds, water, and technical assistance.

- The beginning of a process of adjustment to the new economic and institutional rules by ejidatarios and by the ejido as a form of organization.

In particular, changes in the legal statute codifying the use and ownership of ejido land had by 1994 already activated the land rental market, but they had not yet resulted in any privatization of ejido farm plots that could be observed in the survey. The survey also precedes implementation of direct income transfers through PROCAMPO, introduced to compensate for a drop in the price of corn which was expected to result from trade liberalization under NAFTA. However, by 1994 the reforms had already liberalized individual and community initiatives, allowing numerous adjustments in the production system, in household income-earning strategies, and in the organization of the ejido—adjustments that had been prohibited before the constitutional reforms or that had been introduced illegally.

What we observed between 1990 and 1994 was thus an ejido sector in crisis, at the initial stages of a long process of adaptation and transformation. The obvious difficulties that ejidatarios confronted were thus partly contextual and structural symptoms, but they were also symptoms of a difficult and protracted process of transition toward economic and political liberalization.

The observations in this study in no way pretend to offer a judgment about the wisdom of the reforms undertaken under President Salinas. More time must elapse before making such a judgment, until the reforms come to stabilize a transformed ejido system. However, the reforms have already triggered important adjustments and a process of differentiation in the social sector, and they have also created serious difficulties for large numbers of ejidatarios whose livelihood and continued access to land are threatened. It is consequently important to give attention to these problems in order to help the government of Mexico design complementary reforms and differentiated interventions to improve the process of adjustment.

The main conclusions deriving from our analysis of the data collected in the two surveys are presented below.

Profitability Crisis and Decapitalization

As a sector, the ejido is going through a profitability crisis and a serious process of productive and social decapitalization. This crisis threatens the very permanence of many households in the sector, creates incentives to migrate, and induces more extensive patterns of land use and delays in the processes of modernization and diversification that should be part of agriculture's adjustment to the macroeconomic reforms. This crisis is partly a product of appreciation of the real exchange rate and the elimination of subsidies. But, as we argued at the beginning of this study, it also emerges from the coinciding processes of political and economic liberalization which generate an institutional vacuum and thus reduce the opportunities for ejidatarios to maintain or increase productivity and adjust the pattern of productive activities.

The symptoms of this crisis are plentiful. Some abandonment of the smallest farms and a concentration of land toward the medium-sized and large farm classes is observed in the North, Center, and South Pacific. There is also an acceleration of the process of land rentals. Those who rent land to others are mostly those with smaller land plots. These marginal farmers are heavily involved in off-farm activities and migration. Liberalization of the ejido now allows them to rent out their land without losing their property rights in the ejido. The operational area of small farms thus decreases through land rental and migration. Land titling and further liberalization of the land market can be expected to further accelerate this abandonment of the smallest farms, which had been restrained by government regulation.

The number of ejidatarios with access to credit increased through the intervention of PRONASOL, but the total amount of credit to which the ejido sector has access decreased. Access to larger loans from BANRURAL and commercial banks is confined to a small minority of better endowed ejidatarios. Credit for investment, which is essential to support the productive reconversion of the ejido, is almost nonexistent. The general scarcity of credit is manifest in the fact that 70 percent of ejidatarios do not use credit from any source, neither formal nor informal, and 92 percent declare that they are constrained in their access to credit.

Access to formal insurance virtually disappeared. This is also the case with technical assistance. Combined with the profitability crisis, the result was a strong fall in the use of fertilizers, hybrid seeds, and chemical products for production. There was also a fall in the use of machinery (especially tractors), particularly in its use for beans and cultivation of the next most important crop after corn and beans. In many cases, it was manual labor that replaced machines. Local seeds were substituted for improved seeds, except among the most technified producers. The technological panorama is thus not encouraging. It is a symptom of the profitability crisis affecting the sector as a whole, lack of institutional support, and incomplete adjustment to the new context established by the economic reforms.

Another symptom of the crisis of the ejido sector is the large increase in corn cultivation between 1990 and 1994, including an increase on prime irrigated lands. This increase, in spite of a fall in the real price of corn, indicates the absence of other productive options and the constraints on adjusting cropping patterns toward higher-value-added activities. Diversification toward crops with a higher value and with comparative advantages in the context of trade liberalization has thus been delayed. In 1994, corn covered 52 percent of the cultivated rainfed land, 38 percent of the irrigated area, and 49 percent of the total cultivated area. Expansion of the area planted in monocropped corn occurred in rainfed areas (a 15 percent increase) but above all in irrigated areas (70 percent). Almost all of this expansion was on farms larger than 5 ha NRE: on rainfed land, 65 percent of the increase in monocropped or intercropped corn occurred on these farms; on irrigated land, this increase was 91 percent. On these larger farms, when there is irrigation, it is monocropped corn that expanded most. On rainfed land, intercropped corn expanded most.

The area sown with fodder also increased, a symptom of the increase in cattle raising. The opportunity costs of this expansion of corn and fodder were a fall in the area planted in wheat and oil seeds, as well as a plowing under of fallow lands and natural pastures. On smaller farms, the area planted in intercropped corn increased on both rain-fed and irrigated land while monocropped corn changed little, evidence of increasing differences in farming systems associated with farm size.

High flexibility in the combination of different forms of corn production—a strategy that is clearly preferred in the ejido sector, on both smaller and larger farms—would have been impossible without the weakening of institutions that had been instrumental for political control, particularly BANRURAL, SRA, SARH, and CNA. Each of these institutions systematically repressed certain productive strategies of the ejido, such as intercropping and technological change. Restrictions that made resource management inflexible were part of the arsenal of instruments used by these governmental institutions to achieve political control, since productive inflexibility generally made the rural producers dependent and vulnerable, and even more so if their resources were insufficient for consumption and accumulation. For this reason, the deregulation and the scaling down of a public sector that had been the basis of the government's control strategy have caused a relative liberation of peasant producers amidst the serious stagnation of the rural sector, partially compensating for the unfavorable economic and institutional environment by allowing a greater scope for individual initiatives.

Liberation of a Repressed Peasant Economy

The weakening of state controls that had caused economic repression in the ejido is allowing the emergence of a typical peasant economy. This economy is characterized by reliance on family labor; peasant farming systems with intercropping; selective integration to the product and labor markets; international migration; an increase in cattle raising, partly through access to common-property pastures for the few who had the capacity to capitalize in this period of economic crisis; and forms of mutual support for access to labor and insurance. Because it is closely integrated into a variety of markets, the emerging peasant economy cannot be called Chayanovian or autarkic. As such, it could not be conceptualized by returning to the "campesinista" positions that prevailed in Mexico in the 1970s, as advocated, for example, by Díaz-Polanco (1977).

In some sense, particularly for the smaller landholders and members of indigenous communities, the ejido sector serves as a refuge economy, with households searching for complementary opportunities outside the ejido and using it as a platform for migration while maintaining reproduction of the family on the land and in the agrarian community. It affords these households lower survival costs and more security as they face high risks on the labor market and in migration. The ejido sector can thus be envisioned as a modern embodiment of the concept of functional dualism (de Janvry 1981).

The principal sign of the emergence of this peasant economy on small and medium-sized farms and in rainfed areas is the expansion of intercropped corn. The emergence of peasant production systems is complemented by other systematic changes. There has been an increase in peasant cattle raising that is distinct from the increase in cattle ranching that occurred in Mexico during the economic boom of the 1970s, where the livestock economy was based on the cultivation of sorghum and oriented toward changes in urban consumption associated with rising disposable incomes. During the 1990s, the increase in cattle raising in the ejido was principally achieved by ejidatarios with medium-sized and large land plots whose successful off-farm activities gave them the ability to accumulate capital. The percentage of ejidatarios who own cattle increased. Livestock expansion created an increased use of common-property lands for grazing. This, in turn, exacerbated environmental pressures on these common-property lands, where a strong tendency toward overgrazing exists because the members of most ejidos are unable to cooperate in restricting the number of animals for a socially optimal management of pastures.

Another feature of the peasant economy is the increase in activities for family consumption, such as the backyard activities in which a rising share of ejidatarios engage. Market integration was also uneven, foreshadowing a differentiated impact of policy reforms across classes of households. In 1994, a high percentage of ejido households were either self-sufficient in corn or buyers of corn: 31 percent of the households were self-sufficient and 27 percent only bought corn, leaving 40 percent of ejidatarios as corn sellers. Among those who sell corn, 12 percent sell and buy corn as part of a stock optimization strategy when they have privileged access to CONASUPO. If the price of corn falls as a consequence of NAFTA, the 41 percent of ejidatarios who sell corn would be negatively affected. By contrast, the self-sufficient households would not be affected directly, and buyers would benefit. The impact of NAFTA on corn producers should thus be highly differentiated across households, making generalizations about the impact of trade liberalization on peasant welfare meaningless (de Janvry, Sadoulet, and Gordillo 1995).

Access to credit and insurance also acquired more evident peasant features. The number of families with access to credit increased through the PRONASOL program of credit without collateral, which enabled many households that did not have access to credit in 1990 to obtain it in 1994. The modest amounts of this type of production credit are only enough to support traditional technology on traditional crops—in other words, for peasant production systems. They are not sufficient to allow modernization of traditional crops or diversification of production. The decrease in access to formal insurance also forced households to rely more on traditional forms of protection against adversity, such as using livestock as a security buffer; resorting to informal loans from relatives, friends, and moneylenders; and obtaining mutual insurance with community members. The important presence of informal organizations, in which one-fourth of the ejidatarios participate, is another symptom of a peasant economy. These organizations are more important in regions with indigenous populations, in frontier areas, and generally in more risky rainfed agriculture.

Finally, this peasant economy is strongly inserted in the labor market and in national and international migration. We have observed that the least educated migrate more to other parts of Mexico, while those with intermediate levels of education migrate more to the United States. Those with the highest educational levels migrate mostly within Mexico, where they have greater opportunities of valuing their human capital.[1] The degree of participation in international migration is astonishing. In the states of the Center, North Pacific, and North regions, typically between 15 and 23 percent of the household adults have migrated to work in the United States. The pace of this migration is accelerating, with more adults under 35 years of age having migrated than adults over age 35. Migration also increasingly extends toward the South Pacific, with 10 percent of the adults in Guerrero and 5 percent of those in Oaxaca having participated. This is the region where the acceleration of migration is highest. Abandonment of the smallest farms is undoubtedly connected to this acceleration of migration and to liberalization of the right to rent land.

Entrepreneurship and Social Differentiation

Despite the context of profitability crisis and institutional gaps, the deepening of a process of social differentiation within the ejido was observed as a small, relatively successful entrepreneurial sector emerged, fostered by liberalization from state controls. Because of the

---

[1]For a similar finding based on a detailed case study from households in Pátzcuaro, Michoacán, see Taylor 1987.

adverse economic and institutional context, the exercise of entrepreneurship resulted less frequently in successful capital accumulation than in innovative approaches toward coping with the crisis. We identified four types of successful entrepreneurs: producers of monocropped corn in the fall–winter season, producers of fruits and vegetables, ejidatarios with more than 10 ha NRE and more than 5 head of cattle, and small farmers with less than 2 ha NRE but who participate in migration to the United States. It is to be expected that this process of differentiation will accelerate when the economic and institutional context for agriculture improves and when adjustment to the reforms is more advanced.

We have analyzed the characteristics of these four types of entrepreneurs with the goal of identifying who they are and what main determinants compose their success. This, in turn, is suggestive of policy initiatives for the diffusion of these successful patterns of behavior toward other households. We have seen that successful entrepreneurs have a wide range of defining characteristics, opening up an equally wide array of possibilities for successful participation by other households in modernization, diversification, cattle raising, and migration. For instance, different regions display different characteristics. In the Gulf, South Pacific, and North Pacific, modernization through corn is dominant; in the Gulf and North Pacific, diversification toward fruits and vegetables is more common; in the Center and South Pacific, capitalization in cattle is frequent; and in the Center and North, migration is an important factor. For modernization of corn production and capitalization in cattle, farm size and access to irrigation are important; for diversification, access to irrigation, not farm size, is what matters most. The modernization of corn production and the increase in cattle raising are mostly taking place on farms above 10 ha NRE, while diversification happens more frequently on medium-sized farms between 2 and 10 ha NRE.

For the few small farmers who can pursue them, both modernization and diversification help prevent abandonment of the land, but these are difficult strategies to follow for small farmers and indigenous community members because of their limited access to investable funds and to necessary institutional services. Each of these four paths depends on superior access to credit, a factor that makes their diffusion conditional upon reconstruction of rural financial services accessible to ejidatarios. Furthermore, those who are more successful have more access to irrigation, making diffusion further conditional upon continued public investment in developing and rehabilitating irrigation systems and upon effective devolution of irrigation management to users. Finally, education level is important for successful modernization and diversification, requiring a serious effort to improve the currently very low educational levels in the social sector, particularly among the indigenous population.

We also observed that migration and participation in the labor market are factors that hinder agricultural modernization, calling upon rural development interventions to make the modernization of farming compatible with participation in these off-farm activities. Success in migration is determined less by individual than by social and regional characteristics, emphasizing the fundamental importance of migratory capital and the social networks to which potential migrants belong. This implies that rural development interventions intending to slow down emigration out of the ejido should focus on geographical areas where migration capital is still weak, most particularly the Gulf and South Pacific. Where migration capital is well established—that is, in the older areas of migration such as the Center, North Pacific, and North, where virtually every potential migrant has access to family members who have migratory experience or are already located at the points of destination—migration is basically impossible to stop. Success in migration in turn allows smallholder households to capitalize in livestock, taking advantage of access to common-property pastures. Instead of being used in livestock, remittances could be channeled through local financial institutions into the modernization and diversification of agriculture and the setting up of decentralized microenterprises. For this purpose, local financial institutions need to be developed and technical assistance provided to local initiatives for new investments.

In conclusion, ejido households can follow these paths of entrepreneurial opportunity according to their particular asset endowments and geographic location. However, we have seen that, in all cases, access to credit, technical assistance, and irrigation are fundamental. Thus the reconstruction of institutional and organizational support for the ejido is very important if these entrepreneurial success stories are to spread. Above all, the relative access to these institutions and organizations determines the relative competitiveness of ejido families. The possibility of consolidating a middle class of ejidatarios who are successful in at least one of these entrepreneurial paths— instead of witnessing the elimination of this class for failing to be competitive in their use of the land—thus requires the promotion of institutions and organizations to which this middle class can have access as rapidly as possible.

The Ejido as an Organization in Support of Production

The ejido comes out of the process of reforms, not as a decaying institution, but as an institution with new functions supporting peasant

production and with the potential to help ejidatarios adjust to the reforms. For example, this role was observed in the substitution of the
social sector for the public sector in accessing modern inputs and machinery. During the four years that were analyzed, access to machinery through collective ownership increased by 37 percent, particularly
access to tractors (41 percent), trucks (96 percent), and pickup trucks
(150 percent). Access to chemical products, fertilizers, and technical
assistance was also increasingly obtained through the social sector.
The ejido, therefore, is an important part of institutional reconstruction, allowing access to services formerly provided by the state.

Membership of the ejido in formal organizations such as the ARIC
and ejido unions reinforces the capacity of the ejido to receive services, particularly agricultural inputs, machinery, and equipment. In
this case, the ejido mediates the relationship between ejidatarios and
these formal organizations, which are usually sponsored by the government itself. Despite being strongly hierarchical, and having a cen-
tralized leadership and a clientele more than a participatory membership, these organizations are important instruments in support of
modernization and diversification.

The objectives that motivate ejidatarios to organize have changed.
Participation in formal credit organizations has declined, partly as a
consequence of the tendency of banks to individualize credit and to
shun collective forms of organization. The waning of organizing to
seek access to credit as an objective is also related to the crisis of institutional credit and the perception that PRONASOL's credit without
collateral is the main form of channeling public resources to individual peasants. The solidarity committees are more often perceived as
support mechanisms for agricultural production and input acquisition than as a means of access to credit. Credit without collateral has a
cost below the market interest rate. Repayment rates have been relatively high, and funds are generally returned to the same users in the
next agricultural cycle or channeled to social investments in the community. The motivation to organize is thus shifted toward supporting
agricultural production. It is also displaced toward improving infrastructure, whether through peak organizations that group a number
of ejidos or through informal mutual assistance organizations. Directly or indirectly, the ejido is thus an important organizational medium for improving the competitiveness of ejidatarios in the context
of the new market and institutional rules. This role of the ejido remains, nevertheless, seriously below potential and in need of systematic efforts to promote the emergence of new organizations using
the ejido or subcoalitions within the ejido (particularly when it is very
large) as their basis.

Despite the forthcoming privatization of individual farm plots under the reform of Article 27, the ejido will remain an instrument of

access to common-property resources. These resources are important since, on average, 68 percent of the total area of ejidos is common-property land, of which 67 percent is in pastures and 24 percent in forests. These resources are important for cattle raising. While cattle raising has the potential to improve income among those with less land, it in fact benefits principally those ejidatarios with more land, human capital, and migration assets because they are better able to capitalize in animals. Indeed, we observed that inequality in the use of collective resources for cattle raising largely parallels inequality in the sizes of individual land plots. However, smallholders with success in migration have also been able to take advantage of access to common-property pastures to capitalize in cattle the remittances they receive from migrants. With the increase in cattle raising during the four years surveyed, the percentage of ejidatarios who use the ejido's common-property pastures has increased. The environmental pressures on these fragile lands, many of which are already seriously degraded, have increased, while the capacity of the ejido to organize to protect these resources from predatory use by outsiders and to regulate grazing by ejido members remains weak and underdeveloped.

Finally, the collective resources of the ejido are sources of revenue that support investment in public services, social welfare activities, and, in some cases, investment in productive projects. Efficiency in the management of these resources has generally been low due to the ejido leadership's lack of credibility and inability to coordinate individual initiative. At the same time, this cooperation gap offers the opportunity for significant efficiency gains that could be achieved through improved cooperation, thus increasing efficiency and welfare in the ejidos.

Poverty in the Social Sector

With 47 percent of its households below the poverty line, the social sector is an important national reservoir of poverty. This compares to 25 percent of individuals below the poverty line in the urban sector and 34 percent nationally (INEGI 1990–92). With an extreme poverty line set at 57 percent of the poverty line, 34 percent of the social sector households are in extreme poverty, a much higher share than the incidence of extreme poverty in the urban sector. While part of this poverty is transitory, linked to climatic vagaries in rainfed agriculture and to the profitability crisis of agriculture, most poverty is chronic, associated with the structural problems of Mexican rural areas. Poverty in the social sector is thus an important issue both for national welfare and for political sustainability of the economic model put in place by the economic reforms, including NAFTA and the scaling down of the role of the state in support of the ejido sector.

Inequality is also an important issue in the social sector, even if land is relatively equally distributed compared to the private sector. Most of the inequalities in land endowments are associated with inter-community differences, as opposed to intra-community inequalities. Across the five farm classes that we have used as a typology of producers, the ratio in average farm size between the largest and smallest farm groups is only 3.5 to 1, a remarkably egalitarian pattern of endowments. However, this hides other sources of inequality. Because other assets also matter in the determination of income, the income gap between poor and nonpoor households is 12 to 1. It is 13 to 1 between the second and fifth income quintiles.

A striking feature of household incomes in the social sector is the high diversity of sources. In 1994, 60 percent of the households derived more than half of their total income from off-farm or nonagricultural activities. This rises to 63 percent in the indigenous community, which is consequently less agrarian than usually presumed. Important sources of income include participation in the labor market and in domestic and international migration. Indigenous communities, in particular, have a high percentage of households with migration as their main source of income. This suggests that, for many households, the farm is a base of operation from which to reach other sources of income, implying a household division of labor that combines agricultural subsistence activities (often largely female based) with participation in the labor market and migration. Lack of a continuous presence of men has important implications for the modernization of agriculture and for decision making at the community level regarding the management of common-property resources. The high diversity of sources of income also suggests that there are many routes available to escape poverty and that a rural development program to reduce poverty in the ejido sector needs to focus on potential sources of income beyond agriculture, particularly in the ethnic community and in those ejidos least endowed in land.

Chronic poverty is primarily associated with lack of access to all classes of assets, with ethnicity, and with geographical region. Among assets, key are land and irrigation, human capital (number of working-age adults and educational levels), and migration capital. Improving the asset position of households in poverty, and improving the productivity of labor given access to assets, should thus be the primary focus of rural development interventions. Due to the complexity and local specificity of potential sources of income, this requires a coordinated, multipronged approach that needs to be managed in a decentralized and participatory fashion to be effective (de Janvry et al. 1995). Success of the land reform in progress thus fundamentally depends on the ability of the Mexican government to help put into place an ambitious program of rural development that complements the multidimensionality of rural households which have differentiated potential sources of income. To date, this broad-based approach to rural development is yet to be defined in Mexico, even though the country has a long and rich history of experiments in rural development and many elements of such a program are already in existence in a dispersed fashion.

Political Control and Counter-Reform

The results of the 1994 survey, and comparison with the 1990 data, can be used to speculate about whether the ejido's historical role as an instrument of political control is likely to disappear amidst the economic and political reforms, and about the forces that may militate to restore this former role. As we have shown above, the weakening of the model of political control allowed the consolidation of a typical peasant economy that was always present in the ejido but had been repressed by state control. Following this first phase of liberalization, and the many responses to it that have been analyzed in this book, we now ask how the model of political control has weakened, what remains, and what new elements have emerged that could potentially generate a new form of relationship between the ejido sector and the state.

The model of political control over the ejido had been constructed on the basis of a particular legal framework and specific interventionist practices. The compatibility between state logic and peasant logic had been achieved, however imperfectly, through the existence of a variety of secondary markets and tolerated illegal practices. The legal reforms of 1991 and 1992 radically modified this framework by allowing greater flexibility in the ejido's use of its three basic land components: parceled agricultural land, common-property land, and land in urban settlement. The reforms also weakened the authority of the executive committee of the ejido, and instead reinforced the role of the assembly as the highest authority within the ejido. All the above led to a weakening of secondary markets and hence of the very mechanisms that had made the logics of the state and peasants compatible.

However, what remains from the old model of political control are the very same agents that had implemented the interventionist practices and organized the secondary markets. Even though they were sustained by the old legal framework, these markets and practices had never been formally codified. Thus these informal coercions and practices, and the agents that embody them, constitute the basic nucleus of a potential conservative resistance to the reforms, and they could be the platform from which the old system of political control could reconstruct itself, although in a manner adapted to the new political and economic context.

There are, however, two powerful processes that operate against this potential conservative restoration. The first consists of two phenomena. One is a strong demographic transformation within the ejido as a consequence of generational changes, the notable increase in the settler population attached to the ejidos (*avecindados*), and the role of migratory flows. The other phenomenon is a wave of peasant mobilizations which emerged twenty years ago but have persisted with differing intensities and with redefined objectives (Hernández 1994). These phenomena made much more complex the peasant population over which the ejido was to serve as an instrument of political control. They have also generated higher incentives for direct peasant political participation and induced the emergence of new leaders among ejidatarios, making it difficult to return to the old order. Greater political participation and changes in leadership also make it difficult for the old political bosses to block or abuse the process of land titling and registration (DeWalt and Rees 1994; Gordillo 1992).

The second process operating against conservative resurgence is documented by the 1990 and 1994 ejido surveys: a peasant economy inserted in markets has emerged with the potential to adapt to the reforms by using the comparative advantages that the ejido as a form of organization of production offers. These advantages include the use of family labor, access to common-property resources, diversification of income-generating activities, specific mechanisms to confront risk and weather crises, and reconversion of the ejido as an organization in support of competitiveness of peasant production. As the analysis in this book has shown, successful modernization and diversification of this peasant economy hinges upon the existence of a favorable macroeconomic context, reconstruction of a network of institutions supportive of production in a smallholder sector, delivery of public goods in support of private investment, and promotion of organizations in support of the competitiveness of ejidatarios, most particularly through adaptation of the ejido as a form of organization and political representation to assume functions in support of ejidatario competitiveness.

Rapid success in this economic transformation will be key in fending off pressures to return to the old system of political control. Urgency in achieving economic success is all the greater given that the ejido remains a vast reservoir of poverty—with 47 percent of households below poverty line, the poor concentrated in specific regions, and a clear association between poverty and ethnicity, all of which threaten to destabilize the progress of reforms not only in the rural sector but in the economy at large. The unresolved tensions in

Chiapas over access to land offer vivid evidence of this threat and its cost to the economy as a whole. Until this economic transformation has been achieved, the temptation to restore the ejido as an apparatus of political control will remain, however more unlikely this possibility may become as time passes.

Conclusion

We conclude by observing that the outcome of the second Mexican agrarian reform initiated by President Salinas is still far from certain. Liberalization of the ejido has unleashed numerous individual and collective initiatives that have produced visible adjustments, showing the ability of this vast sector to respond to incentives. At the same time, the overall context of economic crisis in agriculture and de-institutionalization of the rural sector have reduced the economic benefits that the reforms could have yielded, and hence the scope of modernization and diversification that was expected to follow. The main step in the reforms—namely, the individual titling of some of the ejido lands—had not yet become a reality in 1994. And the ultimate outcome of the reforms is tied to the resolution of much broader economic and political questions with which Mexico is currently struggling: on the economic side, restoration of economic growth, maintenance of a competitive real exchange rate, and employment creation; on the political side, implementation of participatory democracy, decentralization of governance, and enforcement of the rule of law.

What is certain is that the second agrarian reform offers major opportunities to improve efficiency and welfare in this sector. Years of neglect and cumulative contradictions between the functions of the ejido as a mechanism to simultaneously achieve political control over the peasantry, represent peasants, and organize production by smallholders had created a huge efficiency gap that is now open for capture. We have analyzed a number of success stories that help identify the measures that must be pursued to fill this gap. They include a favorable macroeconomic environment, institutional reconstruction, promotion of organizations (in particular through the ejido system), and public investment in irrigation and education. The land reform initiative needs to be complemented by a comprehensive program of rural development in support of the land reform beneficiaries, a program that still needs to be put into place in Mexico (de Janvry et al. 1996). Because of the high level of heterogeneity of farm households, a rural development program for the ejido should focus not only on agriculture but also on the other sources of income accessible to ejidatarios. This implies the ability to coordinate interventions by a whole range of public and private institutions. Unless these measures are rapidly implemented, the majority of smallholders in the ejido sector are unlikely to be competitive, and they risk being displaced, through the land market, by the best endowed entrepreneurs in the ejido and the private sector. Failure to be competitive would thus lead to massive displacement of smallholders and to pressures on the urban labor markets and the border to the north. In the interest of global economic efficiency, the welfare of a large segment of the Mexican poor, and political stability, it is thus urgent that the agrarian reform in progress be complemented by a broader range of initiatives to help the agrarian reform beneficiaries achieve competitiveness in the new economic and institutional context before titling is completed and the market for land sales is activated by the reforms.

List of Acronyms

AGROASEMEX   Aseguradora Agrícola Mexicana / Mexican Agricultural Insurance Company

ALBAMEX   Alimentos Balanceados de México / Balanced Feeds of Mexico

ANAGSA   Aseguradora Nacional Agrícola y Ganadera, S.A. / National Agriculture and Livestock Insurance Company

ANDSA   Almacenes Nacionales de Depósito, S.A. / National Warehouses

ARIC   Asociación Rural de Interés Colectivo / Rural Collective Interest Association

ASERCA   Apoyos y Servicios a la Comercialización Agropecuaria / Support Services for Agricultural Marketing

BANCOMEXT   Banco Nacional de Comercio Exterior / National Bank for Foreign Trade

BANRURAL   Banco Nacional de Crédito Rural / National Rural Credit Bank

CAM   Consejo Agrario Mexicano / Mexican Agrarian Council

CAP   Congreso Agrario Permanente / Permanent Agrarian Congress

CCI   Central Campesina Independiente / Independent Peasant Central

CEPAL   Comisión Económica para América Latina y el Caribe / Economic Commission for Latin America and the Caribbean

CIDA   Comité Interamericano de Desarrollo Agrícola / Inter-American Committee for Agricultural Development

CIOAC   Central Independiente de Obreros Agrícolas y Campesinos / Independent Central of Agricultural Workers and Peasants

CNA   Comisión Nacional de Agua / National Water Commission

CNA	Consejo Nacional Agropecuario / National Agriculture and Livestock Council
CNC	Confederación Nacional Campesina / National Peasants' Confederation
CNG	Confederación Nacional Ganadera / National Livestock Confederation
CNPR	Confederación Nacional de Productores Rurales / National Confederation of Rural Producers
CONASUPO	Compañía Nacional de Subsistencias Populares / National Basic Foods Company
DDR	distrito de desarrollo rural / rural development district
FERTIMEX	Fertilizantes Mexicanos / Mexican Fertilizer Company
FIDEC	Fideicomiso para el Desarrollo Comercial / Trust Fund for Marketing
FIFONAFE	Fideicomiso Fondo Nacional de Fomento Ejidal / National Trust Fund for the Promotion of the Ejido
FIRA	Fideicomisos Instituidos en Relación con la Agricultura / Trust Funds for Agriculture
FIRCAVEN	Fideicomiso para la Reestructuración de la Cartera Vencida / Trust Fund to Restructure the Overdue Portfolio
FIRCO	Fideicomiso de Riesgo Compartido / Trust Fund for Shared Risk
FOCIR	Fondo de Capitalización e Inversión del Sector Rural / Capitalization and Investment Fund for the Rural Sector
FONAES	Fondo Nacional de Empresas de Solidaridad / National Fund for Solidarity Businesses
INEGI	Instituto Nacional de Estadística, Geografía e Informática / National Institute of Statistics, Geography, and Informatics
INIFAP	Instituto Nacional de Investigaciones Forestales, Agrícolas y Pecuarias / National Institute of Forestry, Agricultural, and Livestock Research
INMECAFÉ	Instituto Mexicano del Café / Mexican Coffee Institute
NAFIN	Nacional Financiera / National Development Bank
NAFTA	North American Free Trade Agreement

NRE	national rainfed equivalent
PACE	Programa de Apoyo a la Comercialización Ejidal / Support Program for Ejido Marketing
PRI	Partido Revolucionario Institucional / Institutional Revolutionary Party
PROCAMPO	Programa de Apoyo Directo al Campo / Direct Rural Support Program
PROCEDE	Programa de Certificación de Derechos Ejidales y Titulación de Solares Urbanos / Program for the Certification of Ejido Land Rights and the Titling of Urban House Plots
PRONASE	Productora Nacional de Semillas / National Seed Company
PRONASOL	Programa Nacional de Solidaridad / National Solidarity Program
RAN	Registro Agrario Nacional / National Agrarian Registry
SARH	Secretaría de Agricultura y Recursos Hidráulicos / Ministry of Agriculture
SEP	Secretaría de Educación Pública / Ministry of Education
SRA	Secretaría de la Reforma Agraria / Ministry of Agrarian Reform
UAIM	Unidad Agrícola-Industrial de la Mujer / Agro-Industrial Unit for Women
UGOCM	Unión General de Obreros y Campesinos de México / General Union of Mexican Workers and Peasants

References

Bromley, Daniel. 1991. *Environment and Economy: Property Rights and Public Policy.* Cambridge, Mass.: Blackwell.

Bustamante, Jorge. 1994. "Migration and Immigrants: Research and Policies." Tijuana: El Colegio de la Frontera Norte.

Cancian, Frank. 1992. *The Decline of Community in Zinacantan: Economy, Public Life, and Social Stratification, 1960–1987.* Stanford, Calif.: Stanford University Press.

CEPAL (Comisión Económica para América Latina y el Caribe). 1982. *Economía campesina y agricultura empresarial.* México, D.F.: Siglo Veintiuno.

———. 1989. "Magnitud de la pobreza en América Latina en los años ochenta." LC/L.533. Santiago, Chile: CEPAL.

———. 1990. "Magnitud de la pobreza en América Latina en los años ochenta," *Notas sobre la Economía y el Desarrollo* 494/495 (July–August).

COPLAMAR (Coordinación General del Plan Nacional de Zonas Deprimidas y Grupos Marginados). 1982. *Geografía de la marginación: necesidades esenciales en México.* México, D.F.: Siglo Veintiuno.

———. 1983. *Necesidades esenciales en México. Geografía de la marginación.* 2d ed. México, D.F.: Siglo Veintiuno.

Córdova, Arnaldo. 1973. *La ideología de la Revolución Mexicana.* 2d ed. México, D.F.: Era.

Cornelius, Wayne A. 1992. "The Politics and Economics of Reforming the Ejido Sector in Mexico: An Overview and Research Agenda," *LASA Forum* 23 (3): 3–10.

Corona Vázquez, Rodolfo. 1994. "Remesas enviadas de Estados Unidos por los migrantes mexicanos." Tijuana: El Colegio de la Frontera Norte.

Cortés, Fernando, and Rosa María Rubalcava. 1992. "Cambio estructural y concentración: un análisis de la distribución del ingreso familiar en México, 1984–1989." México, D.F.: El Colegio de México.

de Janvry, Alain. 1981. *The Agrarian Question and Reformism in Latin America.* Baltimore, Md.: Johns Hopkins University Press.

de Janvry, Alain, et al. 1995. "Reformas del sector agrícola y el campesinado en México." Rome: IFAD.

de Janvry, Alain, Elisabeth Sadoulet, Benjamin Davis, and Gustavo Gordillo. 1996. "Ejido Sector Reforms: From Land Reform to Rural Development." In *Reforming Mexico's Agrarian Reform*, edited by Laura Randall. Armonk, N.Y.: M.E. Sharpe.

de Janvry, Alain, Elisabeth Sadoulet, and Gustavo Gordillo de Anda. 1995. "NAFTA and Mexico's Maize Producers," *World Development* 23 (8): 1349–62.

Deininger, Klaus, and Ayo Heinegg. 1995a. "Poverty in Mexico." Washington, D.C.: Latin America 2 Division, The World Bank.

———. 1995b. "Rural Poverty in Mexico." Washington, D.C.: The World Bank.

Dennis, Philip A. 1976. "The Uses of Inter-Community Feuding," *Anthropological Quarterly* 49 (3): 174–84.

DeWalt, Billie. 1979. *Modernization in a Mexican Ejido: A Study in Economic Adaptation*. New York and Cambridge: Cambridge University Press.

DeWalt, Billie, and Martha Rees. 1994. *The End of Agrarian Reform in Mexico: Past Lessons, Future Prospects*. Transformation of Rural Mexico Series, no. 3. La Jolla: Center for U.S.–Mexican Studies, University of California, San Diego.

Díaz-Polanco, Héctor. 1977. *Teoría marxista de la economía campesina*. México, D.F.: Juan Pablos.

Durand, Jorge, and Douglas Massey. 1992. "Mexican Migration to the United States: A Critical Review," *Latin American Research Review* 27 (2): 3–42.

ECLAC (Economic Commission for Latin America and the Caribbean). 1994. *Social Panorama of Latin America*. Santiago, Chile: ECLAC.

Eswaran, Mukesh, and Ashok Kotwal. 1986. "Access to Capital and Agrarian Production Organization," *Economic Journal* 96: 482–98.

Fernández y Fernández, Ramón. 1973. *Cooperación agrícola y organización económica del ejido*. México, D.F.: Secretaría de Educación Pública.

Fletcher, Peri, and J. Edward Taylor. 1992. "Migration and the Transformation of a Mexican Village House Economy." Davis: Department of Agricultural Economics, University of California, Davis.

Foster, George. 1942. *A Primitive Mexican Economy*. Seattle: University of Washington Press.

García-Barrios, Raúl, et al. 1995. *Case Studies of Ejidos*, México, D.F.: Centro de Investigación y Docencia Económicas.

Gledhill, John. 1991. *Casi Nada. A Study of Agrarian Reform in the Homeland of Cardenismo*. Austin: University of Texas Press.

Goldring, Luin. 1992. "La migración México–EUA y la transnacionalización del espacio político y social: perspectivas desde el México rural," *Estudios Sociológicos* 29: 315–40.

Gordillo, Gustavo. 1988. *Campesinos al asalto del cielo: una reforma agraria con autonomía.* México, D.F.: Siglo Veintiuno.

———. 1992. *Más allá de Zapata.* México, D.F.: Cal y Arena.

Hernández, Luis. 1994. "The Mobilization of Corn Producers: From the Struggle for Fair Prices to Integrated Rural Development." In *Economic Restructuring and Rural Subsistence in Mexico: Corn and the Crisis of the 1980s,* edited by Cynthia Hewitt de Alcántara. La Jolla: Center for U.S.–Mexican Studies, University of California, San Diego.

Hewitt de Alcántara, Cynthia. 1976. *Modernizing Mexican Agriculture: Socioeconomic Implications of Technological Change 1940–1970.* Geneva: United Nations Research Institute for Social Development.

Hinton, Thomas. 1972. *Coras, huicholes y tepehuanes.* México, D.F.: Secretaría de Educación Pública/Instituto Nacional Indigenista.

INEGI (Instituto Nacional de Estadística, Geografía e Informática). 1990–92. *Encuesta nacional agropecuaria ejidal, 1988.* Vol. 1: Resumen General. Aguascalientes: INEGI.

Lamartine Yates, Paul. 1981. *Mexico's Agricultural Dilemma.* Tucson: University of Arizona Press.

Lustig, Nora. 1993. "Poverty in Mexico in the 1980s: The Answer My Friend. . . ." Washington, D.C.: The Brookings Institution.

Matus, Jaime. 1994. "Competitiveness of Crops under Trade Liberalization." Chapingo, Edo. de México: El Colegio de Postgraduados. Manuscript.

Osorio, Sergio, Rodolfo Stavenhagen, Salomón Eckstein, and Juan Ballesteros. 1974. *Estructura agraria y desarrollo agrícola en México.* México, D.F.: Fondo de Cultura Económica.

Rello, Fernando. 1987. *State and Peasantry in Mexico: A Case Study of Rural Credit in La Laguna.* Geneva: United Nations Research Institute for Social Development.

Rose, Donald. 1992. "Planning for Nutrition in Rural Mexico: A Case Study in Household Food Consumption Behavior." Ph.D. dissertation, Department of Agricultural and Resource Economics, University of California, Berkeley.

Sanderson, Susan W. 1984. *Land Reform in Mexico: 1910–1980.* Orlando, Fl.: Academic Press.

SARH–CEPAL (Secretaría de Agricultura y Recursos Hidráulicos–Comisión Económica para América Latina y el Caribe). 1992. "Primer informe nacional sobre tipología de productores del sector social." México. D.F.

———. 1994. "Tipología de productores agrícolas de los ejidos y comunidades en México." México, D.F.: CEPAL.

Schultz, T. 1993. "Investments in the Schooling and Health of Women and Men: Quantities and Returns." Economic Growth Center Discussion Paper No. 702. New Haven, Conn.: Yale University.

Taylor, J. Edward. 1984. "Migration Networks and Risk in Household Labor Decisions: A Study of Migration from Two Mexican Villages." Ph.D. dissertation, University of California, Berkeley.

———. 1987. "Undocumented Mexico–U.S. Migration and the Returns to Households in Rural Mexico," *American Journal of Agricultural Economics* 69 (3): 626–38.

Warman, Arturo. 1980. *We Come to Object: The Peasants of Morelos and the National State.* Baltimore, Md.: Johns Hopkins University Press.

Whetten, Nathan. 1948. *Rural Mexico.* Chicago, Ill.: University of Chicago Press.

Zedillo Ponce de León, Ernesto. 1996. *Segundo Informe de Gobierno.* México D.F.: Presidencia de la República.